Roots Music in America

ROOTS MUSIC
IN AMERICA

Collected Writings of Joe Wilson

Edited by Fred Bartenstein

CHARLES K. WOLFE MUSIC SERIES
Ted Olson, series editor

The University of Tennessee Press
Knoxville

The Charles K. Wolfe Music Series was launched in honor of the late Charles K. Wolfe (1943–2006), whose pioneering work in the study of American vernacular music brought a deepened understanding of a wide range of American music to a worldwide audience. In recognition of Dr. Wolfe's approach to music scholarship, the series will include books that investigate genres of folk and popular music as broadly as possible.

Library of Congress Cataloging-in-Publication Data

Names: Wilson, Joe, 1938–2015. | Bartenstein, Fred, 1950– editor.
Title: Roots music in America: collected writings of Joe Wilson /
edited by Fred Bartenstein.
Description: First edition. | Knoxville: The University of Tennessee Press,
[2017] | Series: Charles K. Wolfe music series |
Includes bibliographical references and index.
Identifiers: LCCN 2016049351 (print) | LCCN 2016052137 (ebook)
| ISBN 9781621903154 (pbk.) | ISBN 9781621903260 (pdf)
Subjects: LCSH: Folk music—United States—History and criticism.
Classification: LCC ML3550 .W55 2017 (print) | LCC ML3550 (ebook) | DDC
781.62/13—dc23
LC record available at https://lccn.loc.gov/2016049351

JOSEPH T. WILSON
March 16, 1938–May 17, 2015
· ·

CONTENTS

FOREWORD

Remembering Joe Wilson

Joseph Thomas "Joe" Wilson is remembered for his extensive knowledge of American vernacular culture, for his central role in promoting a wide range of roots music acts, and (primarily during his long stint with the National Council for the Traditional Arts) for his informed and accessible, if often irascible, voice in the public discussion about the meanings and values of tradition.

This book—in offering a representative and generous sampler of his writings on American roots music—showcases Wilson's broad base of knowledge, his astute insights into the music he loved, and his gift of gab. If his sense of aesthetics was complex, his mission was simple: "Folk art is something that is preserved and handed on because you like it," said Wilson. "Some things you ought to like just because they're good." When asked what drove him to spend his life delving deeper into traditional forms of artistic expression, Wilson said simply, "I try to get to the source. I want to get close to the soul."

Wilson's vernacular, nonacademic writing style was informed by early experience as a professional journalist and was infused by his politically engaged temperament and a distinctive, sometimes barbed sense of humor. Whether addressing a major topic in American roots music, such as the origins of bluegrass music or the history of the folk fiddle, or assessing the careers of well-known music figures such as Doc Watson or overlooked folk masters like Brownie Ford, Wilson's writings were honest and direct because his work was of the people, by the people, for the people. In other words, his perspectives were not formed in an ivory tower, but through constant engagement with performers and their fans.

Wilson often plied humor and irony when writing about his chosen topics, but he was unafraid to treat them with pure unabashed awe. Being "of the people" of Appalachia, Wilson knew that music was one way to express wonderment at a puzzling and sometimes frightening universe.

When asked by a journalist about the more difficult themes in Appalachian music, Wilson said: "My folk have a lot of songs about death. Some people say it's morbid, overly emotional. But we can't afford any headshrinkers down there. It's about the uncertainty and the tragedy of life and that's how we work things out." Wilson drew from a deep well of experience growing up in a traditional culture, and his understanding of how traditional worlds work was organic, part of who he was.

Wilson was reared in the small mountain hamlet of Trade, the easternmost community in Tennessee. He loved where he grew up, but embraced the opportunity to enter the larger world, attending nearby Lees-McRae College (in Banner Elk, North Carolina) for two years; his subsequent plans to transfer to East Tennessee State University were foiled by his financial situation. He left the mountains to find work, yet remained a true autodidact, learning and doing interesting things in all the places he subsequently lived.

During the first phase of his adult life, Wilson was an independent producer and writer within Nashville's music industry, and at one point he was a press agent for country music hitmaker Marty Robbins at the pinnacle of the singer's career (the early 1960s). During the height of the civil rights movement (1962–65) Wilson worked as a journalist in Birmingham, and he was often outspoken about the inequities of race relations in the South. Subsequently, with a family to take care of, he gravitated to New York City to serve as a senior executive with Oram International Corporation, a Madison Avenue consulting firm.

In 1976, Wilson made a career change, and it was then that he began to reshape the landscape of American music. Over the next twenty-eight years, he served as Executive Director of the National Council for the Traditional Arts. Based in Washington, D.C., he created major festivals in twelve states, and organized twenty-one national tours by musicians and dancers from many ethnic and racial backgrounds. Additionally, Wilson created seventeen international tours that visited nations in Asia, Eastern Europe, and the South Pacific.

In this role Wilson helped musicians associated with all genres of American roots music to find gigs and audiences, and many of those musicians have acknowledged their appreciation for his unflagging support. For instance, in his 2013 memoir *Kentucky Traveler: My Life in Mu-*

sic, Ricky Skaggs publicly praised Wilson for helping a young bluegrass musician from eastern Kentucky to get noticed during the 1970s. Wilson was committed to helping well-established if overlooked musicians as well as emerging superstars; for instance, he was instrumental in obtaining public recognition for melodic banjo stylist Carroll Best by including him on the *Masters of the Banjo* tour in 1993 and 1994. In 1995, Best died tragically, and Wilson continued his tribute to Best's art by releasing the first retrospective compilation of recordings of that banjo master. (In early 2014, when I produced a subsequent collection featuring recordings of Best, Wilson was the first person interviewed for the album notes; when I mentioned that we would host a Carroll Best tribute concert in Best's western North Carolina home county in September 2014, Wilson immediately volunteered to speak at the event out of respect for his late friend.)

Throughout his years with the NCTA, Wilson worked tirelessly in the planning and staging of numerous local and regional festivals. His many accomplishments included working with folklorist Archie Green and others in lobbying the US Congress to create the American Folklife Center at the Library of Congress, and in creating the Folk Arts Program at the National Endowment for the Arts. And Wilson was recognized for his work, receiving a National Heritage Fellowship from the National Endowment for the Arts, a National Treasure Award from the Library of Congress, and an Honored Friend award from the Smithsonian Institution.

For years, Wilson maintained a second home in Trade, but upon his retirement from the NCTA in 2004 he moved to the town of Fries in the mountains of Southwest Virginia. He founded and raised funds—approximately 13 million dollars—for the Blue Ridge Music Center (dedicated to the furtherance of traditional Blue Ridge music; this facility is located at Milepost 213 of the Blue Ridge Parkway and is programmed by the National Park Service). At this same juncture, Wilson teamed with Todd Christensen, then Associate Director for the Virginia Department of Housing and Community Development, to create The Crooked Road: Virginia's Heritage Music Trail. An effort to enhance cultural tourism in Southwest Virginia, The Crooked Road was intended to provide literal access to music-related heritage sites and figurative access to the stories related to those sites. To help people understand the stories associated with this popular music trail, Wilson wrote *A Guide to the Crooked Road: Virginia's Heritage*

Music Trail. The success of this project as an agent of economic development in a rural region owes much to the depth of Wilson's original vision for the project and to his effective application of the music trail concept. Wilson simply knew how to get things done, and he did so with a keen sense of humor, a deep sense of respect for tradition-bearers and their traditions, and an unflagging commitment to the worthiness of his endeavors.

While Wilson never got to attend East Tennessee State University, he made his final public appearance there. On March 27, 2015, just weeks before he died, Wilson participated as a panelist in an Appalachian Studies Association roundtable discussion about Appalachian music (the annual, rotating ASA conference was held in Johnson City that year). The session, which I organized, featured a stellar cast. Wilson, who was one of the invited panelists alongside musician/scholar Stephen Wade and musicologist Ron Pen, surprised everyone in attendance that afternoon by bringing with him banjo-player extraordinaire Tony Ellis. Wilson, during his section of the program, conveyed anecdotes about serving as a promoter and interpreter of music from Appalachia, and Ellis performed fragments of original banjo compositions whenever cued by his friend. Wilson's testimonial of his years of service to Appalachian music sounded to me—and to others in attendance—like a love letter to his native region. But he explained to the audience that in his roles as music promoter, he had championed music from other American regions as well as Appalachian music, and he cautioned scholars and students that it is essential to know the historical contexts behind the music. That was Wilson's great gift: introducing talented musicians from disparate vernacular music genres while making sure that audiences appreciated the full complexity of those musicians' art.

Wilson loved vernacular American music, both traditional and popular, and he recognized that music has the power to unite people. His musical tastes were eclectic and his knowledge of American music was extensive—even beyond the scope of what he ultimately wrote about. The only kind of music he did not like, frankly, was phony music (to Wilson, that meant music that was blatantly commercial without the redeeming quality of emotional honesty or social responsibility). Wilson was never hesitant to speak his mind about the music he loved or the music he hated, and his comments—whether during informal conversation, at conferences, for interviews, or within published works—were legendarily candid. Wilson was always matter-of-fact in his honesty, and it was always evident that his opinions were deeply felt and not for show or posturing. His assessments of music came from a deep and informed wellspring. Wilson meant what he said and he said what he meant—and people respected him for that.

As *Roots Music in America* reveals, Wilson, who was largely unaffiliated with the world of academia, often articulated unorthodox reviews of music-related scholarly publications (for example, his response to Robert Cantwell's book *Bluegrass Breakdown* offered an uncommonly commonsense critical reaction to a controversial academic book that, in Wilson's view, misinterpreted that misunderstood genre of commercial music by over-intellectualizing it). In his own writings, Wilson seemed to effortlessly balance objective and subjective observations of traditional culture and thus avoided the pitfall of one-dimensionality he felt was associated with much writing about roots music. Wilson wanted to understand and to publicly discuss the music traditions he promoted, but he also wished to know them and to feel them—as if he was part of those traditions, which in a sense he was.

Fred Bartenstein's editorial work for *Roots Music in America* is worthy of comment. In this book, Wilson's various writings are organized by theme rather than chronology; this approach underscores Wilson's depth and uniqueness of thinking about various genres of music. To help the reader make connections across the book's different sections, Bartenstein occasionally inserts bracketed comments; these are judiciously done and rarely intrusive. In his Preface, Bartenstein provides a clear rationale for his editorial decisions in compiling disparate pieces into a book.

Roots Music in America will appeal to Joe Wilson's many friends, colleagues, and admirers, as well as to serious scholars and longtime fans of vernacular American music. But the book has the potential to reach and influence another audience: a new generation of readers—younger fans of American roots music—who can learn much from Wilson's authoritative voice, his idiosyncratic intellect, his eclectic interests, and his passion for promoting the people and the cultures that he loved.

This book represents half of a larger project in which Joe Wilson participated during the final year of his life. A related book entitled *Lucky Joe's Namesake: The Extraordinary Life and Observations of Joe Wilson,* likewise published by the University of Tennessee Press and edited by Fred Bartenstein, compiles writings by Wilson that are of an autobiographical nature or that reveal his thinking about cultural issues beyond music. Wilson saw these two books as opportunities to continue past his lifetime a vigorous dialogue with others about American music and culture. The books will ensure that Wilson will remain for a long, long time a central figure in that ongoing dialogue.

TED OLSON
East Tennessee State University

It was 1972. I was twenty-one and a college student in Massachusetts when I first edited Joe Wilson's writing. He was thirty-four and a New York-based fundraiser, indulging—as a moonlighter—his gift for writing and his love for the roots music he grew up with in Tennessee. I published "Bristol's WCYB: Early Bluegrass Turf" in *Muleskinner News*, which I edited from 1969 to 1974. I believe he sent the piece unsolicited. Two years later, we commissioned and ran his stellar Doc Watson profile. (Both articles are included here.)

Fast-forward a decade and a half. I was living in Ohio when Joe started bringing National Council for the Traditional Arts concert tours, such as *Masters of the Folk Violin* and *Masters of the Banjo,* to Dayton for the local arts organization, Cityfolk. Joe and I were delighted to encounter each other again. We subsequently worked together to bring the National Folk Festival to Dayton (1996–1998) and on strategic planning for The Crooked Road: Virginia's Heritage Music Trail (2006). Joe contributed the foreword (included here) to *The Bluegrass Hall of Fame: Inductee Biographies 1991–2014,* which I co-wrote and edited for the International Bluegrass Music Museum.

Editing Joe again—after so many years and experiences—triggered a brainstorm. It would be fun to assemble a book-length anthology filled with Joe Wilson's brilliant published writing for magazines, concert program books, and album liner notes, along with his sizzling online posts, letters to the editor, and privately circulated unpublished writing. I phoned Joe, left a voicemail, and he called back a few days later full of enthusiasm. That same day (October 10, 2014), waves of e-mail attachments and brown envelopes began to barrage my mailboxes. Joe's wife, Kathy James, said the project energized him like nothing else, as a series of health challenges sapped his strength, constrained his travels, and led to his untimely death on May 17, 2015.

Soon Joe's many friends caught wind of the anthology venture and began to suggest must-include pieces, including incendiary personal correspondence. Since Joe had grown up in Tennessee, and because the University of Tennessee Press had a series named for Joe's friend and collaborator Charles K. Wolfe (1943–2006), I approached Ted Olson (series editor) and Thomas Wells (an editor at the press). After letters of support from folk music scholars Neil Rosenberg, Howard Sacks, and David Whisnant, the publisher enthusiastically jumped on board.

The more I worked with Joe's material, the clearer it became that it called for *two* books: a collection of pieces on roots music (the subject on which he was most prolific), and a volume focused on Joe's extraordinary life and eclectic observations. In the last eight months of his life, Joe was intensely involved in selecting material and reviewing my edits for the anthologies. After his passing, the decisions were mine, although I received valuable input from Joe's friends and associates, and from early readers in my own circle.

Several editing issues are worthy of comment:

1) Joe regularly recycled content for his various writing projects, often with revisions, cuts, and expansions. In preparing the anthologies, I tried to use his most colorful and complete language, even if that meant drawing upon more than one source for a single article. Conversely, I removed duplications whenever the same or similar material appeared in original versions of several articles.

2) In editing the two volumes, I tightened and occasionally resequenced Joe's prose for clarity's sake, and because, in the format of an anthology, some of his extended tangents—such as "Minstrelsy (or Why Blacks Gave up the Banjo)" (included here)—could have their own article.

3) Mark Twain famously said, "Never let the truth stand in the way of a good story, unless you can't think of anything better." Joe was a consummate storyteller. Wherever I could correct his facts without damaging his story, I did so. Although we had a few arguments about matters of historical accuracy, Joe usually came around in the face of confirming evidence. I'm not aware of any egregious misstatements in these volumes, but I did not painstakingly check every one of Joe's facts.

4) Joe had many talents, but filing and archival preservation were not among them. His papers were kept in piles whose order wasn't

entirely clear to him, and when he did find something he was looking for, it was usually to lend it to someone who may not have
gotten around to returning it. When he changed computers, many
of his old files failed to make the transition. In his last years, he
adamantly recalled pieces he had once written, with just enough
clues to send me, Kathy, and friendly research librarians, on wild
goose chases that snagged some of the articles in this volume. I'm
sure there's more great Joe Wilson writing out there, but I don't
know where to find it.

Kathy told me that Joe's retirement plans included writing several
books on historical topics. He wanted to author a volume on Virginia's
Great Road (articles in both *Roots Music in America* and *Lucky Joe's Namesake* contain early results of that research). She urged him to write a book
on the origin stories of well-known songs and tunes. "The Wild Horse at
Stony Point, with a Salute to Peter Francisco and a Bow to Jenny Lind";
"Rachel and the Eighth of January"; and "Durang's Dance and Hoffmaster's
Tune" (all included here) are samples of how that book would have turned
out. But in retirement Joe lacked the stamina, and the access to research
associates, that such major projects would have required.

Joe Wilson spent the bulk of his life and energy as a doer and a change
agent, and the country and world are much the better for it. It is fortunate
that his considerable talents as a writer and scholar found sufficient expression to leave a published legacy. I am proud to have made a contribution
to that enterprise, and thoroughly enjoyed my time of intimacy with Joe's
extraordinary voice.

FRED BARTENSTEIN
Yellow Springs, Ohio
March 2016

ACKNOWLEDGMENTS

Many people and organizations helped in the preparation of this volume of Joe Wilson's writings. First among them, of course, is Joe Wilson himself. He spent seventy-four years amassing the experiences and observations contained here; in his last eight months, he was a most enthusiastic collaborator.

I received valuable input from early readers, including Joy Bartenstein, Richard Brown, Carolyn Fuller, George Holt, Kathy James, Mary Mathews, Elaine Morris Roberts, Neil Rosenberg, Howard and Judy Sacks, Richard Spottswood, and Andy Wallace. In addition to writing the Foreword, Ted Olson gave most helpful advice in shaping the project. Denise Jarvinen provided major assistance with the index, and Grant Hackett and Dick Spottswood made helpful suggestions.

A number of sources generously granted permission for the reprint and revision of pieces that originally appeared elsewhere. They include *Bluegrass Unlimited*, The Crooked Road: Virginia's Heritage Music Trail, the International Bluegrass Music Museum, *Journal of Country Music* (the Country Music Hall of Fame and Museum), Kathy James, Ken Landreth, *Mugwumps*, *Muleskinner News*, the National Council for the Traditional Arts, *The Old Farmer's Almanac*, the Publore Listserv, University Press of Kentucky, Walt Saunders; the Alligator, Arhoolie, Copper Creek, County, Cracker Barrel, Rounder, and Smithsonian Folkways labels; and a variety of personal correspondents. (Take just a moment to reflect on who other than Joe Wilson could have published in all those places!)

Research librarians Aaron Smithers at UNC Chapel Hill and Amy Margolin at the Greene County, Ohio Public Library went beyond the call of duty in tracking down articles, sometimes with only the slightest of clues. Andy Wallace—Joe's long-time right-hand man at NCTA—was great about digging through files there, and Kathy James was indefatigable in chasing down paper, computer files, and photos in her and Joe's Fries, Virginia, home.

HISTORICAL SOURCES
OF AMERICAN
VERNACULAR MUSIC

The Blue Ridge

A Place Near the Heart in American Musical History

The Blue Ridge has a special place in the musical history of the United States. The music of this region is historic, known by millions of Americans. Its roots are grounded in the British Isles, in Europe, and in Africa. Its fruits are obvious in many contemporary American musical forms.

But knowledge of exactly what is historic about the musical art of this region and why it was important in the formation of our national culture is flawed by an incredible amount of misinformation. No subject in our national history seems to have been subjected to more misinterpretation.

Local color writers of the popular press began writing about the Blue Ridge and its special music shortly after the Civil War. Unfortunately, many relied upon vivid imaginations for their information. By the mid-1920s, national stereotypes about musical mountaineers were firmly established. They still confuse popular understanding.

Adapted from *The Blue Ridge Music Center: A Place Near the Heart*, National Council for the Traditional Arts, 2000; Introduction to *A Guide to the Crooked Road: Virginia's Heritage Music Trail*, Copyright 2006 by The Crooked Road: Virginia's Heritage Music Trail, John F. Blair, Publisher, 2006; and the tour program book for *Music From the Crooked Road: Mountain Music of Virginia*, National Council for the Traditional Arts, 2010.

The story of what actually happened is far more interesting than the myths and stereotypes spread for a century by the entertainment industry. This is a place where an American culture had important beginnings. Those beginnings are still obvious in the living culture of this place. The people of the Blue Ridge have kept an amazing array of music with roots in colonial times. This music has had an impact upon the culture of Americans that is surprisingly strong, given the relatively small population of the Blue Ridge.

Many historians believe that its distance from ports made the Blue Ridge the first mini-melting pot for a strongly American-flavored cultural stew. Others note that the Blue Ridge was settled just as several European-derived groups and African-Americans were becoming culturally more comfortable with each other.

Speculation about which factors most influenced cultural blending in the Blue Ridge will probably go on forever, but it is clear that a remarkable number of American musical forms have roots in this phenomenon and in this place. Moreover, their musical echoes can still be heard in Blue Ridge communities. Blue Ridge residents have kept these older arts in good health by performing them for their own enjoyment for two and a half centuries. This music is awfully tough and resilient. It has survived the movements of time and place. It has survived being ignored and disparaged. It has also survived the vicissitudes of becoming an international fad.

ENGLAND MEETS AFRICA IN VIRGINIA

In interpreting this history, it seems especially important to take note of the cultural influence of African Americans, to understand that they were important participants in the making of what are now often considered the oldest and most "white" of American arts. A fourth of the population of Virginia in 1710 was of African ancestry; most were born in Africa.

In the early years, few records were kept of how Africans and the English learned music and dance from each other. They were busy with tobacco, indigo, and cotton. They were trading with Indians, and shipping furs to Europe and ginseng to China. But there are occasional incidental reports of cross-cultural learning from before the American Revolution.

In 1773–74, Philip Vickers Fithian, a young tutor educated at Princeton, came to Virginia to teach the seven children and the nephew of wealthy Westmoreland County planter, Robert Carter III. Though very fond of two of his teenage charges, Ben and Harry Carter, Presbyterian professor Fithian had difficulty preventing their high jinks and their delving into forbidden black music and dance. Two examples from Fithian's journal tell of his struggles to convert the sociable young Carters into stiff aristocrats:

> Sunday, January 30, 1774—This evening the Negroes collected themselves in the School-Room & began to play the Fiddle and dance—I was in Mr. Randolph's room; I went among them, Ben & Harry were of the Company—Harry was dancing with his coat off—I dispersed them however immediately.
>
> Friday, February 4, 1774—This Evening in the School-Room, which is below my Chamber, Several Negroes & Ben & Harry are playing on a banjo and dancing!

Like his offspring, Robert Carter III was much devoted to music. He was also sympathetic to the condition of his slaves. In later years he freed all of them—more than 500, the greatest emancipation until Abraham Lincoln.

Among those who observed early black-to-white musical interchange was President Thomas Jefferson. In his book *Notes on the State of Virginia* (1781–1785), Jefferson said of black residents of the Blue Ridge, "The instrument proper to them is the Banjar, which they brought hither from Africa." Jefferson was a fiddler who seems to have had his hands on a banjo, because he explained the instrument and how it was tuned.

There are other incidental references showing that slave and indentured servant musicians provided much of the music for Virginia dancing for generations and left an indelible imprint on the music of both black and white players of later times.

THE BEGINNING PLACE

The Blue Ridge Mountains were at one time the end of the world. The people who settled along the Chesapeake knew about them, and eventually Indian traders with packhorse trains reached beyond the mountains. But these mountains were at first a barrier—a place where the unknown began—and were spoken of in fearful tones.

The Blue Ridge also became the beginning of a new world. Eventually the tide of settlement reached the mountains, and swirled beyond them, but they made a subtle difference to all who crossed.

They were an American blender. You could see London from Baltimore or Richmond, but not from Gap Creek or the Meadows of Dan. The Blue Ridge was reached 170 years after the first European settlements on the Eastern Seaboard. There was something final about crossing this first chain of hazy blue mountains. It brought changes in religion and in religious singing. The old authority did not reach that far.

THE VALLEY ROAD

The most important of America's historic national roads parallels for more than 300 miles the Blue Ridge Mountains in Virginia and North Carolina. The major colonial and early American route to the unsettled West, the Valley Road followed old Indian trails for most of its total length of some 700 miles, from near Philadelphia, Pennsylvania, through the Shenandoah Valley, to the Piedmont of North and South Carolina along one fork, and into southwestern Virginia and eastern Tennessee via another.

Beginning in the early eighteenth century and continuing for more than 100 years, tens of thousands of migrants traveled the Valley Road in search of fame, fortune, and personal and religious freedom. One estimate is that fully one-fourth of the present population of the United States—including many of the original settlers of Illinois, Indiana, Kentucky, Tennessee, Missouri, Arkansas, and Texas—has ancestors who traveled the Valley Road.

Some were on the road or its extensions for a generation or two. Abraham Lincoln's family lived in Pennsylvania, Virginia, Tennessee, Kentucky, and Indiana before arriving in Illinois. Some early Ohio settlers traveled the road, moving northward after they arrived in Kentucky.

The Great Valley Road began at Germantown, Pennsylvania, just west of Philadelphia, and entered the Shenandoah Valley north of Hagerstown, Maryland. In Virginia it traversed the lower valley portion of the Shenandoah in a southwesterly direction, along a route now roughly followed by U.S. 11 and Interstate 81.

In the early years, many travelers turned east toward the Virginia and North Carolina Piedmont at Buchanan (then Looney's Ferry), using the James River gorge to cross the Blue Ridge and reach the relatively flat area east of the mountains. They then continued southward, settling much of North Carolina and South Carolina. The 703-mile Great Wagon Road terminated at Augusta, Georgia.

After the American Revolution, travelers on the road continued down the valley past Roanoke to far southwestern Virginia. As many as 10,000 migrants passed through Abingdon in 1805, a year in which the population of the entire nation was only two million.

Contrary to myths of rugged individualism on the frontier, the pilgrims who came down the Valley Road traveled in groups, for no cause creates community more quickly than shared adversity. People moving great distances—toward nameless dangers—band together for safety and assistance.

These groups brought cultural traits, skills, and learning from many lands, and from diverse sections of those lands, but few have been preserved intact. As people moved and settled together, their cultural attributes blended with those from other cultures and were further developed and refined in this country.

The southward movement began in 1730, when Adam Miller led a community of Germans to an area near today's Luray, Virginia. The Germans were largely from the Palatinate, a region beset by religious wars. Invited to settle in Pennsylvania by William Penn, they were pacifist Anabaptist Protestants: Dunkards, Brethren, Mennonites, and others. They were the first Europeans to settle in the Shenandoah.

The Scots-Irish were also refugees from Europe, but were motivated more by economic opportunity than by religion. They were Protestants from Ulster (Northern Ireland), where they had lived for a generation or two. King James of England had first settled Scots lowlanders and English "border people" on his plantations there, exacerbating difficulties with the native Irish that have continued. More arrived during the reign of Oliver Cromwell. They were actually of Scots and English ancestry. The term "Scots-Irish" is an Americanism, not used anywhere in Europe.

The Scots-Irish were a restless people, and a fondness for migration was only one of their characteristics. In 1923, Tennessee historian John T. Moore had this to say about them: "If abused, they fight. If their rights are abused, they rebel. If forced, they strike. If their liberties are threatened, they murder. They eat meat and always their bread is hot."

In Ulster, these new settlers grew weary of the Crown's demands that they produce only raw materials for British manufacturing. By 1730 they were pouring into Pennsylvania, where they initially flourished. A generation later, cheap land was in short supply for their children. The younger generation of Scots-Irish began saying of Pennsylvania what their parents had said of Northern Ireland, "The only good roads lead out."

At first, the Europeans were a bit wary of each other in Virginia. There's a diary entry by a German Moravian preacher who was traveling north along the road from North Carolina to Pennsylvania. He told how he and his companions "gave thanks to God . . . that we have passed safely through the Irish settlements."

And where were these rude Irish settlements, this place of lurking evil the pious brothers so dreaded? It was Staunton, Virginia, and its environs, now wonderfully sedate and genteel, a town that is a gem of the Shenandoah Valley.

On the eastern slopes of the Blue Ridge, the Germans, Scots-Irish, Irish, and a smattering of other Europeans—Huguenots, Dutch, and Swedes—soon met the African Americans and their English owners moving westward, as land closer to the coast was worn out by the unrelenting planting of tobacco.

So it was that Europeans, Tidewater African Americans, and Anglo-Americans met in the Blue Ridge and became more comfortable with each other. All were minorities in one way or another. In many counties, the Germans became the largest population group, but academicians believe the culture that emerged in the area was largely Scots-Irish. This may be true in a narrow political sense, as these movements occurred in a revolutionary time and the Scots-Irish were experienced in revolution. Soon the groupings that mattered most to them were Whigs and Democrats. Virtually all worked family farms that were largely self-sufficient.

All brought music with them. The west-flowing English and blacks had already created the string band, with its driving fiddle and banjo. Violins were expensive and relatively rare, but all these people were singers. The travelers from Ulster had ballads and ditties galore, and the Germans had a rich tradition of religious singing. Musical concepts from many places met and new blends emerged.

WHERE DID THE MUSIC COME FROM?

Music heard today in the Blue Ridge came from everywhere. Some of it is very old. Asked to play "Billy In The Low Ground," a local fiddler or flatpicker is likely to oblige but not know where it originated. The tune celebrates King William's victory over King James at the Battle of the Boyne, fought in Ireland in 1690.

Practically all singers of older ballads know a beautiful one called "Barbara Allen." A diary-keeping employee of the British navy, Samuel Pepys, took note of it in 1662, calling it "a little Scotch song."

The melody "Greensleeves" is ubiquitous but obscure. It was composed by Englishman Richard Jones, and registered in London on September 3, 1580. It was popularized by lutenist John Dowland at various European courts, including that of James I.

Juba dance is sometimes called "hambone" and has African origins. One participant beats out a rhythm with his hands, mixing the slapping of chest, legs, and hands to create a rhythm, while another dances on a board, keeping the rhythm with his feet. Lyrics are sometimes sung: "Juba this and Juba that, and Juba killed a yellow cat."

Most ballads were carried in memories handed down in generations, but the "ballit" of a song is its written lyrics, kept in families generations before they came to America. After the invention of movable type, these were sometimes printed and sold on the street or in shops.

There were songsmiths putting current news—especially murders and other tragedies—into warning lyrics. Among them was Benjamin Franklin, who told that he wrote a song and sold it on the streets of Boston "about the drowning of Caption Worthilake and his daughters . . . in the wretched Grub Street stile."

The common mountain gospel song "I'll Fly Away" is a 1929 composition by Ozark songwriter Albert Brumley. It was spread in the paperback song hymnals purchased annually by rural churches in the 1930s and 1940s. Other religious songs are of considerable antiquity. One of the best known is "Amazing Grace." A repentance poem, it was written in 1748 by a former English slave ship captain—John Newton—after his ship—the Greyhound—survived a storm, through what Newton believed was divine intervention. But "New Britain," the Scottish melody commonly used with the song, is even older.

The music of the Blue Ridge has at times been influenced by popular trends, but more often has been the launching platform for other genres of music. Now nearly 400 years old, it is still influencing America and is in a state of vigorous health.

Country Music in Tennessee

From Hollow to Honky-tonk

• •

Among the less jarring opinions of Tennessee's fire-breathing Parson Brownlow—editor, governor, and Rebel "ventilator"—was that the state would "ever be plagued with fleas and fiddlers, singers of morose songs, and the depredations of Old Scratch." Though he clearly disapproved of it, the sour parson was right: Tennessee's favorite music is tenacious. It came in folk form with the first settlers and continues to the present in a variety of styles and contexts, from country taverns to Nashville recording studios. An historical example illustrates the linkage from the earliest folk styles to the country music of today.

George Dotson and Henry Skaggs were among the first 18th century "long hunters" to view the sunny glades and hazy ridges of what is now East Tennessee. Today, a community called Meat Camp in Watauga County, North Carolina, takes its name from the spot in the Blue Ridge where each fall these far-ranging hunters salted and stored meat before it was carried to settlements east of the mountains. One of the lowest gaps

From the program book to the *1986 Festival of American Folklife*, presented by the Smithsonian Institution and the National Park Service in the Alleghenies, the one they called the "Trade Gap," is five miles from Meat Camp.

Henry Skaggs sought furs beyond the Trade Gap, and his explorations reached 150 miles west into Kentucky. Daniel Boone was a later traveler here and was assisted by Skaggs and his brothers. George Dotson remained near the Trade Gap and made a farm on the Bulldog Branch of Roan's Creek. Some of his descendants still live in Trade, the easternmost community in Tennessee.

George's son Reuben was born in Trade in 1765 and lived there for 104 years. Among remembrances carried by descendants is his comment: "I've lived in four states but have never moved and live in the house I was born in." (Ill-defined boundaries led the first settlers to believe they were in Colonial Virginia, while actually they were in North Carolina, which in turn became the short-lived State of Franklin, and ultimately Tennessee.) Reuben loved "the singing of hymns, the old ballit songs, and the playing of the fiddle."

How well he loved fiddling and dancing is documented in the minutes of the Cove Creek Baptist Church. Reuben and his wife, Sarah Green, so offended the stern brothers and sisters that they were "sited to meeting" five times between 1811 and 1820. Their promises to sin no more were accepted but, in 1823, "a report taken up against Brother Reuben Dotson and Sister Dotson his wife that they both went to a frolic and stayed all night" resulted in their exclusion from the church. This conviction, that the fiddle is the devil's box, continues among some Tennesseans, but others have resolved the ancient dispute. Among them is prominent Nashville country musician Ricky Skaggs, a devout Christian and descendant of Henry Skaggs.

The anglicization of names has masked the ethnicity of Tennessee's first carriers of country music. In contrast to the widely held view that the early settlers were all of "the purest English stock," George Dotson was of Ulster Irish extraction, and Henry Skaggs was descended from an English mariner. Many who crossed the mountains with the Scots-Irish and English were of German or French Huguenot descent. The latter included Tennessee's first governor, John Sevier, who, like Reuben, was a devotee of balls and frolics.

The Appalachian dulcimer, derived from the German *Scheitholt* and now almost an emblem of Tennessee mountain culture, was actually rare until the craft revivals of the 20th century. It was the fiddle that remained the favorite Tennessee instrument until recent times, but highly skilled fiddlers who could play classics like "Rack Back Davy," "Arkansas Traveller," and "Forked Deer" have always been uncommon. On the other hand, the "ballit book" and religious songbook were open to all.

Huge outdoor camp meeting revivals that began in 1801 sent a knowledge of hymnody and printed songbooks throughout the Volunteer State. Within five years, these songs and a new way of singing spread throughout the nation and even to Ireland and England—Tennessee's first musical influence beyond its borders.

Tennessee country folk have long been in contact with commercial forces that have modified the old ballads, fiddle tunes and sacred music. Tennessee fiddling was modified by popular influences during the second half of the 19th century, principally through traveling circuses and stage shows that featured musical performers. Improved communication brought popular sheet music to the state. But the most important of these influences was the wave of minstrel performance that began in the 1840s and continued into the 20th century. Handmade banjos fashioned after slave prototypes were in Tennessee before the minstrels, but blackface performers improved on the instrument and developed new ways of playing in ensembles that featured several instruments. The old-time string band—as well as its modern manifestation, the bluegrass band—is heir to minstrel instrumentation and repertoire.

Tennesseans and other Americans were "busking" for coins and selling song "ballits" generations before technology made possible a country music industry. That technology was first applied to the music of rural Americans in the 1920s and soon created audiences for recordings, radio broadcasts, and stage appearances. At first, Nashville was less important than Atlanta and Chicago as a country music center and largely ignored in the field recording forays of commercial record companies when rural musicians first found their way onto major labels in the 1920s.

A single institution, the Grand Ole Opry, made the Tennessee capital a music center. Begun in 1925 and broadcast on the static-free, clear-channel 50,000-watt signal of WSM, it reached much of the United States. Opry founder George D. Hay chose his acts carefully and with a concern for variety. The first was Uncle Jimmy Thompson, a fiddler with a 19th century style and repertoire. Hay soon added Dr. Humphrey Bate's "hell-for-leather" string band, the minstrel-influenced banjoist Uncle Dave Macon, barbershop quartets, and—beginning in the 1930s with the addition of "western" to country music—a variety of pseudo-cowboy style bands. Although the Opry in the early years paid virtually nothing to its artists, performers could sell stage appearances and recordings throughout the South, Mid-Atlantic states, and much of the Midwest. Membership in the Opry became the apex of country music success.

Increases in the expendable income of rural and urban blue-collar workers encouraged an annual growth of country music as an industry throughout much of the late 1940s and early 1950s. Because so many musicians "worked out of Nashville," the first recording studios were built there. Country music—with its folk roots—was at first viewed as a specialty item, worth doing but not significant in the overall business of major companies. The best that could happen to a country music "hit" was a "cover" by a popular artist that would increase song publishing royalties.

The immediate popularity of the rockabillies and the later emergence of commercial rock 'n' roll showed recordings produced in Tennessee to be far more than specialty items. Part of what came to be called "the Nashville sound" was influenced by a small group of musicians in Memphis in the mid-1950s. The best known were Elvis Presley, Jerry Lee Lewis, Johnny. Cash, and Carl Perkins. Their "rockabilly" recordings merged rural black blues and white "hillbilly" styles with an electric studio sound. They—and black artists such as Howlin' Wolf, B.B. King and Rufus Thomas—were recorded by Sam Phillips and his associates at Sun Records.

As country music in general moved further from its folk roots, the production of a Nashville record became formulaic. Sharp edges were eliminated, while the goal became a recording that could "cross over" to pop and youth markets. String sections and "doo-wah" choruses were used along with session musicians whose motto was, "Play as little as you can as well as you can."

Today's country music—the modern synthesis of blues, balladry, and string band music—is still largely the music of working class whites. Its development continues, but the past is recalled, especially by well-known traditionalists such as Ricky Skaggs and Bill Monroe [1911-1996]. Perhaps more important, much of Tennessee's country music is still for the consumption of local folks—distant from the recording industry—in fiddle contests, church meetings, house parties and honky-tonks.

Ballads
Music from the Mists

• •

A ballad is a narrative poem, a story told in a song. It may tell of lost love, a great tragedy, a fairy tale, or a humorous event. Passed aurally from generation to generation, the original composer is often hidden in the mists of time. Ballads are the oldest extant genre of song in the English-speaking world.

Francis James Child (1825–1896), a professor at Harvard, collected and published *The English and Scottish Popular Ballads* in 10 volumes, between 1882 and 1898. Child defined and enumerated, with examples, 305 ancient ballads, including textual variations. Variations are important, as they are evidence that the song is very old and has been shaped by generations of singers.

The 305 songs, which have come to be known as "Child ballads," are usually sung a cappella. The best remembered ancient ballad kept by American singers is "Barbara Allen" (Child #84), which London diarist Samuel Pepys called an "old song" in 1663.

From the tour program book for *Music from the Crooked Road: Mountain Music of Virginia,* National Council for the Traditional Arts, 2010.

Among the pioneering collectors of folk songs in the southern Appalachians were Olive Dame Campbell (1892–1954) of Asheville, North Carolina, and British ballad and dance collector Cecil Sharp (1859–1924). Campbell told of her initial meeting with ballad singer Ada Smith:

> Never shall I ever forget it. The blazing fire, the young girl on her low stool before it, the soft strange strumming of the banjo—different from anything I had heard before—and then the song. I had been used to singing "Barbara Allen" as a child, but how far from that gentle tune was this—so strange, so remote, so thrilling. I was lost almost from the first note, and the pleasant room faded from sight; the singer only a voice. I saw again the long road over which we had come, the dark hills, the rocky streams bordered by tall hemlocks and hollies, the lonely cabins distinguishable at night only by the firelight flaring from their chimneys. Then these, too, faded, and I seemed to be borne along into a still more dim and distant past, of which I myself was a part.

Campbell collected over 200 ballads and songs. She invited Sharp, founding father of the folksong revival in England, to come to the mountains. He had been collecting ballad texts from working people in England, and was fascinated to hear from Campbell that "the inhabitants of the Southern Appalachians were still singing the traditional songs and ballads their English and Scottish ancestors brought out with them at the time of their emigration."

During 1916–1918, Cecil Sharp and his collaborator Maud Karpeles collected ballads in Virginia, North Carolina, Tennessee, and Kentucky. The American cognoscenti have long needed Englishmen and other Europeans to tell them their folk culture was good before they accepted it, and Sharp's work helped make ballad collecting respectable.

Among the singers Sharp and Karpeles met was Joe Blackard, of the Meadows of Dan in Patrick County, Virginia. Blackard was a banjoist and bandleader, as well as a keeper of ballads. Nine years later, he was recorded by Ralph Peer for Victor Records. The Meadows of Dan is a tiny but richly musical place, located in a county where nine families have dominated music since colonial times. Among those Sharp met were families named Spangler, Shelor, and Bowman. (Well-known bluegrass banjoist Sammy

Shelor is from the Meadows of Dan and is related to three of those nine families, including the Blackards.)

Among the places where balladry has been brilliantly kept is Smyth County, Virginia. Three of America's greatest ballad singers of the golden era of collecting were from there. Texas Gladden was from Saltville; famed collector Alan Lomax called her the best singer he ever met. Blind ballad-eer Horton Barker was from Chilhowie and was recorded by Karpeles, among others. John M. "Sailor Dad" Hunt was from Marion and was a famed keeper of old songs. He had run away to sea from the mountains as a youth. Returning home in retirement, he recorded a treasury of sea shanties as well as some ballads.

There are still ballad singers in Smyth County. Among them is young Elizabeth LaPrelle of Rural Retreat, a member of a family of singers and a keeper of ballads. During his travels in Appalachia ninety years ago Cecil Sharp was surprised to find that many of the finest singers were young. They still are.

The Wild Horse at Stony Point, with a Salute to Peter Francisco and a Bow to Jenny Lind

• •

During the past forty years, scores of old songs and fiddle tunes have become firmly lodged in the bluegrass repertoire. Some of these originated in the last century; a few reach back two or three centuries. That the songs are old is often obvious; they carry in their lyrics some hint of their antiquity. Many tell a sorrowful story: the betrayal of Jesse James; the assassination of President McKinley; or the slaying of Ommie Wise, Ellen Smith, and the Knoxville Girl (known as the Wexford Girl in that ballad's English ancestor).

The composers of many of these songs are unknown, but fiddle melodies tend to be even more anonymous; they carry no hint of their age or why they were composed. Although the tune is performed frequently, its story is forgotten. Though it is difficult to generalize about differences between songs and tunes, there tends to be another: many of the older fiddle tunes celebrate a happy event or a greatly admired person.

Three venerable fiddle tunes commemorate events and personages of America's early history. Two of them, "Stony Point" and "Jenny Lind," are

From *Bluegrass Unlimited* magazine, September 1988.

relatively common. The third, "Peter Francisco," is rare but just as traditional. There are at least two tunes called "Jenny Lind," and Bill Monroe
learned one as "Jenny Lynn" from his Uncle Pen. I know of only one recording of "Peter Francisco"—by the Fuzzy Mountain String Band—but
it is a fine old tune and there's a wonderful story behind it.

"Stony Point" celebrates an epic fight of the American Revolution:
"Mad" Anthony Wayne's spectacular midnight capture of the British
stronghold at Stony Point, on the Hudson River in New York on July 16,
1779. Wayne took the fort with a bayonet charge, and the victory came
when American morale was low and a victory sorely needed.

"Mad" Anthony was a general on Washington's staff who was noted
for his courage. His nickname came from a deserter's complaint: he was
willing to follow a reasonable commander but could not endure the risks
taken by a madman. Wayne's friends gleefully took up the nickname, and
it was to follow the Pennsylvania-reared general for the rest of his life.

Washington and Wayne completed the planning for an assault upon
Stony Point on July 6, 1779. Wayne's response to Washington's question
about the feasibility of the action was, "General, I'll storm hell if you will
only plan it."

Stony Point was thought to be nearly impregnable. Wayne and his
officers prepared wills before the assault. During the attack, Wayne was
hit in the head by a musket ball. Stunned, unable to walk, and blinded by
blood, he put his arms around the shoulders of foot soldiers and ordered
them to carry him forward into the fight.

British loyalist historian Thomas Jones said the taking of Stony Point
was totally unexpected. "The commandant of the fort and a select company were devoting themselves to pleasure, and pouring down large liba-
tions . . . when Wayne entered the room and made them all prisoners."

News of the victory swept the nation. The Continental Congress had a
medal struck in Wayne's honor, and many poems and melodies were composed praising Wayne and his men. One of them, "Stony Point," survives
in living tradition. It is widespread and found under many other names:
"Kelton's Reel," "Walk Along John," "Pigtown Fling," and "Rocky Mountain," among others. Dan Emmett used the tune for his 1844 minstrel song
"Old Dad," and some southwestern Virginia musicians still call it by that
name. It is possible that the tune existed before the battle at Stony Point.

The first recording I know is by Uncle Am Stuart of Morristown, Tennessee. Stuart called the tune "Nigger In The Woodpile" on his 1925 Vocalion 78. Two years later Kentuckian Doc Roberts recorded the tune as "Buck Creek Gal" on his 1927 Gennett disc.

But the most common alternative title is "The Wild Horse."[1] Sometimes the two titles are combined to create "The Wild Horse at Stony Point." There's a restless back-and-forth quality to one strain of the tune that could have given rise to the "The Wild Horse" title. But it could also be another foot soldiers' name for the hyperactive commander that others called "Mad" but General Washington addressed as "Brave Anthony."

Like General Wayne, Peter Francisco was a soldier of the American Revolution and noted for his courage in battle. And, like Wayne, he was a favorite of General Washington. But there the similarity ends. Peter Francisco was a private but the most remarkable private in the Revolution, one whose feats of strength and courage made him a hero to thousands of other private soldiers.

Francisco's origins are shrouded in legend. Sometime in the 1760s, a mysterious ship—some say a man-of-war—sailed into Virginia waters and sent a boat to the dock at City Point. The sailors who rowed to the dock put a baby on it. They then returned to the ship, which hoisted its sails and left, never to return.

The baby seemed to be about a year old and could speak a few words in a language no one understood. The baby knew its name: Peter Francisco. Peter was reared by the Anthony Winston family of Buckingham County, Virginia, and at one time was apprenticed to a Judge Henry, a relative of Patrick Henry.

Francisco grew into a man of giant physique. When the Revolution came, he was a teenager and nearly seven feet tall. He first came to public attention when he was subjected to taunts by six British soldiers in a Virginia tavern and killed all six with a broadsword.

Peter became legendary while serving in the Southern Campaign, as a member of General Nathanael Greene's army. There's a memorial to him at the Guilford Courthouse [North Carolina] battlefield, and his shoes are preserved there. Greene sent Peter to General Washington to bear news of the North Carolina victories.

Francisco became a favorite of Washington and General Lafayette. When Peter complained that regulation swords were too small for him, Washington ordered that a suitable weapon be made for him.

After the Revolution, Peter served as the doorkeeper of the Virginia House of Delegates. There are folk stories from Virginia commemorating Peter's strength. In one, Francisco was irritated by a man on horseback who had come to challenge him to a wrestling match. Peter picked up horse and rider and set them over a fence and off his property.

That anyone would wish to engage in fisticuffs or wrestle with a man of Peter's size and reputation seems incredible, but the stories say that Peter was often challenged. The post-Revolutionary Peter was a man of peace and, in his later years, a devout Christian.

The earliest printed source I know for the fiddle tune "Peter Francisco" is G.P. Knauff's collection, *Virginia Reels, Vol. 2*, published in 1839. I have encountered the tune just once in living tradition. The late Willet Tarrey, of Trade, Johnson County, Tennessee, performed it during the late 1940s on drop-thumb banjo as "Peter The Giant."

There is one recording in print. The Fuzzy Mountain String Band from North Carolina derived their 1972 version from the Knauff collection, transposing the tune from F to D. It is found on their fine LP *Summer Oaks And Porch* on Rounder Records.

"Jenny Lind" is also a commemorative tune, but the woman it celebrates is a manufactured heroine, a subject who had more in common with Elvis Presley and the Beatles than with Anthony Wayne or Peter Francisco. She was a Swedish singer, born in 1820 and trained in opera. She had become highly successful as a popular singer in Europe before her introduction to the United States by P.T Barnum in 1850.

Barnum was a great master of advertising, show business, hype, humbug, and snake oil. Lind's tour made him rich, and the attention he focused upon "The Swedish Nightingale" makes the mania generated a century later by Presley and the Beatles seem almost trivial by comparison. Barnum biographers doubt that the showman ever uttered the phrase most often attributed to him, "There's a sucker born every minute." But he proved the comment true so often as to make immaterial whether he said it or not.

Born in 1810 in Connecticut, Phineas Taylor Barnum had been hood-winking the gullible thousands at his American Museum in New York before Jenny Lind came to his attention. Displaying what he called a "Feejee mermaid"—the fused body of a monkey and fish, dried and shellacked—he treated the nation to the spectacle of learned doctors of science arguing in the newspapers over the authenticity of this humbug.

Barnum's biggest success before Lind resulted from his exploitation of a twenty-five-inch-tall Connecticut midget named Charles M. Stratton, whom he renamed "General Tom Thumb." Barnum hired Stratton and his mother and father under a long-term contract, for the sum of seven dollars a week and board. He dressed Tom Thumb in a Napoleon-style suit and sword, put him in a tiny carriage, and taught him light conversation so he could talk in public. Taken on a national tour, Thumb was a sensation, a fountain of paid admissions.

In Salt Lake City, the diminutive general conversed with Utah governor and Mormon patriarch Brigham Young. The small easterner plied the leader of the Saints with questions about his state and religion. But he got his comeuppance when he commented, "Governor, all this seems understandable except the polygamy. I don't understand why you would want twenty-six wives." To which Young responded, "Son, when I was your size, I didn't understand it myself."

In 1845, Barnum took Tom Thumb on a European tour that was more successful than his American tours. He was especially successful in France, bamboozling the King and showing that, although Paris had a vaunted reputation for sophistication, it then seemed to be as well populated with suckers as Omaha.

Barnum had never seen or heard Jenny Lind before bringing her to the United States. He knew her only in press accounts from Europe, where she had been popular since 1844. In Prussia, students unhitched horses and pulled her carriage themselves. Royalty fawned upon her, led by Britain's Queen Victoria and Prince Albert. Composer Felix Mendelssohn was her patron and carefully denied a love relationship.

And Barnum had the Elssler example. Fanny Elssler was a dancer from Vienna who had toured America between 1840 and 1842. Her dancing bordered on what was then considered risqué—it would be reasonable to call her America's first sex goddess, in a line that led to Clara Bow, Marilyn

Monroe, and Madonna. She'd been a huge success, the first to endorse products for a fee. There were Elssler shoes, stockings, garters, fans, cigars, shaving soap, bootjacks, and bread. Barnum saw Elssler in New Orleans, and borrowed pages from the book of Elssler's promoter, Stephen Price.

Jenny Lind had endorsed hats, coats, cigars, and oysters before she arrived in the United States, and the gush of merchandising in her name was not to be equaled until the Mickey Mouse mania of the 1930s or the football endorsements of the 1980s.

"Not a day passes," wrote a contemporary New York diarist, "without some article lauding her talents until Jenny Lind is in every mouth . . . everything is Jenny Lind. When she arrived on Sunday from England, thousands of people swarmed the docks eager to glimpse the 'Divine Creature.' Her carriage to the hotel could hardly make its way through the dense crowds. At night she was serenaded and by day the Irving House was besieged by men, women, and children eager to peek at her."

The newspapers estimated the crowds milling about her hotel at 30,000. They reported a street fistfight that resulted from a struggle to possess a peach stone she supposedly dropped from her balcony. One enterprising speculator secured what he claimed to be one of her gloves, dropped from her carriage, and charged twenty-five cents to kiss the outside of it and fifty cents the inside.

Barnum showed his skills at bagging the bird *boobus Americanus* with a gush of articles that praised Lind's beauty, her goodness, her wondrous skill as a singer, and her generosity. Of course, Jenny's generosity was also organized by Barnum. He said she wanted to give money to fire departments and orphanages. When the firemen and orphans came to see Jenny, he selected the recipients and made sure the press was there. It was much cheaper than paid ads and far more effective.

For her first New York concert, tickets were auctioned at $225. Boston scorned such emotionalism, but soon $625 was paid for the first ticket at its own auction. This was only six years after Barnum had contracted to pay $7 a week to Tom Thumb's family for the labors of mother, father, and Tom.

The national uproar over Jenny Lind attracted the attention of the British press. Reflecting an age-old British tendency to view Americans with a mixture of envy and contempt, editorial writers worried that the mania exposed an American weakness that some future political madman might exploit. How quickly they'd forgotten how "Jennymania" had earlier felled the British upper classes, and that their august Queen and consort had been suckers before Barnum took the prize in hand.

Were all Americans taken in? Not all. From the beginning, there were jokes about Phineas and the nuts he was rooking.

What was Jenny Lind really like? Despite all Barnum's praise for her divine form and matchless beauty, daguerreotypes reveal a pleasant but rather plain appearance. And her voice? The consensus of knowledgeable listeners was that it was very good, but certainly not flawless. The well-known Scottish critic Thomas Carlyle said that her voice had "little richness of tone" and that her program was "mere nonsense to sing and act."

But Jenny's real program was money. During her nine-month tour of every major city, she gave 95 concerts, with gross receipts of $712,161. From that amount, Jenny got $176,675. Barnum's profits were in the half-million range, a fabulous fortune at the time. Measured in constant dollars, it is still by far the most financially successful entertainment tour in American history.

Is there a lesson in all this? Actually, there are six.

1. Not all commemorative fiddle tunes celebrate real heroes.
2. "Celebrities" can be defined as a class of people who are recognizable to everyone, although they may never have done anything useful for anyone, including themselves.
3. People who do not know what they like—and who are willing to enrich some oily-tongued fad-making rogue to decide for them—have been around for centuries.
4. "Thundering herd mania" can improve the profits for a music, but not its sound.
5. If you ever find yourself greatly admiring the newest and most popular, it is a good idea to be tested for imbecile fever.
6. Not even Barnum would have been able to figure out how to make big money from bluegrass, so it is okay for him to be dead.

NOTE

1. *Bluegrass Unlimited* editor's note: The Stanley Brothers, during the early to mid '50s, did a variation of the tune, which they called "Wild Horse." It was recorded while they were under contract to Starday Records. In order to correspond with its flip side, "Christmas Is Near," the tune was renamed, "Holiday Pickin'." Flatt and Scruggs also did a variant, which they recorded on the *Flatt and Scruggs at Carnegie Hall* LP as "Fiddle and Banjo."

Rachel and the
Eighth of January

. . . .

The sprightly little tune called "Rachel"[1] honors the memory of a musician. She was a musician notable for courage, great beauty, and for a considerable posthumous influence upon the political affairs of the United States. A later title for her tune is "Texas Quickstep."

Rachel Donelson was born in the Yadkin Valley of North Carolina in 1767. Her family crossed the mountain to what would become eastern Tennessee when Rachel was twelve. During the hard winter of 1779–80, they built rafts and floated down the Holston and Tennessee rivers to middle Tennessee, then at the raw edge of the frontier. There are stories from this time of Rachel's courage, beautiful singing, and dark beauty. Her father, John Donelson, became one of the founders of Nashville.

Rachel married Kentuckian Lewis Robards, and was soon unhappy. She moved back to her family home and then fled to Natchez, Mississippi, to escape the threats of the man she called "a beast." Divorce was then so rare as to be nearly unthinkable. It required an act by a state legislature, but Rachel was living in a territory. Robards applied to the Virginia assembly for a divorce, and a frontier newspaper reported that it had been granted.

From *Bluegrass Unlimited* magazine, May 1988.

In 1791, Rachel married Andrew Jackson—Nashville lawyer, politician, speculator, militia leader, and friend of her family. Two years later, Andrew and Rachel learned that no divorce had been granted, and that Rachel was living in bigamy. They quickly had the matter rectified, but this incident—which would be considered trivial today—was to follow them and Jackson's political career throughout their lives.

While only a boy during the Revolution, Andrew Jackson received a saber cut from an intemperate British officer. He then lived in South Carolina, but moved west with the frontier, first to the eastern then to the middle portion of what was to become the state of Tennessee.

Jackson held to an ancient code of honor, one that reasoned that a fight to the death was appropriate whenever matters of principle were in serious dispute. In 1806, he and Charles Dickinson quarreled over a horse race, and a challenge to a duel was issued. In that duel, Jackson was wounded and Dickinson was shot dead.

The chilling prospect of seeing the red hair and cold blue eyes of Andrew over the business end of a pistol had stilled criticism of the marital status of Andrew and Rachel Jackson in Tennessee. But lies, rumors, and innuendos were unearthed and embellished when Jackson ran for the presidency in 1824 and 1828. In this arena, there was little that Andrew could do to protect the reputation of the woman that he loved with such single-minded, fierce, and gentle devotion. In political broadsides, Rachel was described as a strumpet or worse. There was general agreement that, if Andrew were elected, she would never be accepted in Washington's genteel society, which was then dominated by office-holding aristocrats from cotton states.

Rachel died shortly after Andrew was elected to his first term in 1828, and before he took office. He believed that a factor in her demise was the raft of sly suggestions so unfairly heaped upon her for so long. Some biographers believe that he swore revenge upon her grave.

One of the most beautiful of Southern antebellum mansions is The Hermitage, the home that Jackson built for Rachel between Nashville and Lebanon, Tennessee. There's a curious curve in the road that approaches the mansion. From the upstairs porch, one can see that the road is built in the shape of a guitar, the mansion set at the end of the sound box and floral plantings showing the place of the sound hole.

Those expert in the diffusion of musical instruments in America will tell you that there were no guitars that early in Tennessee, but the Jackson family had one, and it was played by a daughter-in-law: Sarah York Jackson, wife of Andrew Jackson, Jr. He was Rachel's nephew and was adopted by the childless Jacksons. The guitar was made in France and brought by Sarah from Philadelphia to Tennessee. It is still at The Hermitage, and on display in the back parlor.

There's also an old banjo at The Hermitage, one that has been there since the mansion was in the Jackson family. Was it played by one of Jackson's slaves or by a member of the family? There is unfortunately no documentation of who the player was and—given the period—it could have been either. Embedded in this question is a reminder that, for its first 200 years on these shores, the banjo was a black man's instrument. Accounts of banjo playing in the 1700s by travelers and others invariably describe blacks.[2]

Andrew Jackson was the first president from west of the Blue Ridge, and the first non-aristocrat. He had become a man of considerable wealth in Tennessee, a speculator in slaves, land, and horses. He was often an advocate for the interests of land speculators, and an opponent of poor land seekers and squatters.

His alliances did not change as president. The infamous "Trail of Tears" removal of the southeastern Indian tribes from their lands to Oklahoma, a land grab of epic and horrible proportion, was made possible by his administration. Among the very few in public life who opposed that removal—as well as most other works of Andrew—was his bitter political enemy, Tennessee Congressman David Crockett. But though the presidency was usually identified with men of means, cotton states aristocrats saw Jackson's election as the coming of the rabble—the great unwashed— Alexander Hamilton's worst and snobbish predictions realized.

Wives of Kitchen Cabinet members—led by the aristocratic Mrs. John C. Calhoun, wife of the vice president—snubbed Peggy Eaton, the wife of Jackson's Secretary of War. The beautiful Mrs. Eaton was the daughter of a Washington innkeeper, and the great ladies found it impossible to accept a person of such gritty origins. Moreover, there were rumors that she had been intimate with her husband before their marriage. Who would wish to associate with such a terrible person? This social flap made Jackson recall the unfair treatment accorded Rachel, and his blood boiled. When the Cabinet members were unable or unwilling to control the social slights of their wives, Jackson fired the Cabinet.

Jackson also had difficulties with the husband of the *grande dame* Calhoun. At that time, the vice president was not beholden to the president for his election, and could be a separate political power in government. Vice President Calhoun was a native of South Carolina, where resistance to a strong national government was bubbling.

When Calhoun created a social occasion to test him, with toasts praising states' rights and the doctrine of nullification, Jackson was ready. He heard twenty-one toasts praising the dissolution of the union, then arose to his six feet and one inch, glass in hand, ramrod thin and straight, and spat a seven-word response that shook the cotton states: "Our federal union: it must be preserved!" It was clear that the first populist president would raise an army and a gallows and make short work of a rebellion and its leaders. (Rebellion would have to wait a generation for the coming of the bumbling Buchanan, a president with no fire in his belly.)

After two terms as president, Jackson still had Rachel's Bible, her portrait and the house he built for her. He lived for seventeen years after her passing and never remarried.

The association of the melody "Rachel" with the memory of Rachel Donelson Jackson is based, in part, upon an anecdote told by East Tennessee fiddler Charlie Bowman.[3] Bowman had learned some of his tunes between 1910 and 1915, in Sullivan County, Tennessee, from an older fiddler named Ford, a veteran of the Civil War. And Ford had learned his fiddling from his grandfather, an early resident of the Blountville area. Bowman was living in Union City, Georgia, when he was interviewed in June 1959.

> Old Ford told me that his grandpa was in Blountville when Jackson went north to be president. They came up the old coach road, a bunch of them. They stopped and there was speeches, and he played the two Jackson pieces. One was "The Eighth of January." You know that. That's the day Jackson beat the Englishmen, away back yonder [January 8, 1815]. The other one was "Rachel." That was for the woman Jackson married. He said that the president come over and shook his hand and thanked him.

"Eighth of January"[4] has the same tune as "The Battle of New Orleans." The words of the latter song are new, composed by James Morris (Jimmy Driftwood) of Timbo, Arkansas, during the 1950s. But the tune is old and in the public domain, and has been recorded with some regularity since the Arkansas Barefoot Boys recorded it with two harmonicas in 1930. There's even an unrelated second tune called "Eighth of January," also traditional and found among some Tennessee old-timers. It was recorded during the 1920s by Grand Ole Opry pioneer Dr. Humphrey Bate and his band.

The date refers to a well-remembered occasion when Andrew Jackson's 5,400 backcountry boys and French freebooters met Major General Sir Edward Pakenham's 10,084 British soldiers. Pakenham kept half of his men in reserve, while Jackson put almost all of his into the fight. It was a mighty American victory, and during the last century the eighth of January was a date as well known and as honored as the fourth of July.

According to one eyewitness, that day's battle left 700 of Pakenham's men dead, 1,400 wounded, and 500 as prisoners. Jackson's losses for the day were 13 killed, 30 wounded, and 19 missing. Jackson's losses for the entire campaign (December 23 through January 17) were modest: 57 killed, 183 wounded, and 93 missing.

A peace treaty had been drafted two weeks earlier in Europe, without the news reaching Jackson or Pakenham. That draft was ratified by the U.S. Senate on February 15 and proclaimed by President Madison on February 17. So some have said that the New Orleans engagement had no effect upon the outcome of the war. But people of the nineteenth century saw the engagement differently, and not because they were unsophisticated.

Since the United States had won its independence, there had been many humiliations for Americans: seamen impressed into the British navy by force, and other jarring reminders of British primacy. Washington had been taken and the White House burned. True independence came when it became clear that meddling in the Americas would have an unacceptably high cost. General Jackson became a hero in every part of the nation by leading the frontiersmen who delivered that message with resounding force.

The Monroe Doctrine that warned European powers against interfering in the western hemisphere was pronounced, a dozen years later, by

President James Monroe (a blood relative of a musician we all know and love [Bill Monroe]), and derived much of its real meaning from Andrew Jackson's work on the eighth of January.

So play these tunes with the knowledge that they honor heroism and the memories of Rachel and Andrew, who shared a deep and enduring love. But a word of caution—we urge you to treat Rachel's little tune gently. Else you may be roused from your sleep by a skinny ghost with the gleam of cold blue fire in his eyes.

Many thanks to the following for their suggestions and assistance: Jim Isenogle of the Jean Lafitte National Historical Park in New Orleans; Bobby Fulcher of the Tennessee Department of Conservation; Fletch Coke and Marsha Mullin of the Ladies' Hermitage Association; and Wayne Shrubsall of Albuquerque, New Mexico.

NOTES

1. Fiddle and banjo versions of "Rachel" have been recorded by Tommy Jackson, Larry Richardson, and Bob Paisley and the Southern Grass, among others.

2. The adaptation of the banjo by whites seems to have occurred over several generations, but after the frontier had moved as far west as the Blue Ridge.

3. During the 1920s Bowman toured and recorded with The Hill Billies, a Washington, D.C. string band, composed of players from the Carolina-Tennessee-Virginia border country. It was this band that gave hillbilly music its name, in a process similar to how bluegrass received its name some thirty years later.

4. Instrumental versions of "Eighth of January" have been recorded by the Fox Chasers, Scotty Stoneman, Chubby Wise, Benny Martin, Eric Weissberg and Marshall Brickman, Tony Rice, Tommy Jackson, and many others.

Durang's Dance
and Hoffmaster's Tune

· ·

It is late in the third set, and the noisy barroom crowd has already yelled most of the requests that Berline, Hickman, and Crary might be expected to play. Dan Crary is tuning his guitar and has an eye on Byron Berline that seems to say a fiddle tune might be expected next. It is time to slip in a different request. "Hey, how about 'Durang's Hornpipe?'"

Berline snaps to attention. "Hey, yourself," he responds. "Now that's a fine tune, Durang's old deranged hornpipe." He fiddles with his fine tuners for a moment, tries his bow once, and eyes Crary, who announces, "For the deranged among you, Byron is about to perform 'Durang's Hornpipe.'" They play the old tune with loving attention, obviously enjoying it.

"Durang's Hornpipe" is one of many historic fiddle tunes that live in the repertoires of better fiddlers. It is not an especially common tune, nor is it particularly uncommon. Nowadays it is more likely to be found at a western musical gathering, but its origins are in the East. It takes its name from John Durang, the first American-born person to win wide recognition as a dancer.

From *Bluegrass Unlimited* magazine, November 1982.

Born in Lancaster, Pennsylvania, in 1768, John Durang began his long career in 1784 at Philadelphia's Southwark Theatre and soon became widely known for his specialty, an acrobatic hornpipe which came to be called "Durang's Dance."

Hornpipes are a type of tune, like rags or polkas. They are very old and take their name from the instruments upon which they were originally performed, flute-like instruments made from the horns of animals. The dances associated with these ancient tunes are lively solo dances, and are antecedents of both ballet and tap dancing. Ballet historians tend to ignore this, preferring to stress the relationship of ballet to dancing in the French courts of the eighteenth century.

In 1785, Durang and his fellow dancers and players moved to New York City, where they were met with a hostile reception. Theater and dancing had a bad local reputation; these had been favorite preoccupations of the British garrison during the city's occupation. The companies in which Durang worked incorporated patriotic themes, and, as opposition to theater eased, the dancer toured widely, ranging from Quebec to Washington City, although he danced most often in Philadelphia and New York.

During his first season in New York, Durang commissioned the writing of a tune for his dance by a well-known New York fiddler, a three-foot-tall German dwarf named Hoffmaster. During the season of President Washington's first inauguration [1789], the capitol was in New York, where Durang's company was then located. The President attended this theater frequently. In 1794, Durang participated in the premier of *Tammany*, one of the first operas written in America with an American theme. Durang's part was an "Indian dance."

Durang was also a pantomimist, actor, manager, and director. When well-schooled European ballet companies flooded the American stage in the late eighteenth century, he survived the competition and learned ballet. He played the role of Harlequin in harlequinades; danced hornpipes "on thirteen eggs, blindfolded without breaking one;" and was a featured member of Ricketts' Circus troupe.

John Durang's father Jacob, a native of Alsace Lorraine, had served in the York County Militia during the American Revolution. John and two of his sons, Charles and Ferdinand, served in the Pennsylvania Militia during the War of 1812. Charles was in the embattled battery at North Point, Baltimore, where Francis Scott Key was inspired to write "The Star Spangled Banner." It was Ferdinand who arranged these words to the tune of the English song "Anacreon in Heaven" to make our national anthem. Ferdinand was the first to sing the new song in public, at the Holiday Street Theater in Baltimore, while Charles led the chorus.

As Byron finished the old tune I glanced out the window to the rainy parking lot. Leaning against a pickup was a small fellow, about three feet tall, playing the fiddle, while a handsome fellow in sailor costume danced on the tailgate. The dancer caught my eye and said something. The glass was thick and he had to say it again, but this time I read his lips. He said, "It didn't all begin in 1945" [a reference to the year in which the classic edition of Bill Monroe's Blue Grass Boys was assembled].

John Dee Holeman
Juba Dancer

● ●

John Dee Holeman, a native of North Carolina, is one of a very few remaining practitioners of juba dance, and by far the most skilled. He is
also a talented blues musician and "toast" speaker. I ask that you give particular attention to his dancing skills and consider his music and toasting
as frosting on a very fine cake.

The use of complex handclap rhythms to provide timing for dancers
is an ancient technique practiced by Africans and African Americans for
at least three-and-a-half centuries. The best compilation of early accounts
of it is found in a meticulous study of black music prior to the Civil War,
Sinful Tunes and Spirituals: Black Folk Music to the Civil War, Dena J. Epstein,
University of Illinois Press, 1977.

African handclapping to give timing for songs and dance was reported
by early European travelers to that continent. Richard Jobson's 1621 account of enslavements and the transport of victims includes a description
of handclappers providing rhythms for dance.

Nomination for the National Endowment for the Arts' National Heritage Fellowship, awarded
in 1988.

Many of those brought to the slave pens and the ships waiting offshore were skilled in the use of drums to make complex music. Their captors learned to fear drums and drumming. They might call people together. They carried messages. They could help unify people.

On September 9, 1739, a slave named Jemmy led a rebellion at Stono, South Carolina, and his "seventy-five to eighty" followers marched to the sound of two drums. A few months later, the South Carolina Slave Act of 1740 was enacted, banning drums and drumming. Drums had been prohibited even earlier in other locations. Later insurrections strengthened the bans and extended them throughout the slaveholding states.

The prohibition of this important instrument undoubtedly influenced the course taken by black music. One development seems beyond question: much of the rhythmic complexity of drumming was taken up by the juba handslappers and dancers. Among the arts of black people, juba has a singular distinction: no one seems to have ever claimed that it came from anywhere other than Africa or was developed or influenced by anyone other than African Americans.

The first academic notice of juba came in the 1830s, when American poets became interested in the metrical complexity of these rhythms. Juba was the subject of correspondence between Edgar Allen Poe and other poets. Poe's friend, Thomas Holly Chivers, called it: "a Jig which must be accompanied by a measured clapping of the thighs and alternately upon each other. . . . there is no such rhythm in Greek poetry—nor, in fact, in any nation under the sun. There is no dance in the world like that of Juba . . . the very climax of jocularity."

In 1880, poet Sidney Lanier used juba as an example in discussing the uses of pauses in poetry: "I have heard a Southern Plantation 'hand,' in 'patting juba' for a comrade to dance by, venture upon quite complex successions of rhythm, not hesitating to syncopate, to change the rhythmic accent for a moment, or to indulge in other highly specialized variations of the current rhythmus."

Born in 1929 in Orange County, North Carolina, Mr. Holeman learned juba rhythm and dance at country dances. When the musicians took a break, it was customary for males to engage in competitive solo dancing to handslapped rhythms. Mr. Holeman knows the term "juba," but "slapping" or "patting" were more common terms for the rhythm in his area.

The dance done to the juba rhythm is also called "buck dance," "bust down," "jigging," and (infrequently) "flatfoot" when performed to music from instruments, but Southern country dance terminology is very elastic and changes with place. Mountain "flatfoot" differs from Piedmont "flatfoot."

Juba is both the complex hand rhythms and the dance traditionally done to them. The relatively familiar "hambone" is a bit of juba-like rhythm that takes its name from a rhyme ("Hambone, Hambone, where you been . . ."), common since the heyday of the minstrel troupes.

Those who have written the history of vernacular dance in our nation have tended to rely heavily upon their imaginations. This is in part because of the complexity [of the dance art]. Scores of folk and popular dances have appeared, flourished briefly, then disappeared—often through combinations with newer dances or movements. Those skilled in dance notation have only recently become interested in these dances. That juba is the primary precursor of tap dance is obvious, and a fine summary of the process was given by tap dancer Willy Smith in 1939: "Its just the old Southern 'bust down' put on a stage. People have been doing that thing forever."

Like all truly great traditional folk performers, Mr. Holeman has selected and shaped his repertoire with a keen sense of self. It matters little whether an item is old or new, black or white, popular or not. What matters is whether it fits. Recently he reacted to a bluesman friend, performing a song he had not heard before and liked, "Now let me try that on. I might want to take it with me!"

Mr. Holeman's first blues influences were the players who lived nearby; he first heard blues on store porches and at house dances. Nearby Durham was a center for the Piedmont blues style and home of Blind Boy Fuller, the hero of all Piedmont players. Mr. Holeman performs many Fuller pieces, but not exactly like Fuller performed them. He is of the second generation of players, those exposed to traveling bluesmen from other areas and to recordings from the Delta and Chicago.

Mr. Holeman also heard and interacted with white country music performers. Uncle Dave Macon is as much a part of his early "listening to radio" memories as Mississippi John Hurt.

He recalls the first time he saw the juba dance and heard the rhythm. "I was little, but it hit me: Lord, if I could do that, I'd always be all right."

Dance All Night

· ·

with Ken Landreth

D ance is an integral part of the rich musical culture of Southwest Virginia. When music fires up at fiddler's conventions, concerts, or on porches, slapping feet are not far behind. The exciting rhythm of flatfoot dancing originated with early settlers from England, Ireland, and Scotland, and evolved alongside old-time fiddle tunes in mountain communities. Dancers are as much a part of America's musical heritage as fiddlers and banjo players.

Settlers from the British Isles brought with them a unique brand of step dancing, descended from ancient dances that go back into the dim mists of European history. It was marked by rhythmic slapping of the feet—to create a percussive rhythm—while the frame of the dancer remained relatively motionless. In the Virginia backcountry, English clog dancers melded their dance steps with those of Irish step dancers and African buck dancers. The resulting amalgam became known as "flatfooting" or just "dancing."

Dancing became as vital a part of musical gatherings as a good fiddle tune. Like fiddlers who introduced regional variations, flatfoot dancers

Adapted from the program book distributed at the Abingdon (Virginia) Crooked Road Music Fest, October 5–7, 2012.

developed unique styles, reflecting the local preferences of their mountain communities. Fancy steps were added, given unusual names, and passed to the next generation. Jay Burris, one of the best dancers ever to grace a Galax [Virginia] dance floor, called a particular dance step "cutting the pigeon-wing." (The famed early American show dancer, John Durang, a favorite of President Washington, had also used that step and term.)

Flatfoot dancing was competitive in early America, and remains so. Youthful dancers compete for the attention of suitors at social events, and all ages compete for prizes at contests across the Southeast. The best musicians are often the best dancers, so dance competition categories were added to community fiddle contests in colonial times, and the winning dancer is as respected as the champion fiddler.

Flatfooting was common in homes before electronic entertainment interfered. Music and dancing were part of rituals such as corn shuckings and holiday gatherings. In early times, the fiddler might be strategically seated in the "dogtrot" entryway between two cabins under a single roof, with dancers in both cabins. An up-tempo tune might lead to vigorous dancing, causing the split round logs of a puncheon floor to break down and spill the dancers. Thus, any fast tune became a "breakdown."

In 1928, Bascom Lamar Lunsford presented flatfoot dancers at the Mountain Dance and Folk Festival in Asheville, North Carolina (the first event to be billed as a "folk festival"). At first these were individual dancers, but choreographed dances with flatfooting were soon added to square dance routines, and team dancing received its own competition category. In 1939 one such dance team performed at the White House during a visit by the king and queen of England. The queen remarked on the similarity of the dance to English clogging, and "team clogging" got its name.

Today's dancers and clogging teams excite audiences with newer steps and exaggerated body movements. Dudley Culp formed the Green Grass Cloggers, the most influential of these teams, in 1971. Culp had attended the Union Grove [North Carolina] Fiddlers Convention and learned clogging steps from Evelyn Farmer, a musician, singer, and dancer from Fries, Virginia. The Green Grass team devised energetic routines with high kicks, unconventional steps, and choreography based on four-couple western square-dance figures. Dressed in flowing calico dresses, jeans, and black hard-sole brogan shoes, they toured widely and brought clogging to audiences worldwide.

Nowadays, hundreds of precision clogging teams emulate and build upon the style, costumes, and steps introduced by the Green Grass Cloggers. Exciting as it is, the new form differs significantly from traditional Appalachian flatfooting, a solitary dance where the body remains relatively motionless, and feet stay close to the ground.

But don't worry about "saving" this fine old dance tradition. Bright-eyed young dancers, eager to compete, still line up at fiddler's conventions. And traditional flatfooting can still be seen—on porches, at family holiday gatherings, and every night of the week at community jams—along Southwest Virginia's Crooked Road.

The Toby Character

When Bluegrass Bands Needed Lightning Rod Salesmen

● ●

There was a time when bluegrass faintly resembled ballet or, perhaps, modern dance, with musicians ducking in and out and executing near pirouettes in order to reach the one microphone. During that time, one member of the band often wore baggy pants, a silly hat, and had blacked-out teeth. Most such comedians belong to a category called Toby clowns.

Toby has a long and complex history in American entertainment. His antecedents made people laugh in the 1790s, when Scotsman John Bill Ricketts ("Ricketts' Hornpipe" is named for him) organized the first American circus and laced it with comedy and hornpipe dancing, along with equestrian acts and acrobatics.

In some of those early shows, Toby was called Brother Jonathan. His humorous comments, reflecting American political opinion during the post-Revolutionary era, made him a symbol of the young nation. Cartoons from that period show Brother Jonathan tall, gangling, and earthy, with pants and waistcoat too short, wearing a battered hat. Printed jokes attributed to Brother Jonathan reveal him to be a sharp-tongued wit, with inci-

From *Bluegrass Unlimited* magazine, October 1982.

sive views on matters social or political. His depiction contrasted sharply with the effete contemporary portrayals of European national figures. (Our familiar Uncle Sam character draws upon Brother Jonathan, but arose in a later period.)

Small traveling circuses were an important entertainment medium in the 1800 to 1850 period, and Toby was found in many of them. As national interests changed, he became less political but remained pointedly rural and unabashedly all-American in outlook.

The Toby character was greatly influenced by the blackface minstrel phenomenon. Minstrel shows began in the 1840s and continued to be a major force in American popular entertainment until the 1890s—to some degree, even into the 1950s.

Toby took to the vaudeville stage, the touring tent variety show, and the medicine show early in their existence. As he made his way through the decades, Toby acquired his name and a more or less standardized costume, which usually included baggy pants and an oversized wide necktie. There were other elements that the individual Toby could add if he wished: a shaggy red wig, a battered hat, an oversized loudly checked shirt or coat, blacked-out teeth, giant shoes, or perhaps an oversized bow tie.

Along with the costume came an attitude: Toby was a bold rube with a quick wit who unabashedly said what many in his audience could only think. He was grateful for any opportunity to insult the boss or any other high and mighty folks who might be around. He had trouble with his girlfriend, the weather, and the boll weevil, but had figured out ways to master them and a plan to put himself on top. His jokes and banter are familiar to modern audiences from their television use by Red Skelton. Other popular comedians who borrowed parts of their act from Toby include Charlie Chaplin, Emmett Kelley, Buster Keaton, and Charlie Weaver.

Toby has been a good musician, too. During the minstrel period he became a banjoist, and comedy became closely associated with banjo playing. Hence the comment attributed to banjoist Uncle Dave Macon when he first saw the young Earl Scruggs: "He plays good, but he ain't a damn bit funny."

Perhaps the best-known banjo-playing Toby nowadays [1982] is South Carolina banjo patriarch Snuffy Jenkins, who influenced Earl Scruggs's complex banjo rolls if not his comedy. Another Jenkins banjo student,

Don Reno, was more tractable in learning comedy. Reno's portrayal of the outrageous Chicken Hot Rod was Toby comedy at its best.

Toby has played other instruments. Country music pioneer Gid Tanner was a fiddling Toby. The influential early country guitarist Sam McGee delighted audiences in his Toby role. Clell Summey (Cousin Jody) played steel guitar and brought Toby to southern audiences via filmed television segments of the Grand Ole Opry during the 1950s.

Toby's infatuation with the banjo continued into the 1940s and 1950s. In blackface, old-time banjoist Clarence "Tom" Ashley brought his minstrel-based Toby to Charlie Monroe and the Stanley Brothers' live acts until the mid-1950s [see "Clarence 'Tom' Ashley"].

Let's stop in on the Charlie Monroe show and see one of Ashley's "Rastus Jones from Georgia" skits, with all the band members playing roles. Charlie is a fine actor as a harried executive, too bothered by loafers and salesmen to finish his work. His office is behind a door at the side of the stage, and there Rastus knocks, seeking employment.

Charlie emerges, enraged by still another interruption. Rastus responds to the dressing down he receives by offering to be paid to keep everyone else away. That puts a new light on matters, and Charlie carefully examines Rastus as a potential employee. In his examination, Charlie opines that Rastus's pants seem a bit too short. "No," responds Rastus, "I'se just down in 'em too far."

Hired for the munificent sum of five dollars a day, Rastus finds a huge wooden club, seats himself, puts his feet up on a table, and tells the audience that his ship has come in and that this job is better than various ones he's been fired from recently. He waves the club and tells what he'll do to anyone who might cause him to lose this one.

Charlie has made it clear that one interruption is one too many, and nobody is important enough to interrupt him today. Then the band members begin arriving, each with an urgent and important reason to see Charlie. One is a lazy brother-in-law, there to borrow money. Another is a lawyer, bearing news of an inheritance Charlie is to receive. Rastus's position is delicate. He is black, so, despite earlier threats, he really can't chase them away. He resorts to strategies that include outrageous lies.

He welcomes the brother-in-law, telling him that Charlie will be out soon, that he is busy preparing a list of the work he wants the brother-in-law to do. Rastus describes the various jobs in sweaty detail, and the lazy brother-in-law soon flees.

The lawyer bearing gifts is turned away by Rastus's comments about Charlie's intense dislike for his deceased benefactor and his lack of need for the money. To be sure the point is not missed, Rastus makes it clear: "Dat man need another $10,000 like I need another hole in my socks."

The final visitor is an aggressive and abusive lightning rod salesman. Rastus is reduced to physically blocking the path to Charlie's door. In desperation, Rastus mentions that he has a house and is scared of lightning. Diverted by this new victim, the salesman immediately begins writing a contract and loudly demanding a down payment. Rastus has only a nickel, and he drops it on the floor. It rolls under the table, and the greedy salesman is quickly on his hands and knees, scrambling for the nickel and presenting a broad posterior (stuffed with a pillow) to the audience.

Rastus picks up his club and asks the audience with signs if he should hit the inviting target. There is a unanimous roar of approval, and Rastus goes into an elaborate and hilarious batting preparation. The audience is surprised by the mighty lick he eventually delivers, loudly shattering the club, which has been carefully sawed in advance.

Possibly because Earl Scruggs had transformed the banjo away from a comedy instrument, Toby most often became a bass player in early country and bluegrass bands. He also lost his name; he became Cousin Wilbur, Uncle Josh, Cousin Jake, Old Dad, Humphhammer, Cousin Winesap, Uncle Snort, Mutt Highpockets, or Cousin Mort. He sang in quartets and—as in the past—had a keen eye for pretty girls and suffered an accident-prone existence.

When bluegrass was slicked up for city people, the renamed Toby characters disappeared from the bands. Toby had great appeal to children, but they did not come to the city bars or college concerts. City girls didn't squeal and run when Toby leaped from the stage, vowing to kiss "every dadburned one of them." But beneath the veneer, which passes for sophistication among the less perceptive, there still lurks a delight in the broad humor and extemporaneous banter Toby has brought us for nearly two centuries.

The Hicks and Related Families
Carriers of Tradition
· ·

S tanley Hicks (1911–89) was a good woodworker, and was also well known as a musician, dancer, and storyteller. He learned banjo and dulcimer making from his father, Roby Monroe Hicks (1882–1957), and from his grandfather, Samuel Hicks (1848–1929)—also a respected banjoist and singer. It is not clear whether or not Samuel's father, Civil War veteran Andrew Hicks (1829–1901), was a banjoist, though members of the family assume he was. But Andrew's father, Samuel "Little Sammy" Hicks, Jr. (1798–c.1860), and his grandfather, Samuel "Big Sammy" Hicks (1753–c.1835), were banjoists and singers, according to family historian and taleteller Council Harmon (1806–1890), who said he learned from them. Those members of the Hicks family lived south of the Virginia line in Watauga County, North Carolina, but the family was descended from many generations of Virginians.

Council Harmon, a Hicks grandfather, was a banjoist and singer and the source of the famous Appalachian "Jack tale" stories. Though often assigned to British tradition, these stories are German, arising from the same

From the *Masters of the Banjo* tour book, 1993, National Council for the Traditional Arts [see also "Stanley Hicks"].

oral tradition as those collected by the Grimm brothers. Harmon told his grandchildren that he learned his music and stories from his Hicks relatives. He was a nephew of "Little Sammy" and grandson of "Big Sammy," and lived with them during his formative years.

Council Harmon's posthumous fame as a singer and storyteller spread beyond his family and community when, in 1916, English song collector Cecil Sharp collected sixty-four songs from Jane Gentry of Hot Springs, North Carolina. Harmon was Jane Gentry's maternal grandfather. Other grandchildren in Virginia also proved to be keepers of "Old Counce's" trove of songs and stories.

"Big Sammy" Hicks moved to the Watauga River area of the Blue Ridge in 1780 with his father, David Hicks (then often spelled "Hix"). They had lived farther east in North Carolina, but were born in the Tidewater area of Virginia in Goochland County. No one knows when banjo making and playing became a Hicks tradition, but the family had lived among Tidewater black families for many generations.

The first in this line of the Hicks family was Samuel Hix, who came from England to the Rappahannock River area of the Virginia colony as an indentured servant. He arrived in 1637, when the first English-speaking colony in North America had a population of about 5,000. Between 200 and 300 of these were Africans, most born in Africa. This was before the chattel enslavement of black people was a fully accepted concept in Virginia.

After completing his servitude, this first of many Samuels moved southward. Several generations of his descendants lived along Tuckahoe Creek, in what became a large Hicks community in the Goochland/ Hanover/Amelia County area. This is near the Tuckahoe manor house, built by Thomas Randolph in 1712, and near the Randolph School that Thomas Jefferson attended as a boy with his Randolph first cousins.

In the Tidewater, marriages between the upper-crust Randolph, Jefferson, and Eppes families were frequent. The nearby Hicks family owned much less land, and its members did not attend the Randolph School, but they were also given to intermarriages—with the Harman (also spelled Hamann or Harmon), Holtzclaw, Goulden, and Ward families. These families moved together—to the North Carolina Blue Ridge, the Tennessee Cumberlands, and other areas—as an extended family. In fact, it would be reasonable to refer to them as "the Hicks and related families."

The Harman and Holtzclaw families were of German ancestry. This may explain the Grimm-style stories. It may also account for how the *scheitholt* (from the German *scheitholtz*, a musical instrument from northern Europe now called the Appalachian dulcimer) came into the construction and performance repertoire of the Hicks family. All of the banjo makers discussed above also built and played dulcimers.

Hans Jacob Holtzclaw came to Virginia in 1714 as an indentured servant, along with his family and 11 other German families skilled in iron-working. They were imported from Nassau-Siegen in Westphalia by colonial governor Alexander Spotswood. In 1729, Jacob acquired 680 acres near the Hicks settlement.

A German brought to Henrico County, Virginia, as an indentured servant by Captain William Byrd in 1675, Henry Harman was the first of his line. At that time, at least two members of the Hicks family worked for Byrd at the trading post he operated at the falls of the James River near Richmond.

Did the extended Hicks family leave their black Tidewater neighbors behind upon moving westward into the Blue Ridge? Not quite. "Big Sammy" was listed as the owner of four slaves in 1800. I believe that Council Harmon would not have misled his grandchildren—that he really did learn banjo playing from "Little Sammy" and "Big Sammy," and that their playing precedes the minstrel fad.

I'm indebted to my friends John Henry and Mattie Hicks and to Barnabas B. Hicks for much of the information used in this essay. The 463-page book they co-authored and personally published in 1991, *The Hicks Families of Western North Carolina* (Minor's Printing, 1991), is an excellent documentation of one of the nation's oldest and most artistic families.

Minstrelsy
(or Why Blacks Gave Up the Banjo)

● ●

While black players brought the banjo from Africa to Virginia and were its primary players for over 200 years, they began abandoning it shortly after the Civil War. There are only a handful of black players now. Virtually all banjoists in Virginia and elsewhere are white.

This is a result of minstrelsy. The minstrels in blackface beat black people over the head with the banjo for some seventy years, using it as a foil as they made African Americans the butt of an endless series of cruel and insulting jokes.

Much comedy is not funny if subjected to analysis, and the theatrical comedy and music that was minstrelsy was especially crude. The first big-time minstrel, T.D. Rice, had seen an aged black man with a pronounced limp. His "dance Jim Crow" imitation of the limp was a key part of a black-face song-and-dance routine that he performed in ragged clothing. Thus, the first minstrel and his audience were laughing at the handicapped and the poor. Matters did not improve much in the ensuing decades.

Excerpted from the Introduction to *A Guide to the Crooked Road: Virginia's Heritage Music Trail*, copyright 2006 by The Crooked Road: Virginia's Heritage Music Trail, John F. Blair, Publisher.

Minstrelsy excused slavery. It depicted blacks as endlessly foolish, the unspoken conclusion being that they were subhuman—needing to be owned and told what to do. Yet minstrelsy became the first internationally popular cultural fad to sweep the world. Its effects were so far-reaching that they can still be felt.

The first hugely successful musical group of this pop form was the Virginia Minstrels, formed in New York in 1843. Their show, like all minstrel performances, was a stage production with five carefully rehearsed men in blackface in a row, using banjo, bones, fiddle, vocals, and set-piece jokes. Like later groups, they claimed to have learned their songs from plantation "darkies," but their repertoire was in fact far more Anglo-Scots than black.

One member, banjoist Joel Walker Sweeney, was from Virginia, but the other members were Yankee veterans of the theater. The "Virginia" in their name was yet another claim to plantation origins, a reach for authenticity. A pivotal member of the group, Daniel Decatur Emmett, the composer of "Dixie," "Old Dan Tucker," and scores of other songs, had learned banjo from a white man named Ferguson, a native of "western Virginia."

A huge hit in New York, they were invited to London, where they were also very popular. On their way home, they toured Ireland and helped to inspire the creation of the Irish ceili band. This most traditional of Irish ensembles originated as an imitation of a minstrel band, creating a considerable amount of historical confusion. Today's musicologist, hearing an Irish melody that he has also heard by Appalachian players, automatically assumes that it came to America from Ireland. Sometimes he is wrong. The Virginia Minstrels, and many groups that followed, left an American repertoire in Ireland.

Minstrelsy lasted until around 1910 as a major theatrical and musical form, and reached most of the world. No other dominant popular-music style has lasted as long as minstrelsy, although rock 'n' roll is getting close.

As with all popular fads, material was left behind after minstrelsy passed. A part of that material is repertoire; many of the old banjo tunes have minstrel roots. Another part is the instrument; the fad spread the banjo to various folk populations who put it to good use. The elite who were attracted to the banjo could afford good instruments, so the construction of the instrument was vastly improved. Some songs from that period were good and continue in use today. Modern African popular musics such as High Life, Palmwine, and JuJu have their roots in a form of minstrelsy that went even to Africa, a proof that life is stranger than fiction.

Fries

Where the Music Began

●●●●●●●●●●●●●●●●●●●●●●●●●●●●●

The town of Fries, Virginia—population 697—is the place where the country music industry began. Located in a sheltered cove of the beautiful New River, tiny Fries has had a major impact on American music. Other places in southwestern Virginia's Blue Ridge Mountain counties of Grayson and Carroll also have a rich musical history, but Fries keeps its heritage in a picture-perfect setting.

Incorporated in 1903, Fries became the epitome of an industrial town. Washington Cotton Mills owned the little white houses where the workers lived and all of the businesses in the town. Workers were paid in scrip that could only be spent in company owned stores. It was named for its founder, Colonel Francis Fries (pronounced FREEZE), a visionary North Carolina industrialist who saw the potential for power generation and industrial profit.

This founding gave rise to an enduring joke, that here one freezes in the winter and fries in summer. But the joke could not be more wrong; Fries is located on a stretch of riverbank high in the mountains, and is wonderfully cool in the summer.

From *Bluegrass Unlimited* magazine, June 2009.

It was in this unlikely utopian setting that the country music business was born. In 1923, loom-tender Henry Whitter, an employee of Washington Mills, became the first singer to record a country music record. He invited himself to New York with his guitar, his shoulder-harness-mounted harmonica, and a new song in the Victorian tragic song tradition: "The Wreck of the Southern Old 97."

Vernacular music had been recorded before, but mainly as vaudeville and light popular music. Whitter took the music to another place—one that better represented rural and small-town America, and the keeping of story songs. His song became an international hit and set off a spirited competition with co-workers at the cotton mill.

Three other Fries millhands soon followed him to New York and recorded in major label studios: Ernest V. Stoneman, Kelly Harrell, and John W. Rector, each with his own band. The surge was fueled by Stoneman's disdain for Whitter's musical skills: "We thought if he can do it, anybody can."

Stoneman brought to New York a homemade autoharp, a harmonica, and another big-selling tragedy song, "The Sinking of the Titanic." In the Galax [Virginia] and Washington, D.C. areas, he raised a family band that became prominent on TV filmed and broadcast out of Nashville during the 1960s and 1970s. His son Scott Stoneman became a brilliant bluegrass fiddler and consummate showman. A daughter, Roni Stoneman, became the first female bluegrass banjoist to record, and a comic on *Hee Haw* as well. She continues [2009] the family tradition of performing, some eighty-five years after "Pop" Stoneman helped create the country music business.

John Rector, a storekeeper in Fries and an accomplished banjo player, traveled to New York to record at Whitter's second session. Days after his return, he ventured with his banjo into a Galax barbershop and helped to make country music history. Led by vocalist Al Hopkins, the barbershop string band that was formed that day also traveled to New York and became famous as the Hill Billies. It was the first time the older term "hillbilly" had been applied to anything musical. They gave an enduring name to the music they performed in vaudeville shows and radio broadcasts, from New York to Washington, D.C., and were for a time the best-known country band in the nation [see "The Hill Billies: The Band that Named the Music"].

Recordings by Fries millhands were on ten major recording labels by 1926, and it is doubtful that any other American workplace can claim as much immediate influence upon the popular culture of the nation. But that prominence was relatively brief, as the Great Depression soon brought the recording boom of the 1920s to a halt.

Whitter returned to recording in 1927 with a brilliant partner, fiddler, and vocalist: Gilliam Banmon Grayson, of Johnson County, Tennessee. Recordings by this duo powerfully influenced the Mainer brothers and the Stanley Brothers, and left major tracks in bluegrass repertoire with tunes such as "Lee Highway Blues," "Train 45," "Rose Conley," "Banks Of The Ohio," and many others [see "Grayson and Whitter"].

The Fries millhands gave country music much of its variety. Kelly Harrell recorded Scots-Irish and Anglo ballads. Grayson and Whitter and Stoneman incorporated parlor-music string instruments and song styles and, like the Hill Billies, brought to the studios fiddle and banjo tunes from the dance traditions of colonial Virginia.

It was Ernest Stoneman who persuaded Ralph Peer to bring his 1927 Victor recording foray to Bristol, a venture that led to the first recordings of the Carter Family and Jimmie Rodgers. That session would have been held in Fries had it possessed the necessary facilities. The railroad came to Fries, but the company-owned hotel had only twelve rooms, and neither Fries nor Galax had a Victor sales outlet. So Stoneman brought his family band to Bristol, and served as an agent for Peer in persuading other musicians from the eastern and central Blue Ridge to come to this noted recording session.

When the Great Depression ended the initial recording boom, music continued in Fries. The outstanding fiddler Glen Neaves worked at the same cotton mill for thirty-eight years. In 1935 he joined other millhands Bill and Everett Patton and three-finger banjoist Raymond Swinney in creating a form of music with a remarkable resemblance to bluegrass, a decade before the emergence of that genre. Swinney's adroit and highly syncopated banjo style is an inconvenient problem for historians of folk banjo styles who like to attribute its creation to later and better known players. The music they played has been internationally heralded as the "Galax Sound."

Brilliant and tragically short-lived guitarist, banjoist, and bandleader Jimmy Arnold was born in Fries and made waves in many genres of music during the 1970s. Influential string bands such as the Spring Valley Boys formed within the walls of the cotton mill. And nowadays the most respected old-time fiddler, singer, and banjoist in the region—Eddie Bond—lives in Fries and continues the tradition. Some of this is on display every Thursday evening at the weekly jam session held in a downtown Fries restaurant and open to all.

Since its beginnings in a bend of the Merrimack River in Lowell, Massachusetts, in the 1820s until its recent removal to the new dormitory towns of today's Wal-Mart China, the cotton mill industry has mixed *lumpen* living and utopian rhetoric as it chased the cheapest wage. The cotton mill that Colonel Fries built shut its doors long ago. The brick walls have been hauled to New Orleans to become street pavers. The power dam—made of hand-cut stones that provided electricity to the looms—remains, creating a spectacular waterfall in a pristine river where local folks fish for bass and muskie.

Fries provides easy access to the New River for bicycling, hiking, floating, and boating. The roadway of the fabled New River Train—the train that once delivered raw cotton to the mill—remains, and has been transformed into a bike trail that can be followed for fifty-seven miles. The grades are gentle and the views gorgeous. (Yes, Fries was the destination in the renowned song "The New River Train," recorded by Henry Whitter in 1923. The song itself is said to be a composition of the musical Ward family of Fries.)

The Fries Fiddlers' Convention remains one of the best showcases of regional talent. It is held annually on the third weekend in August, one week after the larger Galax Old Fiddlers' Convention.

So, along with history, there is continuity in this tiny Blue Ridge Mountain community. The wonderful old-time banjoist and fiddler Glenn Smith, who once graced this place and is immortalized in recordings by the Smithsonian Institution's Folkways label, is now gone from Fries, but his grandson Jesse Lovell conducts the Thursday jam session with grace and gentility. And his great-granddaughter Gin Burris is a favorite ballad singer and keeper of old songs of the region.

The clatter of the looms is silenced in Fries, but its music is a living thing. It continues in Fries families with power and grace, not unlike the ancient New River, that begins its tumble from a spring above 5,000 feet in the high part of the Blue Ridge, crossing much of America before reaching the sea, south of New Orleans.

With thanks to Ken Landreth for information and editing only a native son could provide.

Radio and
the Blue Ridge

. . . .

When we got the first radio that had a speaker, we'd set it out here on the porch and people would come listen to it with us. Sometimes the yard was full. Not long after we got it, an old man from over in Beaver Dams was here listening to a boxing match. When the fight heated up and Dempsey began slamming that Frenchman, he began to get real nervous. He said, "Tip, if you don't turn that dang thing off, he's a-goin to kill that feller."

Tipton Madron, Trade, Tennessee, December 25, 1961[1]

It seemed like magic, this box that could grab voices from the wind and reproduce them on headphones or speakers. Here were the words, songs, and tunes of people who stood hundreds of miles away, words heard instantly as they were spoken—the modulations of voice perfectly audible, the intake of breath heard as if inches away. It was magic, a form of transporting, ancient witchcraft made science; the future had arrived.

Excerpted from Charles K. Wolfe and James E. Akenson (ed.), *Country Music Annual, 2001,* University Press of Kentucky. Joe Wilson wrote: "Professor Wolfe put into one of his collections my analysis of early radio and my conclusion that it had huge influence on the development of country music, far more than recordings."

Nowadays, it is common to equate early radio with early television in assessing impact. This is an error. Nothing like radio had happened before. Radio came before sound films and ignited what was called "a craze." That is an apt term, because one has to go back to the ancient manias in Europe to find anything with the intensity of excitement that radio generated.[2]

Radio was made possible by the superheterodyne, the so-called "tuning circuit" invented during World War I by Edwin Armstrong. That new development brought startling clarity to voices carried by radio. Before the superheterodyne—which roughly translates as "above" (super) "other" (hetero) "force" (dyne)—radio had primarily been a medium for wireless telegraphy messages sent point-to-point in code, the wireless companies decoding and delivering them by messenger boys. Hundreds of amateur radio fans owned receiving and sending equipment before this invention, but the idea of "broadcasting" news and entertainment was unthinkable before the superheterodyne.

Change came with amazing rapidity. The first event that could be called a broadcast happened on July 2, 1921: the heavyweight boxing championship match between American Jack Dempsey and French challenger Georges Carpentier. An estimated 300,000 people heard a blow-by-blow description of this fight, the largest audience that had ever simultaneously heard a single speaker.[3]

Corporations began building radio stations as part of their advertising and public relations gambits. Some selected call letters that reflected their business. Chicago radio station WLS was owned by Sears; its call letters were an acronym for "World's Largest Store." Nashville's WSM was owned by the National Life and Accident Insurance Company, and its call letters reflected the company slogan "We Shield Millions."[4] The number of Americans owning a radio soared: a handful in early 1921, 100,000 in 1922, and 500,000 in 1923. There was one station in 1920, 30 in 1922, and 556 in 1923.[5]

The technology of popular entertainment may greatly accelerate the presentation of older art forms and even "use them up" (for example, the use of older films by television). Among older forms taken up by early radio was blackface comedy. This was a popular form that presented racist caricatures derived from the minstrel stage. Such presentations began around 1840, developed into an internationally popular form, and continued to television in the early 1960s, when the early civil rights movement finally pushed it into obscurity[6] [see "Minstrelsy (or Why Blacks Gave up the Banjo)"].

Though the minstrel form was old, tired, and as unrelentingly racist on radio as it was at its nineteenth-century beginnings, such radio presentations as *Amos and Andy* became hugely popular. Beginning in 1925 as a serialized story of various black stereotypes performed by white actors, the show was syndicated to scores of radio stations. *Amos and Andy* became so popular that restaurants had to put the show on speakers to keep customers when it was on the air. Nothing could compete with it, and the country almost shut down during its weekly broadcast. President Coolidge made plain that he was not to be disturbed during the time it was on the air. That most of the nation listened was a claim so often made that it must be given some credence. The audience grew until the mid-1930s—unprecedented popularity, escapism on a grand, even national, scale.[7]

Blackface comedy was not the only older entertainment form adopted by radio. Sopranos and other classical vocalists, violinists, orchestras, pianists, and poetry reading were also heard. At first, virtually all performance was live. Early radio avoided recordings, viewing the recording industry as competition. Likewise, some record companies did not allow the use of their recordings on radio.

At first, stations were on the air for limited periods. As it became evident that people would listen all day, stations scrambled to find programming to fill the hours.

Exactly when and where older, rural forms of music took to the air is disputed, but it had certainly happened by 1922. Atlanta's WSB put Fiddlin' John Carson on the radio that year, and other fiddlers and singers of traditional American musical forms were soon heard on stations across the country. [8]

Consumers of the arts are often interested in context, and this is especially true of folk arts. The intensity of a typical sports fan's interest in where an important athlete was reared cannot compare with the importance the devotee of fiddle music places on the background of a great fiddler. If, as with folk art, the art arises in a community and reflects it, the audience craves to know that community. This was as true of early radio fans as other audiences, and the producers made much of the origins of the performers of older music forms.

An interest in the "other world" qualities of the southern Appalachians had been growing for more than a half-century before radio became a craze. This interest seems to have had its origin in the North at the time of the Civil War, when major portions of the mountain South opposed the Confederacy and sent many thousands of "Mountain Yankee" troops into Union armies. President Lincoln praised those loyal citizens and, after the war, this national interest was fed by the fundraising appeals of home missionaries and by local-color writers.[9]

A part of the credit (or discredit) for the notion of Appalachia as a habitation or birthplace for traditional music should also be accorded to increased literacy and the boom of popular-press magazines in the post-Civil War period. The new readers wanted action and drama, and they were willing to pay for it. The Texas cowboys, who showed up at the Kansas railheads with new words in Spanish and new workmen's gear, were even more exotic than the mountaineers, and eventually attracted more attention. Cowboys and hillbillies both became popular because of their appeal in the publishing marketplace.

The "other world" attitude toward small Appalachian communities can still be observed. In our own time, people continue to demonstrate a need for an apparently remote, rustic place that is, nevertheless, relatively nearby and where all the good and vanishing things of the past are being kept alive—a living museum. In Ukraine, the keepers of culture are the Hutsuls of the Carpathian Mountains. In Poland, the rural folk of the Tatra Mountains near Zakopane perform this service. In South America, villagers high in the Peruvian Andes do the same. Evidence abounds that it may be a universal human need to have remote, rural keepers of the best of ancient cultures. After all, poor shepherds were the first community to welcome Jesus, while wise men had to travel for days to bring their gifts.[10]

That the southern Appalachians have long been viewed as a place where older forms are preserved can be demonstrated by reviewing the history of bluegrass, a form of country music that began in 1945.[11] Bluegrass was performed on acoustic instruments and—thus sounding older than most other modern forms—was instantly assigned in the public mind to the southern Appalachians.

The founding father of bluegrass was Bill Monroe, reared in central Kentucky (the Bluegrass State). Monroe had been a resident of the Nashville area since the late 1930s and was never a resident of any community in the mountain South. Bluegrass takes its name from "The Blue Grass Boys," Monroe's band. The first of his bands with this name was formed in 1939, but the critical band—the one that created the "bluegrass" sound— was assembled in 1945, and no member of that group had been reared in any of the southern mountain ranges. But when one of the first books was written about bluegrass, some thirty years later, it was entitled *Old as the Hills*.[12]

Why was this new form instantly assigned to antiquity and to the mountains? One answer lies in powerful precedents, many of them derived from radio in the previous two decades.

Fiddlin' John Carson had been performing in and around Atlanta for a quarter century before he took to the WSB microphone in 1922. Where and exactly when Carson was born is not clear but, in his biography of Carson, scholar Gene Wiggins takes note of various attempts to assign the exuberant fiddler to the Blue Ridge Mountains. According to Wiggins, this began as early as 1914, in vaudeville publicity.[13]

Wiggins notes, "Naturally newspapers of the period, when John was a good story, wanted to think he was born near Blue Ridge," a community in Fannin County in northern Georgia. Wiggins reports doubts that Carson actually was born there, and one informant said that when his father corrected Carson, pointing out that he was born elsewhere, Carson replied, "That's right, Joe, but I always say Fannin County. It sounds better."

In a September 10, 1933, article in the *Atlanta Journal* about Carson and other old-time musicians performing on WSB, he is called "the Fannin County mountaineer." The article went on to extol the popularity of the radio shows (the newspaper owned the radio station).

A November 7, 1925, article in the nationally circulated *Radio Digest* magazine about Carson's radio success describes John as a "Blue Ridge Mountain and eight times Champion of Dixie" in its first paragraph. The second paragraph begins, "Fiddlin' John was born and 'jerked up' in the moonshine fastnesses of Fannin County in the heart of the Blue Ridge Mountains."

The writer says that Carson was "one of the most popular radio entertainers in these United States" and notes that he had "given hundreds of concerts at WSB's studio."[14] The unnamed writer also notes that

Carson's radio broadcasts led to his invitation to make phonograph records, and to unprecedented record sales during the mid and late 1920s.

This period has been called a "golden age" of early country recording, and the Nashville-based country music industry traces its origins to
Fiddlin' John's 1923 recordings.[15] The 900-word *Radio Digest* article contains 12 references to the supposed mountain origins of the fiddler. Fiddlin'
John is pictured with his instrument in a natty and stylish business suit,
but a photograph of a log cabin appears adjacent to this portrait, accompanied by the following comment: "Below, Fiddlin' John's wistful look
was probably brought on by a flash back in his mind to the days spent in
his mountain cabin."

The ability of *Radio Digest* editors to read the minds of persons depicted
in photographs, and to rusticate vaudeville performers, is also demon-
strated in an article the magazine published in its issue of March 6, 1926.[16]
The subject is the Hill Billies, a string band then broadcasting from station
WRC in Washington, D.C. (and, at about the same time, on Washington's
WMAL and New York's WJZ).[17]

The prime movers in this ensemble were the Hopkins brothers: Al,
Joe, John, Elmer, and Bill. They were from Gap Creek, North Carolina, in
Ashe County, between Boone and West Jefferson, and distant relatives of
the nineteenth-century western railway magnate, Mark Hopkins. Their
father had moved to Washington in 1904 to work for the Census Bureau.
Al was a professional musician all his life. He organized his brothers into
a vocal quartet and began working in Washington vaudeville theaters in
1910. In 1924, the Hopkins brothers organized a string band with two
men from Galax, Virginia: John Rector and A.E. "Tony" Alderman[18] [see
"The Hill Billies: The Band That Named the Music"].

John Hopkins said that radio brought their music to the attention of
recording companies:

> I doubt that Brunswick [record company] had heard us on the radio, but
> the radio thing came first. The record companies got interested after ra-
> dio showed that a lot of people liked this music enough to pay money
> to see it played. Don't let anybody tell you that some record man woke
> up one morning and believed that this music would sell. They were lis-
> tening to the radio. They knew people were buying tickets. They didn't
> rush into it. We were on the radio for at least two years before records of

music like ours came out. We had a barbershop quartet, with Al playing the piano, for a long time before we got into the Hill Billie business . . . you know, records had been around for a long time. My father bought an old 'talking machine' before I was born. Radio showed the record companies they could make money and they were interested in that.[19]

The Hopkins family lived in a large house in an upper-middle-class Washington neighborhood. They were relatively well-educated and held business, professional, and bureaucratic jobs. One of the Galax men, Tony Alderman, had moved north with Al Hopkins. Alderman was a bright young man with much technical expertise, building radio receivers and transmitting units and working as an X-ray technician part-time.

It is instructive to note how these rather sophisticated musicians are depicted in the 1926 *Radio Digest* article. A vaudeville-style photograph shows them with musical instruments and in costumes. Alderman wears a rube clown getup. Al Hopkins wears a fake goatee, horn rim glasses, and what appears to be a railway conductor's uniform. John Hopkins wears a college-boy straw boater and a gentleman's evening jacket. Joe Hopkins wears a World War I Army dress uniform. Charlie Bowman wears a country costume including rolled-up sleeves, suspenders, and floppy hat.[20] The following caption accompanies this photograph:

> Below is the famous gang of Hill Billies who took the nation's capital by storm. They are, from the left: A.E. Alderman of Carroll County, Virginia; Al, John and Joe Hopkins of 'No'th Ca'lina;' and 'Fox-Hunt' Charlie Bowman of Tennessee. Every one of 'em from the 'mountings' and born with the lingo.

The full-width head for the *Radio Digest* article is "'Hill Billies Capture WRC." A subhead follows: "Boys from Blue Ridge Mountains Take Washington with Guitars, Fiddles and Banjos; Open New Line of American Airs." The first five paragraphs of the article set forth many of the stereotypes about the effect of radio upon the mountain South that are still current:

> Modern improvements make slow progress in the hill country of the South. During the World War it was discovered that some of the more remote communities were living much as they did a century ago.
> But radio has taken hold of the primitive inhabitants with amazing alacrity. Its effect on the development of their education and

communication with the outside world promises benefits untold. They are learning a new language. They are discovering America as it is today. To some, who were born and have grown old within a few miles of the homes of their fathers, it is a revelation. They scarcely associate it as being in reality a part of their own world. They do not all have receiving sets but there is one in the general store, and they come from far and near for the concerts. The storekeeper in many instances has made it possible for individual families to own their own receiving sets.

A few weeks ago Radio Station WRC at Washington, D.C. broadcast a concert by an organization called "The Hill Billies." The response was astounding.

Letters and postcards arrived from the mountains of Tennessee, from the hills of Kentucky and the Carolinas and the Blue Ridge counties of Maryland and Virginia. Phone calls, local and long distance, demanded favorite numbers, and repeats and what not.

A voice with a distinct Georgia drawl asked that they play "Long Eared Mule," and added the significant remark: "You-all caint fool me, ah know where them boys come from. They's Hill Billies for suah. They ain't nobody kin play that music 'thout they is bawn in the hills and brung up thar."

The article goes on at length in a similar vein. The process of pretending that sophisticated persons are rustics has since been dubbed *rusticating*, and mountain residents who take on some of the attributes expected of them are called "feedback hillbillies."

The unnamed writer of this *Radio Digest* article makes two particularly interesting assumptions: first, that readers of this magazine would find it believable that the mountain South was isolated from the "outside world" and was, in fact, a century out of date; and second, that radio was having a greater effect in the mountains than in the rest of the country. The latter assumption is contrary to the findings of Myer Horowitz in his 1931 analysis *America Listens*.

Addressed mainly to advertisers, this statistical work showed that radio had its greatest effect where there was more leisure time. Horowitz noted that the effect of radio was lessened where there were daylight-to-dark work traditions, and where lower incomes restricted the numbers of radios owned. "Purchasing power aside, you simply cannot assume the people in Iowa or eastern Kentucky listen as much or heed what they hear when compared to listeners in Philadelphia, Boston or Chicago."[21]

The point bears mentioning, because early radio signals blanketed an enormous area, making radio enormously attractive to advertisers. In the early static-free days of radio, the night DX (distance unknown) signal of larger radio stations reached far across the country. Tony Alderman said that letters and postcards from Canada to Florida were common, and that many listeners were in the Midwest. He said that he could predict the size of the evening audience in any city or town by the number of radio antennae that were evident.

The Carter Family became a household name thanks to radio. Ralph Peer recorded them first for Victor in 1927, but their late-1930s and early-1940s broadcasts on "border blaster" radio stations helped make the group a household name. The transmitters were across the Rio Grande in Mexico, fed by telephone lines from studios in Texas. They aimed a barrage of bizarre advertising and mail order sales toward the United States. These stations had power far beyond the legal limits in the United States. One reached 500,000 watts, ten times the strength of American stations. It could be heard from the North Pole to the South Pole, and was the hottest spot on the dial throughout North America.

The *Carter Family Good Neighbor Get-Together*, heard nightly on such border stations as XERA, had radio audiences that dwarfed those of WSM's Grand Ole Opry and WLS's *National Barn Dance*. Bands that imitated the Carter Family arose in Peru and Canada. Among those who regularly sent requests to the station were listeners in Sweden and New Zealand.

While 1920s radio producers were skilled in the rustication of rural and small town performers, the greatest rusticators seem to have appeared in the 1930s. Among them was John Lair, first the director of the WLS (Chicago) *National Barn Dance* and later the founder of the *Renfro Valley Barn Dance* in Kentucky. He gave flower names to the women in one all-female group (the Coon Creek Girls) and dubbed other musicians with such rusticated titles as "Arkie, the Arkansas Woodchopper."[22]

Such tactics did not endear radio to all who loved Appalachian music. In 1982, octogenarian fiddler Inez Osborne told why her all-woman band had limited its performances to home and a few annual pie suppers:

I never liked playing for drunks, and I never gave a toot for contests, either . . . the first ones here were run by the Ku Klux Klan, and they were a trashy set. . . . People thought you ought to go play on the radio, but I never could tell that the radio people liked music. They wanted you to talk silly talk or pop your gum and show your bloomers like Lulu Belle [Wiseman]. Now what on earth does that kind of stuff have to do with good music?"[23]

What indeed? But the rusticating of performers on radio was to continue until the mid 1950s.

I will at this point summarize what I have learned:

First, it is clear that radio had a huge effect upon Americans, but it is equally clear that it had no more effect in the Blue Ridge than elsewhere. That some wish to believe it had a greater effect in the mountains is nothing more than a new application of an old myth.

Second, the assigning of what was conceived to be older musical forms to Appalachia was a part of popular culture when radio arose—and it still is.

Third, the producers and artists who engaged in this rustication knew what they were doing and employed it as a show-business tactic. This is as true of some who came from the culture—such as John Carson and Al Hopkins—as it was of vaudeville types.

Fourth, relatively little of the musical arts of the Blue Ridge was ever heard on radio. Concert musics were heard, but very little dance music. Radio was the major factor in converting one form of dance music to bluegrass, a concert form. The a cappella ballads and most of the religious music—the two most prevalent forms—were almost never heard on radio. And because it was never put to radio or commercial recordings, even knowledgeable fans of Appalachian music have difficulty believing that a form as fine as Cherokee fiddling ever existed.

Fifth, local stations—for instance, WPAQ in Mt. Airy, North Carolina—have a long tradition of presenting excellent local artists.

NOTES

1. Tipton "Tip" Madron, interview with the author, Christmas day 1961. "Uncle Tip" had the first radio, automobile, bathroom, electricity, telephone, and refrigerator in Trade, Tennessee, a community eleven miles, as the crow flies, from the Blue Ridge summit.

2. Tom Lewis, *Empire of the Air: The Men Who Made Radio* (New York: HarperCollins, 1993). This is by far the best analysis and the best narrative I have read that is concerned with early radio, its makers, and its amazing effects.

3. H.L. Mencken, "Dempsey vs. Carpentier," *New York World* and *Baltimore Sun*, July 3, 1921. Mencken initially ignored the broadcast, but took note of it later when this piece was reprinted in such collections as *A Mencken Chrestomathy* (New York: Knopf, 1949).

4. Bill C. Malone, *Country Music, USA* 2nd ed. (Austin: University of Texas Press, 1985). First published in 1968, this is a good introduction to country music and how it evolved from folk musics.

5. Lewis, *Empire of the Air*.

6. There are several books concerned with the history of the minstrel business. The best known is Robert C. Toll's *Blacking Up* (New York: Oxford, 1974). But Toll is a fan, and his work is as much apology as analysis. In *Dan Emmett and the Rise of Early Negro Minstrelsy* (Norman: University of Oklahoma Press, 1962), Hans Nathan provides a great deal about the massive business and how it grew, but relatively little about where it came from and why. The role of free northern blacks in creating material and models for the form has been ignored until recently. Howard and Judy Sacks' book about Ohio's Snowden family, *Way Up North in Dixie* (Washington, D.C.: Smithsonian Press, 1993), will help to fill this gap.

7. Lewis, *Empire of the Air*.

8. *Atlanta Journal,* September 10, 1922. WSB is called a "radiophone," and there is an individual photo of Carson, along with a band photograph. This is reproduced in Gene Wiggins' *Fiddling Georgia Crazy*, cited below.

9. How the Blue Ridge and the rest of the southern Appalachian Mountains became a unique place in the minds of Americans is a fascinating and complicated topic. Portrayal of the "blue mountains" as a barrier or distancing place first appears in colonial and early American writing. See *The Memoir of John Durang, American Actor, 1785–1816*, and Thomas Jefferson's *Notes on the State of Virginia*. The writer who has given most attention to the Appalachia-as-another-place phenomenon in recent years is Henry D. Shapiro, and his book, *Appalachia on Our Minds: The Southern Mountains and Mountaineers in the American Consciousness, 1870–1920* (Chapel Hill: University of North Carolina Press, 1978), is highly recommended. Shapiro is very good with the details of the rise of the idea among various popularizers after 1870. Why he chose 1870 is not clear, but he places the entire phenomenon after that date.

10. Extrapolated from New Testament accounts in the Bible.

11. There are two excellent histories of bluegrass: Neil Rosenberg's *Bluegrass, a History* (Urbana: University of Illinois Press, 1985) and Richard D. Smith's *Can't You Hear Me Callin': The Life of Bill Monroe, Father of Bluegrass* (New York: Little, Brown, 2001).

12. Steven D. Price, *Old as the Hills: The Story of Bluegrass Music* (New York: Viking Press, 1975).

13. Gene Wiggins, *Fiddling Georgia Crazy* (Urbana: University of Illinois Press, 1987). This excellent biography is another good offering in the Music in American Life series of the University of Illinois Press.

14. *Radio Digest* had a considerable circulation until the Depression years. Many libraries have the journal in their collections.

15. There were a few earlier recordings, but Carson's were more successful in sales. See Wiggins, *Fiddling Georgia Crazy*, and Malone, *Country Music, USA*.

16. A facsimile of this article appears with other notes enclosed with an LP of reissued recordings by the Hill Billies (A *Fiddler's Convention in Mountain City, Tennessee*). This was compiled by the author and issued by County Records in 1973.

17. Archie Green's article "Hillbilly Music, Source and Symbol," *Journal of American Folklore* (1968) noted that his band was the first to put the term *hillbilly* to a form of music.

The *JAF* later issued this article as a booklet, and it is recommended as a fine example of Green's work, as well as the best introduction to an early country music band. It deals with the complications of such status. Few other works attempt this.

18. Tony Alderman is the source of most of what is known about this band, and he recalled broadcasting on WRC in 1925. But in a telephone conversation in December, 1973, John Hopkins said groups organized by his brother Al began broadcasts earlier, "a couple of years before Tony Alderman came up here." That puts their radio beginnings in 1922, the same year that John Carson began broadcasting.

19. John Hopkins, interview by the author, December 1973.

20. This photograph is part of the facsimile described in the note above.

21. Myer Horowitz, *America Listens* (New York: Champion Press, 1931). This small booklet of statistics was aimed at corporations and others using radio advertising. It was to be a quarterly, but I have found only one copy.

22. This man and his work get considerable attention from country music historians.

23. Inez Osborne, interview by the author, January, 1982.

INSTRUMENTS

The Devil's Box

· ·

L et's get the first question out of the way. You can call it a violin or a fiddle; there's not a bit of difference. Folk and classical performers have used the names interchangeably for more than three centuries.

Violin types and prototypes had existed in a bewildering variety of shapes and sizes before Antonio Stradivari (1644–1737) and his compatriots in Cremona, Italy, turned their hands to the business of improving their sound. The instruments they made were of such a high standard that many claim modern makers have not equaled them.

Folklore concerned with Stradivari has been growing for over a century. There's almost a cottage industry of persons attempting to discover the supposed secrets of the wily Italian who made no two violins exactly alike. One branch of this enterprising effort tends to be campus-based and fostered by learned professors of chemistry and physics. Major new theories emerge every four years, almost without fail. The secret has been

Adapted from *Masters of the Folk Violin* tour program book, NCTA, Fall, 1989; Introduction to *A Guide to the Crooked Road: Virginia's Heritage Music Trail*, Copyright 2006 by The Crooked Road: Virginia's Heritage Music Trail, John F. Blair, Publisher; and the Abingdon [Virginia] Crooked Road Music Fest program book, October, 2012.

found in the varnish, in the effect of this or that on the wood fibers, in displacements, or in Antonio boiling the wood. The respectable press is interested in the activities of this branch. Keep an eye on *The Wall Street Journal*, *The New York Times*, and public television. They are almost certain to report a new and utterly plausible fantastic scientific report about the secrets of old Antonio in a year or two.

But there are other branches: little old men in garrets measuring old violins with calipers and cooking up new varnishes. And near every wall where there's a row of old violins stands a fellow with a different theory about Strad secrets and maybe, just maybe, a real one hanging up there.

There's even a Cajun branch of the Strad fraternity. Eunice, Louisiana, accordion maker and violin friend Marc Savoy has a sign in his window that salutes them. It says, "In his lifetime, Stradivari made 496 violins, 3,000 of which are owned by the Cajuns!"

Marc's sign is a reminder of a statistic from Interpol, the international police. Guess whose name has been forged most often? You got it! Old Antonio signed all 3,000 of those fine instruments for Marc's buddies, and tens of thousands of others. Is imitation still the height of flattery, even after it veers off into forgery?

The shape, sound, and mystery of the violin are major challenges to fine woodworkers everywhere. Yet, no other instrument is made by so many. Major cities have dozens of violinmakers, and even a small rural county is likely to have one or two. One of our favorites is the old-timer near the crossroads at Shouns, Tennessee, who has made over a hundred—and never sold one.

And how good are these violins being made in every part of the country? There are fine players who will tell you that the best violins ever made are being made right now, and here in these United States.

Moreover, there are some distinctive American violins, instruments developed by native peoples who saw the European violin and decided to make their own. These include the one-string Apache violin and a two-string instrument built by the Eskimo.

FIDDLING IN THE NEW WORLD

The fiddle was new and exciting when European emigrants brought it to North America during the late 1600s and early 1700s. In the old country, it was replacing the hornpipe, tabor, and harp at country dances and other rural social gatherings. Part of the excitement resulted from improvements to the instrument and its availability. As early as the 1730s, "Cremona" violins were awarded as prizes at country fiddling contests in Virginia.

The Virginia Gazette contains many advertisements that provide a glimpse of fiddling two-and-a-half centuries ago. A 1736 advertisement tells that among various contests at a forthcoming celebration in Hanover County will be a violin competition, in which twenty players will contend for a violin. Black slaves and white indentured servants did much of the performing at Virginia dances, and Gazette advertisements for runaways sometimes mention that the escapee is a fiddler. In other advertisements, Virginians seeking to buy slaves and indentured servants specified that in addition to the usual qualifications they wanted a musician.

Americans imported fine instruments and paid high prices for them during these years. Merchants offered violins by Cremonese makers, by Jacob Stainer in the Tyrol, as well as good copies of Stainer and Cremona violins.

Among fiddlers in the colonies was Josiah Franklin, a candlemaker who came to Boston from England in 1683. His famous son Benjamin recalled that he was " . . . skilled a little in music and had a clear pleasing voice, so that when he played Psalm tunes on his violin and sang withal, as he sometimes did in an evening after the business of the day was over, it was extremely agreeable to hear."

Another early fiddler was mapmaker and plantation owner Peter Jefferson, born in Virginia in 1708. His son Thomas became the third president of the United States and its first well-known fiddler.

Thomas Jefferson loved all music, but especially that of the violin. By age fourteen he was copying his favorite country fiddle tunes into notebooks, sometimes adding lyrics. His voluminous correspondence and records make it clear that fiddling was very important to him. Among the fiddlers that Jefferson met as a young man was Patrick Henry. They were later bitter political enemies, but Jefferson told Henry's biographer that they spent two weeks playing the fiddle and dancing with other revelers after their first meeting in 1760.

There's a huge trove of Jefferson family music at the University of Virginia. It reflects broad-ranging tastes—classical, popular, and folk—and its well-worn condition is evidence that Jefferson and his family loved and used it constantly. There are items from Bach, Handel, and Purcell, but also well-thumbed copies of "Black-Eyed Susan," "Crazy June," "The Cuckoo" (with lyrics), "The Farmer's Description of London," "Lovely Nancy," and scores of others that give evidence of a family interested in country tunes.

Jefferson practiced three hours a day while he was taking lessons from Francis Alberti, an immigrant Venetian fiddler he met in Williamsburg and persuaded to move near Jefferson's Charlottesville home. Alberti also taught Thomas's younger brother Randolph, and tutored Mrs. Jefferson on harpsichord. According to Jefferson's great-granddaughter, Sarah N. Randolph, local friends thought it would be good to introduce the Venetian to a favorite local music of the upper Blue Ridge—that of the hounds chasing foxes at night. Alberti was taken to a ridge and the dogs loosed. When they were in full cry, he was asked how he liked the music. He replied, "De damn dog make such a noise me no hear de music."

The Jeffersons were wealthy—heirs to vast sums made through the export of tobacco—and could afford lessons, Cremona violins, and more. When Jefferson built Monticello, that amazing residence was at the frontier. But the frontier was shared with others of lesser means, and it moved west.

A glimpse of the violin in the life of another frontier family is provided in a description written by Virginia Pierce Bedford (1791–1882). Born in the Shenandoah Valley, Mrs. Bedford describes her family when it was resident in Missouri, before moves to Colorado and California.

> Papa's violin was among our treasured possessions. It was a battered relic but a sweet tone resided in it. His grandfather had brought it from Ireland to Pennsylvania, and his father had fetched it to Augusta County before the War for Independence.
>
> It brought trade to Papa's mill and store, and got him elected to offices that advanced his business. He called the violin "Her" and "My Old Toll-Getter" for the percentage of the corn and small grain that he kept when it was brought to his mill for the grinding.
>
> We might also have called her "An Old Husband-Getter," for my sisters and I met our husbands while they were guests at dances at our home. There were then, as now, some church ministers, narrow men, who ranted against the playing of the violin and all social gatherings that included dancing. But such opposition is grounded in gross ignorance and envy and we believed most firmly that such persons deserved our pity.

VIOLINIST OR FIDDLER?

As in the case of the instrument, these titles have been used interchangeably for at least three centuries. Those who would make distinctions between them often seize upon superficial or nonexistent differences.

A good example is in how the instrument is held. A few players hold it on their chest rather than under their chin. Classically trained performers almost never do this, so it is said to be a difference. It is not. The vast majority of all performers in all genres hold the instrument under their chin. And we know of one classically trained fiddler who held the instrument on his chest.

A more common myth is concerned with musical literacy. We are told that violinists read music, but so do many fiddlers. The training of fiddlers has not been a subject of concern to many scholars, but we suspect that a well-defined study would show that many—perhaps most—of those who perform publicly read music. Moreover, fiddlers have read music for generations, and those of the past two centuries were as likely to use tune books as those of today. Of course, Thomas Jefferson read music. And so did John Pierce, the fiddling miller and storekeeper who moved west with the frontier. Revered Galax [Virginia] fiddler Emmett Lundy, born in 1864, read music and brought to the modern era tunes from even older fiddlers, who also read music.

There is reason to suspect that musical literacy has declined among fiddlers during the twentieth century, as it has among singers and the general population. Yet one of the major tune books used by fiddlers continues to be very popular. This book of 1,000 tunes—1,050 in some editions—has been in existence, in one form or another, for over a century. It is now published by the M.M. Cole Company of Chicago and called *1,000 Fiddle Tunes*. The title used for the 1883 edition was *Ryan's Mammoth Collection of 1050 Reels and Jigs, Hornpipes, Clogs, Walk-arounds, Essences, Strathspeys, Highland Flings and Contra Dances, with Figures, and How to Play Them*.

The person largely responsible for its compilation was Elias Howe [related to, but not the sewing machine pioneer of the same name]. Born in 1820 near Framingham, Massachusetts, by 1840 he was selling a tune book, *The Musician's Companion*, door-to-door in rural New England. In 1842, Howe operated a music store in Providence, Rhode Island, and, in 1843, another on Cornhill Street in Boston. Howe's tune and instruction books became very popular. Country music historian Charles Wolfe studied the movement of tunes among Howe's books, and concluded that he transcribed the core of them from rural Massachusetts fiddlers in the 1830s.

This huge compilation of tunes has been in print for over a century. It was distributed for many years via the Sears and Roebuck catalogue, which sent it to every corner and crossroads of the South and West, and to the Arctic villages of Alaska and Canada. Moreover, most of its tunes had been in print in other collections for a generation before the 1883 printing. The Cole Company subtitles the current edition *The Fiddler's Bible*, surely an appropriate name for this venerable collection of folk fiddle tunes.

So both fiddlers and violinists tend to read music. Are there areas in which they differ? There's the obvious one of the "violinist" tag nowadays being assigned to an artist trained in the classics at a conservatory. But this is a recent distinction. Older country players in every area of the country called themselves violinists and their instruments violins. Performers in folk violin styles have traditionally received instruction given master-to-student, one-to-one, more personal than formal, catching the music and carrying it on—often a legacy handed from one generation to another. Nowadays, the fiddler may be taking lessons at the community school and learning from friends and recordings, but the process is still a personal one in a small world.

Yet, there is a difference in the way the terms "violinist" and "fiddler" are used. A value judgment is often implicit, and this is a difference that reaches deep into history. When Samuel Pepys wrote his diary entry for May 27, 1663, he entered the tunes performed that evening as "fiddle" tunes; he spoke of enjoying his "fiddling" that night. On most other nights his instrument was called a "violin." The difference for Pepys was in the type of tune performed. The tunes performed that night had been bright and tuneful, very different from the fantasias he'd been performing. When the British antiquarian Captain Francis Grose compiled his dictionary of street terms (*A Classical Dictionary of the Vulgar Tongue*, London, 1785), there were four entries that began with "fiddle," and all seem to express some disregard for our favorite art.

Some historical notes treated it as an antisocial activity. Nero "fiddled" when Rome burned; he did not perform a selection on the violin. (The emperor Nero was actually not a fiddler, but played a predecessor of the guitar.)

When the fine eastern Kentucky fiddler J. P. Fraley took up the violin, his father—a fiddler, but also a trader and worker—pulled him aside for a few words of caution: fiddling should remain a leisure activity. The elder Fraley, concerned that J.P. not let music interfere with his family responsibilities, would have been very proud of the fine way J.P. has served both fiddling and family. But his Dad's concern was a valid one from the perspective of his folk community, and that of many others.

The violin is a most demanding instrument. It rewards those who spend much time with it. It has the power to engross and to mesmerize. It will take all the time invested in it. And for those who do not love it as much as we, it has seemed a powerful instrument for the wasting of time. It has been the "Devil's Box" for many generations of hellfire and brimstone preachers. The author's fiddling uncle had a term for all who expressed such judgments. He called them, "a goddamn bunch of tin-eared Jeremiahs."

STYLE

At one time, the community of musicians was wrapped in a place. Irish old-timers could tell which county—and in many cases which village—a fiddler was from. If you have a sharp ear, you'll discern changes in style as you travel south along the spine of the Blue Ridge and visit its towns and trading areas. Virginia's Patrick County borders Carroll County, but the traditional fiddle music is different in these two counties.

Style grows out of the influence of master performers. The echo of a truly great fiddler may reverberate in a community of musicians for a century or longer. Every musician in eastern Kentucky and southern West Virginia knew that Ed Haley was a towering musician—and absorbed as much of his repertoire as they could—but few outside that area had heard about the blind wizard from Ashland. Nowadays, one can live in Ashland and be largely oblivious to its traditional culture. Fiddling communities are being defined in new ways. Place is still very important, but recordings and the ease of movement have made it possible for a young fiddler to follow a master teacher living in a distant place.

Like all living things, traditional fiddling changes over time. It absorbs and rejects parts of what it encounters. It can thrive on massive social dislocation, such as that caused by war (especially if monotony is a by-product of the dislocation). No event in the history of our nation seems to have been as impactful in expanding fiddler's repertoires as the American Civil War of 1861 to 1865.

Here's a part of what Confederate Edward Worthington in Kentucky wrote to his cousin Amanda in Mississippi, on October 28, 1861:

> We have a lively time here . . . every fellow full of life . . . every night fiddlers are plentiful. . . . When we want something nice we borrow the fiddle and go to our tent. Will tries himself and draws a tent as full as they can stick around in it. . . . I wish you could happen in sometime when Will Mason is playing the violin and see some of our capers.

Two years later, John D. Billings of Massachusetts was in the Union Army and encamped in Virginia, where the red clay stuck to his feet. When a group of new recruits arrived from back home, the fiddler—a veteran—added a verse to his tune:

> I'm a raw recruit, with a bran'-new suit,
> Nine hundred dollars bounty,
> And I've come down from Darbytown
> To fight for Oxford County.

FIDDLE CONTESTS

Fiddle contests were commonplace in England, Ireland, and Scotland; have been held since the 1730s in the Southeast; and are traditional in many Anglo-American communities elsewhere in the nation. Among prizes handed out to winners over the years have been violins imported from Cremona, a two-year old filly, fittings of false teeth, and—since the 1930s revival of the contests—ribbons and cash. A half-dozen contests claim to crown a national champion, and others dub state champions. The people who attend seem to enjoy them, and a few contests—especially those conducted in the state of Missouri—put a strong emphasis on local tradition. The Cajun and Cape Breton fiddling traditions have no history of contests.

Contests have been minor affairs for most of their history. But during the mid-1920s they briefly became a national fad, under the sponsorship of the Ford Motor Company. Henry Ford held contests at his car dealerships to name the "King of the Fiddlers" and to surreptitiously elevate old-fashioned values above the evils he associated with jazz and communism. (That Henry thought fiddling might be an antidote to communism tells much about the agility of his inquiring mind.) Disturbed by black and Jewish influences in vaudeville, he hoped that old-time fiddling would sweep it all away.

Ford crowned two national champions after holding contests all over the country. His champions made records under the best studio conditions, and they sound OK on them, but no better than a dozen other fiddlers who recorded in that era. One of those champions betrayed Ford. He was an old man, but he went off briefly and consorted with the enemy on the vaudeville circuits.

In 1931, a group of enterprising individuals decided to hold a fiddle contest on White Top Mountain, in Grayson County, Virginia. The resulting folk festival was successful beyond expectations. It attracted an ever-growing line of participants to the mountain, particularly because cash prizes were being offered during a time of economic depression. But success has its own demons, and by 1940 the festival had fallen victim to infighting amongst the organizers and ended rather unceremoniously.

The big bang of fiddle contests in Southwest Virginia happened in 1935, when the newly formed Galax Moose Lodge was looking to raise money to support civic activities. After several evenings of debate around the pot-bellied stove at Matthews Hardware Store, the group settled on sponsoring a string-music competition, simply named the "Old Fiddlers Convention." It was a resounding success; the hall overflowed with great musicians who seized on the opportunity to demonstrate their prowess. An audience willing to plunk down an admission fee watched the competition unfold. Contestants and audience members had to be turned away that day, so they held a second Old Fiddlers Convention later that same year.

The Galax Old Fiddlers Convention has grown to be the longest running and largest of the fiddle contests in the United States. Since the 1950s, it has been held in Felts Park on the second weekend in August, and is now a six-day event with a full night of youth competitions. Success of the Old Fiddlers Convention in Galax spawned an ever-growing number of like events across the Southeast, and beyond.

Contests are often viewed with distaste by the better fiddlers, even in communities where such events are customary. Among these was the late

Tommy Jarrell, a legendary fiddler from Mt. Airy, North Carolina. Tommy said, "Music is something you ought to share, not something you contend with."

Many fiddle contests are fund-raising activities for local organizations engaged in charitable activities. But they also have purposes that are not as obvious. For example, many bring together musicians who have traveled hundreds of miles for a musical homecoming. They are intense experiences for fiddlers who learn best in face-to-face situations. They amount to a powerful form of musical community. What other form of artistic presentation from the 1730s is still common in this country?

Origins of the Banjo
in North America

● ●

The banjo is a folk instrument, introduced to the southern American colonies by Africans. It has since been well kept by generations of blacks and whites from that region. The banjo was first defined in the national perspective by two major fads: minstrelsy [see "Minstrelsy (or Why Blacks Gave up the Banjo)"] and early jazz, which used the loud and incisive chords of the tenor banjo for a rhythm that would cut through the sound of brass instruments. The nation's libraries have massive quantities of sheet music and other detritus concerned with these fads.

But on its native turf the banjo has never been defined by faddism. It is a part of the countless things that make up the fabric of life, and it has a history that reaches back nearly 400 years. There is in this a belonging to a place and a people that faddism never achieves. The difference may seem subtle, but it is critical.

Adapted from liner notes to *Masters of the Banjo: A National Tour of Traditional Banjo Styles*, Arhoolie Records, 1994; and the Introduction to *A Guide to the Crooked Road: Virginia's Heritage Music Trail*, copyright 2006 by The Crooked Road: Virginia's Music Heritage Trail, John F. Blair, Publisher.

No one knows exactly when the banjo came to North America, but there's no doubt about where it came from. West Africans brought here to work on tobacco, rice, and sugar plantations introduced banjo-making skills. The instrument had existed in a bewildering array of forms in Africa for hundreds of years, having moved across Africa from east to west.

According to John Rolfe (the husband of Pocahontas), the first Africans were purchased from "a Dutch man-of-warr" at Jamestown, Virginia, "about the latter end of August" in 1619. This was twelve years after the founding of that first permanent English-speaking colony in North America. Some Africans were treated as indentured servants during their initial decades in colonial America. Many of the first European settlers were also indentured, having sold their services for a period of years in order to buy passage to the New World.

The thirty million kidnapped Africans who were jammed wholesale onto fetid, filthy, and dangerous slave prison ships brought nothing more to America than the rags on their backs. But they did not leave their culture behind. They brought musical concepts and styles, and they knew how to build sophisticated drums and several banjo-like instruments.

Just one slave-ship banjo survived, kept today in a museum in the Netherlands. But there are representations that make it clear that Africans built the early Virginia banjo. Among them is a painting, now at the Abby Aldrich Rockefeller Folk Art Museum in Williamsburg, that shows a party of slaves dancing and making music on a plantation in the coastal South—either Georgia or South Carolina. This famous watercolor, our earliest depiction of the banjo in America, was completed between 1777 and 1800. The instrument has four strings, one of them a short drone string. A whiskey jug is in place under the bench where the musicians sit, and the dancers are placed in poses that bespeak African dance. The banjoist is accompanied by a small drum; this tracks Richard Jobson's 1623 account of banjo playing along the Gambia River in West Africa.

Jobson's description appeared in his book, *The Golden Trade, or a Discovery of the River Gambia and the Golden Trade of the Aethopians:*

> The [instrument] that is most common in use is made of a great gourd and a neck thereunto fastened, resembling in some sort our Bandera; but they have no manner of fret, and the strings are such as the place yields. . . .

Notwithstanding, with pins they wind them to agree in tunable notes, having not above six strings upon their greatest instrument.

In consortship with this they have many times another who plays upon a little drumme, which he holds under his left arm, and with a crooked stick in his right hand, and his naked fingers on his left, he strikes the drumme, and with his mouth gaping open, makes a rude noyse.

The "great gourd" soundbox continued to be used in banjo construction in eastern Virginia, but other materials were pressed into use as the banjo moved westward. Handmade wooden banjos, fretless and with groundhog or cat skin rawhide heads, are found in considerable numbers in a relatively small area of southwestern Virginia, eastern Kentucky, northwestern North Carolina, and northeastern Tennessee. Studies of the Hicks (Hix) family of makers [see "The Hicks and Related Families: Carriers of Tradition"] and others show that these skills were developed as those families moved from the Virginia Tidewater in the latter half of the eighteenth century.

The banning of drums by Virginia and other colonies increased the popularity of the banjo. A banjo is after all a drum with strings, and thus a good substitute. The colonies lived in dread of slave revolts, and drums could be used to convey messages. Laws forbidding drums and drumming were passed after the 1739 slave rebellion at Stono, South Carolina, and were strengthened after Nat Turner's 1831 Virginia rebellion.

The European fiddle and the African banjo met in the hands of black players in the Virginia Tidewater. It was the first American ensemble—the root of the root, the beginning of rock, country, jazz, bluegrass, blues, and all the rest. It is clear from travelers' accounts that black fiddle and banjo players, sometimes with other rhythm performers, provided music for dancing in several areas of the Southeast for many generations.

Among the historians to comment on black banjoists was Thomas Jefferson. In a footnote to his book, Notes on the State of Virginia, he wrote, "The instrument proper to them is the Banjar, which they brought hither from Africa. . . ." Jefferson's book was written in French in 1780, while he was the wartime governor of an invaded Virginia. The first English edition was published in 1787 by John Stockdale, a London bookseller. Jefferson kept a Stockdale edition, and added notes to it; the banjo comment is one of those. Exactly when the note was added is not clear, but it was after August 1787. Jefferson and his slaves were then living at Monticello, located on the upper Blue Ridge.

Thomas Fairfax told of an encounter with a Richmond banjoist in his 1799 *Journey from Virginia to Salem Massachusetts*.

> After going to bed I was entertained with an agreeable serenade, by a black man who had taken his stand near the Tavern, and for the amusement of those of his colour, sung and played on the Bangoe. He appeared to be quite adept on this African instrument, which tho it may not bear a comparison with the Guitar, is certainly Capable of Conveying much pleasure to the musical ear.

No one knows when whites took up banjo playing. There is speculation, but guesses vary over a 140-year period from about 1630 to 1770. The earlier dates seem more reasonable. The banjo moved from east to west, and from blacks to whites. That transfer is still in process, though nearly complete. White players have predominated in the twentieth century, but there are still a few black players who learned from older blacks.

Wooden banjos in the Blue Ridge are sometimes explained by my esteemed colleagues in banjo history as copies of minstrel banjos, a result of the minstrel fad that began in 1843. I'm awfully dubious about that explanation. If the fretless wood banjo is an imitation of a minstrel banjo, it is among the oddest imitations ever devised by the mind of man. The Hicks family and several other Tidewater-to-mountains instrument-making families had been living in proximity to black people for 206 years before the first burnt-cork troupe took to the road. Is there anyone who believes that white musicians listened to black players that long without asking, "Hey, could I try that dang thing?"

After 1800, the instrument began to be used by white comics who impersonated black banjoists, creating racist caricatures by using burnt cork to blacken their faces and by wearing ragged clothing. Some of these performers worked in early circus troupes. These self-styled "Ethiopian delineators" told jokes, sang comic songs, and performed on banjo, fiddle, hand drum, and bones. They set off the first international pop-music fad, the so-called minstrel era that lasted until the end of the century. During the minstrel period, an instrument that had been used by an underclass was adopted by an elite. The new upper-class players could afford fine instruments, so banjo construction improved and the instrument as we know it today was created.

As in all popular fads, material was left behind when minstrelsy passed. A part of that material is repertoire; many of the older banjo tunes have minstrel roots. Another part is the instrument; the fad spread the banjo to various folk populations who have put it to good use.

Almost everyone knows the wonderful North Carolina Piedmont folk style that Earl Scruggs and Don Reno burnished and passed to the world during the 1940s and 1950s. Scruggs is the most imitated American banjo player of our time, and possibly of any time. Bluegrass music has become one of the best providers of steady income for banjoists since minstrelsy.

During a six-year period that began in 1958, burr-headed "we-got-together-on-campus" groups singing folk songs were suddenly at the top of the pop music charts. Some used a rudimentary banjo accompaniment. An interest in old-time string band music arose at about the same time. Suddenly kids from Brooklyn to Berkeley were trying to walk, talk, dress, and play string band music like old Tar Heel farmers. This continued until the 1970s [and has revived again since the mid-1990s].

That the banjo was prominent in these "revivals" can be largely attributed to Pete Seeger. A Harvard dropout and union activist with an abiding interest in progressive causes, Seeger made the banjo visible to an intellectual elite. His book *How to Play the 5-String Banjo* has been in print since 1948.

The banjo continues to have regional and ethnic ties. The clawhammer style is still centered in a small area of Virginia and North Carolina. There's a Hawaiian plectrum style, a ragged style on a tiny banjo from the U.S. Virgin Islands, and a rip-snorting new Irish style that is improving the market for good tenor banjos.

Banjo is not currently popular with the larger public, but it is very healthy. This historic instrument is likely to be around when most of the current musical fads have gone to the land of the hula hoop.

Men and Kings
A Mini-History of the Guitar

• •

During the twentieth century, the guitar became the emulsifier of American musical culture, the common denominator between hillbilly and bluesman, rocker and cowboy, jazzman and ethnic. It found its way to the American working class—not because of the political revolution of 1776, but because of the industrial revolution that took place shortly after the Civil War. That revolution dislodged the guitar from its aristocratic perch and gave it to the working people of the republic.

In terms of its origins, the guitar is the polar opposite of the banjo. The banjo percolated upward from the sweat-stained people who hoed tobacco, shucked corn, curried mules, and rocked babies. The guitar traces its lineage to antiquity's royalty and the upper classes and—in the nineteenth century—to a popular fad of the upper-middle class.

The guitar was at first an import, an expensive and fancy instrument totally in the hands of the elite. The Bolsheviks who were reorganizing Moscow University in 1921 forbade guitar playing, thundering that "a

Adapted from *Masters of the Steel String Guitar,* National Council for the Traditional Arts tour program book, 1990.

guitar is not a class-proletarian instrument and is, indeed, an instrument favored exclusively by bourgeois and middle classes."

The guitar has been assigned other symbolic identifications. In 1963, at the height of the Southern civil rights movement in Alabama, an arch-conservative John Birch Society newspaper railed against "outside agitators led by guitar-plinking pinkos." In the nineteenth century, the guitar was almost exclusively a woman's instrument, but by the late twentieth century it had become strongly identified with unabashedly masculine rock 'n' roll.

The guitar is arguably the most forgiving of instruments. A poor beginning crooner who knows but three chords can carry it onstage and escape without sounding half as terrible as a beginning violinist or pianist in similar circumstances. But in the hands of a master player, the guitar becomes a small orchestra. Its six strings encompass more than four octaves, more than half the range of a grand piano. It has a rich singing tone, is responsive to mood, is deeply resonant, and offers rich harmonies. It is a paradox that the guitar is one of the easiest instruments to play but among the most difficult to play really well.

The earliest guitar-like instrument was called a *nefer*. Dating to as early as 1200 BC, these were engraved, painted, and sculpted on objects in Egyptian tombs. A Hittite instrument from 1300 BC has many of the features of a modern guitar: a flat top with sound holes, a long fretted neck that runs the entire length of the body, and a soundbox with in-curving feminine sides. Egyptian Pharaoh Ramses II (c. 1303–1213 BC) married a Hittite princess and erected an obelisk that depicts a guitar-shaped instrument.

Greeks and Romans adopted the instrument. Our word guitar derives from the Greek *cithara*, a type of seven-string lyre. It appeared shortly after the Trojan War (1193–1184 BC) and is found in many Greek myths. The *Iliad* and *Odyssey* of Homer were originally sung with *cithara* accompaniment. Much later, Socrates (469–399 BC) performed with the instrument. Pythagoras, the ancient mathematician and philosopher, helped to create an improved fretboard design.

The instrument underwent many changes in its 1,000 years in Greece and Rome, where it was chiefly used at public games. Nero was not a fiddler but a cithara player; he had himself sculpted in marble with his instrument. In Roman times, as in our own, it vacillated between being a man's and a woman's instrument. Sculptures of instrument-playing women—never men—are found among sarcophagus reliefs of early Christian tombs in Rome.

A description of an anonymous citharist, written in the tenth century by Ikhwan Al-Safa', shows that the virtuoso is timeless:

> "He played them (the strings) in a way that made everyone in the assembly laugh. . . . Then he altered them and played them in another way, and made all weep. . . . Then he altered them again . . . and made everyone go to sleep."

Technical improvements in the early sixteenth century made guitars popular in Europe, and they began to push out the lute. Lute lovers retaliated by claiming that the guitar was undignified and associated with debauchery and sensual abandon. Of course, the more the guitar was identified with such things, the more popular it became.

Soon guitars were in all the new plays, and painters were rendering guitarists galore. This popularity percolated the guitar upward in the social structure to royal families. Henry VIII of England and his daughter Elizabeth I were performers on the *rebec*, a form of guitar. The musicians in *Romeo and Juliet* were also *rebec* players. It became so essential a companion to fashionable young men that when Figaro left his instrument behind in *The Barber of Seville* he exclaimed, "I have forgotten my guitar! I am losing my wits." The leading thief in Ben Jonson's 1621 play *The Gypsies Metamorphosed* calls out, "Give me my gittara: and room for our Chiefe."

But it was Louis XIV of France, the so-called "Sun King," who became the most exalted royal guitarist. Of Louis it was said, "He was never taught anything but how to dance and play the guitar." There was so much praise for Louis's playing that one begins to suspect the praise was not entirely sycophantic boot licking, and that he really was a skilled player. The most incredibly decorated and ostentatious guitars ever created were made in France at the time of Louis XIV. His guitar teacher was an Italian, Francesco Corbetto, the foremost guitarist of his time. Corbetto later went to England and gave instruction to Charles II, who became head of a fashionable guitar clique at the English court.

Colonial and Revolutionary America were well supplied with English and French guitars. Benjamin Franklin was a guitarist; so was Francis

Hopkinson, another signer of the Declaration of Independence. Thomas Jefferson's daughters Polly and Maria took lessons in France while their father was ambassador, and guitars were brought back to Monticello. Here as in Europe it was an instrument of the upper classes, yet some early guitars were taken to the frontier. In the 1820s, Rachel Donelson Jackson, wife of President Andrew Jackson, owned a French-made guitar in middle Tennessee. [See "Rachel and the Eighth of January"]

A tradition of parlor guitar performance by young women of wealthy and upper-middle-class families started in Europe in the late eighteenth century and gained momentum in the early nineteenth. Young ladies from the upper crust learned light classical, semi-classical, and romantic tunes. These were performed in social settings for their suitors and family members. The fad soon trickled down to the urban and rural middle-class masses and became a hugely popular movement. Like other large-scale phenomena, it created a commerce—primarily in sheet music publishing and the sale of new and improved instruments.

The parlor-guitar movement struck the United States with full force in the post-Civil War period. Beginning among the upper class in the Northeast, the fad spread to the middle class and created a demand for guitars. American guitar-making craftsmen used the same kind of woodworking factory methods that had made the violin commonplace a few decades earlier. A huge number of young middle-class women throughout the nation took up the guitar, their interests engaged by instructors, easy-to-learn guitar instruction manuals, the widespread distribution of sheet music, and the availability of fairly inexpensive guitars through such mass-distribution enterprises as the Sears Roebuck catalog. Places as distant from urban centers as rural Mississippi and Hawaii felt the parlor fad.

The mass appeal of the guitar followed hard on the heels of the blackface minstrelsy craze, the first popular-music movement in the history of the nation. [see "Minstrelsy (or Why Blacks Gave up the Banjo)"] The guitar movement offered a more cultivated and nonracist option, of special interest to young women.

The guitar was mostly a one-person phenomenon until the twentieth century. It was a sound for small rooms and small audiences. Parlor styles had become a mass fad, in part, because the parlor was an ideally suited room for guitar—and more families had parlors. Other string instruments were massed and collectivized into banjo, mandolin, hammered dulcimer, and balalaika orchestras—but not guitars.

The instrument was especially well suited to accompanying songs, whose style in those days combined a late-Victorian worldview with epic sweep. Early titles included "The Voortrekker," "Crossing the Pampas," and "The Curtains of Night." The new ragtime tunes could also be played on the guitar. Flat-picking and finger-picking methods were taught, including complex techniques that later became widespread—for example, the use of the thumb as a steady alternating bass, marking the main beats of the piece, while the other fingers syncopate a melody on the treble strings.

Like all popular movements, the late nineteenth-century parlor-guitar phenomenon eventually faded. But American folk-guitar styles continue to be based on instruments and techniques spread by that period's amazing confluence of historical events, technological developments, and growth in communications. Descendants include the black Mississippi Delta and Piedmont styles, the Hawaiian slack-key and slide styles, and the flat-picking and finger-picking styles of country players [see "Kentucky Thumb-picking," and "The Birth of the Blues"].

Its legacy can also be found in open tunings that survive from the parlor era. Black musicians all over the United States call open-D tuning "Vastopol" from "The Siege of Sebastopol," a sheet-music piece published in 1880 that celebrates an episode in the Crimean War. White and black musicians in many areas of the country still call an open-G tuning "Spanish" after "The Spanish Fandango," by far the most popular of parlor tunes, found even today in living tradition everywhere in the nation.

Movement of the guitar from the genteel to the working classes brought striking changes in performance styles. New players began to take the instrument and techniques for playing it away from a slavish reliance upon printed notation and trickle-down faddism. They injected the creativity of streets and store porches, and blended it with sounds of other instruments. Black players were among those who warmly embraced the guitar and subjected parlor techniques to further development. Guitars were also added to the minstrel and string bands of rural whites.

Many technical improvements came to the guitar in the middle and late nineteenth century. Among these were mechanical tuning machines, improved strings of a standard length, and new methods of bracing. Among the modern innovations most beneficial to guitar players was a huge increase in the number of high-quality acoustic music halls at the end of the nineteenth century. The career of the great guitar master Andres Segovia was made possible by advances in acoustic science and the building of halls that would reflect and project soft sounds. Segovia was now able to perform to hundreds of people—in some fine halls to as many as 3,000—rather than to audiences of a few dozen.

Metal-strung guitars have been around for centuries and have a history in several countries, but all the types of steel-string guitars now in use are of American origin and were developed near the turn of the twentieth century. Compared to gut or nylon-string guitars, they offer greater volume and demand a much stronger bracing of the top. They are also preferred for the unique qualities of their sound.

The two major types of steel-string acoustic guitars are the flat top and the arch top. There are fundamental differences in the way they operate. Strings on a flat top terminate at a bridge glued to the top; string vibrations are transferred to the top by a rocking motion of the bridge. Strings on the arch top pass over the bridge and attach to a tailpiece; the top is subject primarily to vertical movement. The soundboard of the flat top needs more bracing, to resist the pull of the strings and to distribute vibrations.

The flat top evolved from earlier gut-string guitars, but the arch top has always been made for steel strings. Orville Gibson, founder of the Gibson Guitar Company early in the twentieth century, was the person most responsible for the development of the arch top. Inspired by the workmanship of Antonio Stradivari, Gibson adapted violin-making techniques to guitar construction, including carved graduated tops. C.F. Martin of the Martin Guitar Company invented the "X" bracing that made it possible to adapt the flat top to new responsibilities in the twentieth century.

The 1920s and 1930s were a heyday for the arch top guitar. Its considerable volume and short sustain made it an ideal instrument for dance bands and jazz orchestras. Played with a pick, it offered an incisive beat for rhythm or fast solo runs.

Beginning in 1916, new flat tops sold by the Martin Company were offered in a new and larger "D" size (named for the "all-big-gun" dreadnought class of battleships) that emphasized the bass frequencies. Many of Martin's shop workers preferred older, smaller models that better balanced volume across the tone spectrum. But the bass emphasis of the dreadnoughts helped to define a new role for the guitar in the string band ensembles that were beginning to emerge.

A third American innovation in guitar construction came from the Dopyera brothers, who in 1926 invented an all-metal resophonic guitar. They were partners in a company called National, and these instruments came to be called "National steel" guitars (actually, the metal was bell brass). These instruments had internal acoustic speakers and were intended to increase the volume of the instruments to serve a vaudeville craze for "Hawaiian" music (which, in many cases, was not actually from Hawaii). The brothers split from National in 1928 and formed the Dobro Company (the name is a contraction of Dopyera Brothers, and a word meaning "goodness" in their native Slovak); they first offered guitars with wood bodies and metal resonators in 1929.

In Hawaii, the open-tuned guitar was sometimes played with a metal bar—the strings not pressed to the frets—producing a wavering tone of variable pitch. This new and exciting sound came to the mainland in the 1890s and was incorporated into such shows as Broadway's *Firebird*. A "Hawaiian" popular music fad was created and continued until the 1930s. Dobro and National steel guitars moved "Hawaiian" sounds into new forms of country and blues music in the late 1920s.

Other innovators had been working on the volume problem, and the introduction of electric guitars soon made the once-popular Dobros and National steels obsolete. But some players liked the tone of the older instruments and began liberating them from the hockshops where vaudeville musicians had left them. Among players who took up the National steel were great blues performers like Bukka White, Blind Boy Fuller, Memphis Minnie, Tampa Red, and Scrapper Blackwell.

Country players who liberated Dobros from pawnshops included Jimmie Tarlton, Howard Dixon, Cliff Carlisle, Beecher Kirby (Brother Oswald), Speedy Krise, Jenks Carman, Shot Jackson, James Kimbrough, Josh Graves, Tut Taylor, and Mike Auldridge. That's almost the whole list of prominent Dobro players from the 1920s until the arrival of a teenaged Jerry Douglas in the 1970s.

The most far-reaching guitar innovation has been the application of electricity to the instrument. In prior centuries, the guitar had often been overwhelmed by other instruments' greater volume. But no more—with the microphone technology of recording and sound reinforcement, even the acoustic guitar could take solo lead "breaks" with ensembles.

Among the innovators who brought electricity to the guitar was acoustic engineer Lloyd Loar, a musician and composer who had earlier helped the Gibson Company develop its famous Mastertone banjo, F5 mandolin, and improved arch top L5 guitar. Loar left Gibson in 1924 and helped found the Vivi-Tone Company, which introduced several electric instruments.

The first electrics seem to have been steel guitars played with a bar, and these instruments were to develop in amazing ways until the 1960s. Equipped with two or three necks and as many as a dozen pedals, each capable of retuning the instrument, the pedal steel guitar became a form of mechanical synthesizer, largely used in country music [see "The Pedal Steel: A Folk Instrument of Our Time"].

It was electricity that moved the jazz guitarist into the limelight. The player who first caught the ear of the nation was Charlie Christian, performing in Benny Goodman's band. Christian was enormously influential, even though he died of tuberculosis at the age of twenty-three. In the 1930s and '40s, French Gypsy Django Reinhardt left a strong imprint on jazz guitar. During the 1950s, the idiom was much enlarged and enriched by a bevy of great players: Tal Farlow, Barney Kessel, Herb Ellis, Johnny Smith, George Van Eps, and Kenny Burrell. Charlie Christian had used the new access to volume to put great guitar solos into jazz ensemble playing. These other players enlarged upon his legacy and made jazz guitar a new and exciting idiom that could stand on its own feet.

The volume problem had weighed heavily upon blues guitar performance until the advent of new and louder steel-string guitars. Those instruments and electric recording technology set off a boom of blues recordings in the 1920s. The new performers were working people. They played in bars and whorehouses. Many had physical handicaps and were wresting a living from the streets with a tin cup, in an era before there was even a beginning of the social welfare net. More than a few died young, among them Robert Johnson—an all-time favorite among blues fans. It was a tough scene for women; Memphis Minnie was the one great early female blues guitarist who left a sizable recorded legacy.

While "Hawaiian" guitar that was not always Hawaiian was being heard in mainland popular music, major changes came to real Hawaiian music. The parlor style of "open tuning" became the basis of a "slack-key" style in the islands. A tune was rendered with as many open strings as possible, so the instrument could resonate freely, then the strings were "slacked" (retuned) so the next tune could also be played mostly on open strings. This picking style has not been heard much on the mainland, but in Hawaii it has always surpassed slide styles in popularity. Among the most influential slack-key players are Gabby Pahinui, Raymond Kane, Sonny Chillingsworth, Atta Isaacs, and Ledward Kaapana.

Country and rockabilly guitar has its heroes, both electric and acoustic. Among the most influential acoustic players during the past fifty years are Maybelle Carter, Sam McGee, Don Reno, George Shuffler, Dan Crary, Norman Blake, Tony Rice, and especially Doc Watson [see "Doc Watson: Just One of Us"]. And there's a Cajun acoustic superpicker: David Doucet.

The list of electric guitar heroes is long: Merle Travis, Jimmy Bryant, Scotty Moore, Chet Atkins, Duane Eddy, James Burton, Hank Garland, and Grady Martin, among others. Their influence reached around the world with the recordings of Elvis Presley, Rick Nelson, and other pop stars. Portions of England became musical suburbs of Memphis and Chicago. Among those who internalized their lessons was young Albert Lee in England. He learned to play both the electric lead and electric steel leads from the Speedy West and Jimmy Bryant recordings—not an easy task, but no one was there to tell him it was impossible. It led to a discipline and drive and an excitement that has endured in his music.

Among pop guitarists, there is a very special place that was carved out by Les Paul—guitarist, technician, composer, and inventor. He started in the 1930s as a country player, known as "Rhubarb Red," before moving into jazz and pop idioms. The first to do multi-track recordings, he also pioneered in the creation of solid-body guitars. These instruments have provided latitude for new forms of showmanship. For example, Jimi Hendrix based much of his act upon tearing his guitar apart—stomping, smashing, and grinding it into the floor.

The best guitars ever made are being made right now, and here in the United States. The application of electricity to hand tools has created a renaissance of instrument making, and the very best instruments are custom made in small shops. These are found everywhere in the country, from Cape Cod to a fine little shop near where the road ends on the north side of Hawaii's Big Island. Rugby, Virginia's, Wayne Henderson is one of the new brand of luthiers. Asked to name his most important tool at a 1977 Smithsonian instrument workshop, Wayne said it was his pocketknife, and that he wore one out every year.

These are the guitar elements that influenced the creation of musics that have spread from our nation to all the world. The Iron Curtain could not shut them out. Their working class vitality is intact. Keep your eye on the guitar. More good stuff is coming.

The Pedal Steel

A Folk Instrument of Our Time

• •

Of the many musical marvels and synthesized electronic wonders developed during the past half century, the pedal steel guitar promises to be one of the longest-lasting contributions to man's music-making tools. Most of the innovations in the development of this new and intricate instrument have come from part-time musicians working in their basements and renovated garages.

The pedal steel is a folk instrument. Its players have learned to play it without recourse to text or formal instruction. Its development has come at the hands of musicians who heard its sound, liked it, and built their own or purchased an instrument from one of the craftsmen building pedal steels—usually another player. There is no accepted method of musical notation for the instrument, and only now [1976], twenty-five years after the early popularity of the pedal steel, have the first rudimentary instruction books begun to appear. These are not sufficient to train a player, although they could conceivably increase the speed of a beginner's learning.

Adapted from *Mugwumps* magazine, Volume 6, Number 1, Winter 1977; this article previously appeared in the National Council for the Traditional Arts publication *Tradition*, 1976.

This is an instrument one learns by listening, watching, and doing; a high degree of musical aptitude and years of practice are required before most players are ready to play in public. Its development from earlier folk instruments resulted from the need to adapt to new performing situations, and from the availability of new technologies.

Early steel guitars (pre-pedal and pre-electric) were nothing more than guitars flipped over and played with a steel bar. A raised nut prevented the bar from pressing the strings into the frets and the instrument was tuned in an open chord. Where this style of playing originated is not clear; it may have arisen in several places. One widespread story holds that the style was developed by a student at a Hawaiian boys' school in 1894, but the story is poorly documented. Some writers have suggested that it developed from Hawaiian slack-key guitar style, but they cite no evidence that slack-key playing came first.

Accounts of the style in Hawaii usually begin with the introduction of the guitar to the Islands by early Spanish sailors, Mexican cowboys, or Portuguese settlers—and then jump to the boys' school story. Such accounts ignore pre-1900 parlor guitar fads, their open tunings, and the existence of mainland-style fretted-instrument orchestras in the Islands. They also ignore a crucial technological development: the introduction of steel strings. Try playing a gut-string instrument with a bar and you'll understand why it was crucial.

Whatever its origin, the style became a fad in Hawaii before 1900 and was spread throughout the U.S. by a vaudeville craze for "Hawaiian" music. By 1907, Victor had recorded fifty-three single-side "Hawaiian" discs. This fad continued until the early 1930s. Some of the players of this style were native Hawaiians, but more were mainland citizens who adopted Hawaiian names and learned such standards of the "Hawaiian" repertoire as "Maui Chimes," "The Hilo March," "Beautiful Isle of Somewhere," and "Beyond the Reef."

Early hillbilly recording artists adopted the instrument during the mid-1920s. Jimmie Tarlton used it first for recording with Tom Darby as Darby and Tarlton. Cliff Carlisle used the instrument in recording with Jimmie Rodgers and for recordings made in his own name.

During this era, black musicians used similar open tunings and techniques to play and record "bottleneck" guitar pieces. Such skills were scattered over a wide area of the South during the 1920s, causing some to wonder whether the style could have migrated from Southern blacks to Hawaii, and thence back to the mainland.

Another plausible explanation is that a guitar tuned in an open chord invites a player to use a bar. Open-chord guitar tunings had widely been used in earlier times, especially during the Victorian parlor guitar fad.

Transplanted to the vaudeville stage, the acoustic steel guitar had serious disadvantages, a primary one being its lack of volume. Attempts to resolve this problem led to the invention of acoustic resonators, installed in instruments constructed entirely of metal—usually brass—during the early 1920s.

The primary inventors in this work were the Dopyera Brothers of California. They were Slovak-Americans who later build a wood instrument with a metal resonator they called a "Dobro," a name now used in a generic sense for resonator guitars played with a bar. The brothers also built mandolins and guitars, then equally popular, but they are now primarily remembered for their contributions to slide instruments. Their instruments were used by then-famous performers such as Jim and Bob, Sol Ho'opi'i, and Roy Smeck.

But volume remained a problem, as even a National brass-body guitar or Dobro could not match the volume of a well-built banjo, violin, mandolin, or guitar. The name of the person who introduced electricity to stringed instruments is not known to the writer, but among the early innovators one finds a familiar name, that of the great acoustic engineer Lloyd Loar. Loar's Electrostatic pickup was developed in 1923 before he left the Gibson Company, and was used in the Vivatone instruments he produced during the mid-1920s. Loar's first electric instruments were a guitar and a bass.

In 1928, Benjamin Messner, associated with the Amperite Company, developed a contact microphone for use on guitars. In 1931, Rickenbacker began making its "frying pan," an instrument some have called the first commercially produced electric guitar. In 1921, the Dopyera Brothers, assisted by Art Simpson, produced a few steel guitars equipped with bar-magnet pickups. The earliest recording of an electric steel guitar is an August 1934 Columbia recording of a Hawaiian musician, Andy Iona.

Hawaiian groups declined in popularity, but the new electric instrument quickly spread to country music performers throughout the South and Southwest. It was adopted by western swing bands, most notably those headed by Bob Wills and Bill Boyd. In his first session for Columbia in September 1935, Wills included electric steel guitarist Leon McAuliffe. A year later, in September 1936, McAuliffe recorded with Wills "Steel Guitar Rag," the tune that is still most identified with the instrument. McAuliffe had learned the tune from a 1928 recording by Roy Harvey and Jess Johnson, and they'd learned it from Sylvester Weaver, a black guitarist who recorded it in 1923 as "Guitar Rag." The common arrangement of this piece seems to have been created by Johnson, a noted fiddler from Wolf Pen, West Virginia, who also pleased fans with lovely arrangements played on a Dobro guitar.

Electric pickups made the sound box of the acoustic steel guitar useless or a hindrance. During the mid-1930s, the instrument became a flat board with six strings, tuning keys, an electric pickup, tone and volume controls, and whatever decorative art the maker cared to add. During this period, some players carried as many as three such "lap steel" instruments, tuning them in different open chords and plugging in the one most appropriate to the tune being played. By 1942, makers were building instruments with two, three, and four necks, and some built instruments with eight strings for each neck.

In 1940, the Gibson Instrument Company produced a steel guitar it called the Electraharp. The instrument was mounted on three legs. Foot pedals attached to cables allowed the player to change the tuning of individual strings. It is likely that Gibson based its design on one developed by an electric steel player, but his name is not known to the writer. The pulling of strings to change the tuning of the instrument was not new— at least one Victorian acoustic guitar had featured that innovation. But it was new to change the tuning of an electrically amplified instrument by means of foot pedals.

The Electraharp attracted relatively little attention. The attention came later, to instruments built by California craftsman Paul Bigsby. He developed a pedal system by which a player could pull to a new tuning whatever strings—usually two—were attached to the foot pedal. Bigsby sold his first one-pedal instruments in 1948. Early 1950s recordings made on these instruments by Speedy West, Bud Isaacs, and others created an instant demand that neither Bigsby nor commercial manufacturers were prepared to fill.

This led to a period of basement innovation, with many players building their own instruments. The most important innovators during this period were two Nashville steel guitar players: Shot Jackson and Buddy Emmons. Their handcrafted Sho-Bud instruments established a new standard for pedal steel construction. Jackson and Emmons brought a high degree of precision to pedal action, as many as fourteen strings per neck, and as many as ten pedals. Three or four knee levers could drop one set of strings, while others were raised by pedal action.

In the early 1960s, Emmons left Sho-Bud to start the Emmons Guitar Company, but Jackson and his son continued the innovations. The instruments they and other craftsmen build today are a study in complexity and potential. A player can adjust his pedals to his liking, pulling or dropping whatever strings he wishes. Most steels are tuned to C6th and E9th, although the two necks can be tuned in scores of other ways. Once a tuning is selected, pedals and levers add new tunings, individually and in combination. Because of this, one steel guitar player usually cannot play another's instrument.

Part of the appeal of the instrument is the sound it makes when a pedal is used to change a chord or to produce a rising note. Even the early one-pedal instruments had this appeal. It was used to good advantage by Bud Isaacs, who helped bring the instrument to national attention on such recordings as Webb Pierce's "Slowly" and "More and More" (both 1954) and Isaacs's own "Bud's Bounce" (1955).

Within five years, pedal steel backup was as necessary for a Nashville country crooner as a cowboy hat or spangled suit made by Nudie's Rodeo Tailors. This has continued until today; while Nashville's current crop of crooners often use doo-wah choruses and string orchestras for recording, many use pedal steel players on the road.

There was a brief heyday of recording of steel guitar instrumentals during the mid-1950s, a period of considerable innovation in the adding of pedals to the instrument. The most notable recordings were by Bud Isaacs, Herb Remington, Noel Boggs, Speedy West, and Buddy Emmons.

At the same time Alvino Rey reasserted his interest in the instrument. A well-known steelman from the late 1930s, Rey married one of the King Sisters [big band and TV stars] and toured with this pop group for some twenty years, but popular music audiences were not attracted to the extent that country people were.

Most players of the electric steel guitar turned to pedals during the 1950s, but three well-known players—Jerry Byrd, Leon McAuliffe, and Don Helms—resisted the trend and continued playing non-pedal steel. Each of these three became identified with a distinctive trademark sound that automatically identified their playing to knowledgeable country listeners. Helms was known for his "wah-wah" effects in the Hank Williams band, McAuliffe for his single-string bar slides with the Bob Wills band, and Jerry Byrd for a long string of Hawaiian-type instrumentals recorded for major labels in a style patterned after early vaudeville players such as Sol Ho'opi'i. But most steel players were delighted with the new pedal and lever technology.

Masters of the pedal steel could be found during the 1950s and 1960s in the bands and recordings of well-known country singers. Ernest Tubb was a devoted fan of the instrument, employing such notable players as Buddy Emmons and Buddy Charleton. (In 1960, Tubb used Charleton on steel and Emmons on take-off electric guitar, reasoning that both needed jobs.) Buck Owens gained his first attention while backed by the driving right hand and lightning pedal work of Ralph Mooney and later by Tom Brumley. During his early years, Ray Price was ably supported by Jimmy Day, and Faron Young never sounded as good after the departure of "Big Ben" Keith.

The commercial work of the better steel guitar players is interesting, but, to take their real measure, it is necessary to hear them in a jam session playing what they prefer. Such outstanding players as Curly Chalker, Doug Jernigan, Lloyd Green, and Buddy Emmons are as likely to take their inspiration from jazz, bluegrass, traditional folk, or classical music as from commercial country.

When Jernigan was afforded the rare opportunity to record what he wished on a recent Flying Fish LP, he chose selections from J.S. Bach, Jimmie Rodgers, and Hank Williams. Why Bach? Perhaps to overcome an inferiority complex by showing that this instrument is now full-grown and as good for playing Bach as any other. Whatever the reason, Jernigan's delivery of Bach has the studied clarity of Julian Bream's lute playing, while other pieces echo the bubbling intensity of jazz guitarist Johnny Smith.

Yet the pedal steel is a folk instrument. When Shot Jackson was developing his important universal pedal system in a tiny East Nashville garage, he kept handy a large square of quarter-inch sheet metal. When a visitor of any kind arrived to gape at his work, Shot's helper distracted the visitor while Shot slipped up behind and dropped the square of metal on the concrete floor. The resulting crash caused jumps and yells, which Shot enjoyed. (This is the same Shot Jackson who worked the country schoolhouse circuit with such performers as the Bailes Brothers, Johnnie and Jack, and Roy Acuff.)

Many of those who jumped and yelled at Shot's practical joke were pedal steel guitar players, visitors who had come down from Hopkinsville or up from Carrollton. They took Shot's instruments to the hillbilly bars, still the best place to hear them.

Stanley Hicks

∙ ∙

D o you know the story of Jack and the Beanstalk? It is only one of the many traditional stories about Jack, most of which had never been recorded until collectors found their way to the Hicks family, of Beech Mountain in Watauga County, North Carolina.

The story came to the Hicks from an ancestor, Council Harmon (1806–1890). In these stories, Jack is a witty lad who serves the king and himself by catching unicorns, lions, wild hogs, robbers, and other dangerous creatures.

The Hicks family has been self-sufficient in far more than its literature. For generations, members of the family have made their own tools, medicine, food, implements, houses, and musical instruments.

Stanley Hicks grew up absorbing these old ways from his father. He helped to distill oils from birch, mountain tea, and sassafras. He gathered and sold roots and herbs. He knew the homemade games children played to pass the long winter nights in the mountains.

From *Mugwumps* magazine, Vol. 6, No. 3, Fall 1978. Joe Wilson wrote: "I was reared six miles from Stanley, and have known him since childhood" [see also "The Hicks and Related Families: Carriers of Tradition"].

Stanley will tell you that he is "from out of the Beech," one of the highest and most remote of the Southern Appalachian peaks. He had to go elsewhere—to the North Carolina Piedmont and even to upstate New York—to earn the money to buy his little farm, but he returned to his mountains when enough had been saved.

Stanley makes and sells fine traditional banjos and dulcimers, grows good burley tobacco, keeps some cattle, and has a big garden. He still tells the tales he learned from his father and grandparents, plays the banjo and dulcimer, and sings songs he learned around firesides as a child. A good fiddle or banjo tune is likely to persuade him to show his skills as a buck dancer.

Each banjo and dulcimer Stanley makes has its beginning when he selects a tree on one of the high ridges near his home. He prefers walnut, but has made instruments from cherry, oak, chestnut, and poplar. The tree is taken to a local mill, sawed, and the boards brought home to dry.

Also drying on the walls of his shop are groundhog skins. Stanley's neighbors are glad to be rid of the pesky animals that dig holes that can break the legs of horses and cattle if they accidentally step into them. Stanley hunts groundhogs with a .22 caliber rifle and shoots them in the head, so as to leave the larger part of the pelt undamaged for use as a banjo head. The animal is skinned, remaining bits of fat are carefully scraped from the hide, and the pelt is soaked in wood ashes and water for a few days, until the hair loosens and can be scraped off. After being stretched and nailed to the wall of the shop for a few weeks, the head turns white and is very tough.

Stanley buys the brass screws, strings, and the wax with which he finishes his banjos. The metal ring inside is cut from a larger piece of metal hanging in his shop and made into a hoop. Everything else is produced on his farm and shaped by his hands. In making a dulcimer, his "outside" material is fret wire. Stanley is a painstaking, careful workman who tells with pride that only one of his instruments has ever come back for repairs—one that had been dropped from a considerable height. He handles wood lovingly, carefully selecting unflawed sections with good grain. He eschews decoration and commercial finishes, preferring to let the beauty of the wood show through careful hand-rubbing and waxing.

Stanley lives only a few miles from two other well-known Southern Appalachian instrument makers: Leonard Glen and the late Frank Proffitt.

His instruments are similar to theirs, but Stanley learned his craft from his father, once the best-known tool and instrument maker in the Beech. He prizes instruments made by his father, and recently made a new banjo to trade with a neighbor for one his father made for $2.50 decades ago.

Stanley's fretless banjos are louder than most, and their tone is exquisite. Of the instrument he plays, Stanley says, "It's just like the others I make." Indeed there is a uniformity in the quality of his work. There are no "top of the line" or economy models; Stanley builds just one model of a banjo and one model of a dulcimer. He prefers to sell his instruments to people who will play them, refuses to deal with middlemen of any kinds, and has found that working alone suits him best.

Stanley avoids craft shows and sells most of his instruments by mail ($125) to buyers who have seen them in the hands of others, or who have seen Stanley at the North Carolina Folklife Festival or the National Folk Festival. He knows that others sell instruments of comparable quality for more, but says, "I don't want to charge more than working people can afford." The waiting period for those who order is always several months, and Stanley refuses to be rushed.

At festivals, Stanley is a consummate, irrepressible showman. His "Jack tales" fascinate children and adults, and are told with antics, male and female voices, and sound effects. His singing voice is strong and he has a plentiful store of banjo and dulcimer tunes native to his part of the mountains. His jack-in-the-box style of mountain dance puts the common-style choreographed clog dance to shame.

If he wished to do so, Stanley could build fretted metal banjos and other modern instruments. He has the tools and the skills to do so. He has lived elsewhere by necessity but returned home. He has seen other models and admired them but prefers his father's.

After I paid for my banjo and prepared to leave, Stanley asked if he could play a tune on it "before I see it go." He played "Johnson Boys," a favorite on the Beech. He sang with the same intensity and humor that he would use on stage, although only he and I were there. I treasure the instrument for many reasons. Among them is the fact that it is a part of Stanley and his father, and the hazy blue ridges where close-grained walnut grows.

OLD-TIME MUSIC

The Hill Billies
The Band That Named the Music

. . . .

This band gave hillbilly music its name. Beginning in 1925, it made the first recordings of many tunes and songs that are now standards, including "Sally Ann," "East Tennessee Blues," and "Nine Pound Hammer." It pioneered the use of the microphone to solo each instrument in country music. It made the first movie to feature country music, was the first country band to tour widely, brought country music to Washington and New York, and played for President Coolidge.

The Hill Billies were from the Blue Ridge of the Southern Appalachians. But the stereotype of the head-of-the-holler band, which they helped to create, does not fit them. The Hill Billies were showmen—they played what they heard and liked, and they traveled widely. Simply put, they were a commercial country music band, the first one to have any real success in show business. Familiar to fans from Canada to Florida, and from the Atlantic coast to west of the Mississippi, they were the first to mix radio fame and incessant touring.

From *Bluegrass Unlimited*, July 2013; and liner notes to *The Hill Billies*, County Records, 1973 and *A Fiddlers' Convention in Mountain City, Tennessee*, County Records, 1972.

Their radio shows, recordings, and shenanigans on vaudeville stages of the mid- and late twenties made The Hill Billies well known—at a time when the recording industry needed a short and highly descriptive name for the music of the rural South that it had just begun to record. But this group left more than a name; it left a legacy of fine recordings and a joyous approach to music.

Tony Alderman said The Hill Billies began in the early spring of 1924. Joe Hopkins brought his guitar into City Barbershop, located on Main Street in the furniture boomtown of Galax, Virginia. Tony laid his scissors down and tuned his fiddle. A two-day jam session began, with other barbershop customers and hangers-on joining the fun.

A lean banjoist with a distinguished aura and tailored suit brought a beautifully honed sense of timing. This was businessman John W. Rector, owner of a store and member of an intense musical community in the nearby cotton-mill town of Fries [see "Fries: Where the Music Began"]. Joe's brother, Al Hopkins, offered a voice with great volume and intensity. A third singing brother, John Hopkins, provided ukulele rhythms and a soaring tenor.

Within weeks, they moved to Washington, D.C. The Hopkins boys were from Watauga County, North Carolina, but their father was a long-time employee of the U.S. Census Bureau. His spacious Washington home on Kennedy Street became headquarters for The Hill Billies. Al was an experienced showman; as early as 1910, he had organized his three younger brothers into what he called the Old Mohawk Quartet for shows at the Majestic Theater, a Washington vaudeville showplace.

Rector had a suggestion for the core group: they should go to New York and record. He had just been there for a string-band session with two Fries neighbors—fiddler Jim Sutphin and guitarist and singer-songwriter Henry Whitter—as the Virginia Breakdowners. He thought the barbershop group could do as well and, anyway, he needed to return to New York to order fall fashions for his store. Six titles recorded during the summer of 1924 for Victor A&R man Clifford Cairns were never released.

The term "hillbilly" had been in print and general use for several decades but apparently had not been applied to any form of music until January 15, 1925, when Ralph Peer of the OKeh Recording Company and Al

Hopkins had to choose a name for the Hopkins-Alderman-Rector band at their second New York recording session.

Self-deprecating humor has long been a mountain staple, and Al Hopkins humorously used a "fighting term" when asked to name the group. "We're nothing but a bunch of hillbillies from North Carolina and Virginia," Al said. "Call us anything." Peer reacted to the self-mocking term by telling his secretary to list "The Hill Billies" on the six titles Al's group had just recorded.

Al Hopkins, who invented the band's bib overall and bandana costumes, knew how to create comedy skits and how to rusticate the press into believing that the band had swung out of the mountains on grapevines. Some of the stereotyped tomfoolery associated with "hillbillies" may have resulted from the antics of this group, and they possibly influenced the development of cartoon strips such as Snuffy Smith and Li'l Abner [see "Radio and the Blue Ridge"].

Actually, the Hopkins brothers came from an upper-crust family from Boone, North Carolina. One of the older Hopkins brothers was a physician who owned a small hospital at Galax. Al Hopkins managed the hospital. Brother Joe worked nearby for a railroad. Fiddler Tony Alderman was skilled in the application of the new emerging technologies in sound, radio, and photography.

Other bands quickly appropriated their name, and Tony Alderman recalled their amazement and chagrin at finding the Ozark Hillbillies playing at a theater in New York that was across the street from their hotel. Faced with the theft of a brand they felt to be their property, The Hill Billies turned to the law and had a Washington lawyer incorporate their name. As a side venture, they issued stock in the group. But the attempt to protect their name was no more successful than the stock, as bands calling themselves "hillbillies" spread, and the name became a term for the music of rural whites from the South.

The Nashville-based Country Music Association had an enormous inferiority complex regarding the term "hillbilly," attempted to substitute "Country and Western" (with some success), and probably wished Al and his friends had been more successful in protecting their property. The disrespect in the band's name still makes some country music fans flinch.

Tony Alderman recalled Al Hopkins' good-hearted dismissal of such objections: "Tell 'em to use more talcum powder."

The Hill Billies recorded for four companies. Their 1924 Victor session was not issued, and they left OKeh in late 1925 for the jointly owned Vocalion and Brunswick labels. Their recordings were released simultaneously on both of these labels, with The Hill Billies listed on Vocalion and Al Hopkins and his Buckle Busters listed on Brunswick. They used both names for personal appearances.

The May 8, 1925, Fiddler's Convention at Mountain City, Tennessee, taught the boys that a huge audience could be attracted to a remote location through radio advertising, the first country music posters, multiple performers, and corporate and social sponsorships. Fiddlin' John Carson, the Fiddling Powers Family, and "Uncle Am" Stuart appeared alongside The Hill Billies. The corporate sponsor was the Buster Brown Shoe Company, and the social connection was the local unit of the Ku Klux Klan. The floor of the high school auditorium almost collapsed in the press of the crowd, and the courthouse and grade school auditorium were opened to accommodate the overflow.

This convention was a watershed in the development of professional country music. It brought together, in a "package" show, four of the earliest groups to pioneer in radio and recording. More importantly, it demonstrated the power of then-new media. The lesson was not wasted upon Al Hopkins, Tony Alderman, and Joe Hopkins of The Hill Billies. They quickly moved to schedule similar events in other towns, and for the first time an organized professional country band reached for an audience beyond its local community.

Thanks to radio broadcasts from Washington, D.C. and New York, The Hill Billies became the first nationally known country music band. "We could tell how big the crowd would be by looking at radio antennas as we rode into town," Tony Alderman recalled. "Lots of antennas meant two shows."

John Hopkins disagreed with the modern assumption that it was the recording men who created the country music industry. "They recorded this music because they were hearing it on the radio" he said. "It was a good-sized business before they got over having the big head about it."

Alderman said The Hill Billies scarcely had time to record. "We played a lot, and we got paid from ticket sales. Radio got us the crowds."

In these early static-free days of radio, tours began extending to the Deep South, to Middle Tennessee, to Ohio, to Pennsylvania, and to New York. Later commercial bands claimed to have introduced country music to New York, but The Hill Billies worked in that city as early as 1927. They played at the Broadway Theatre many times, and were heard on New York's WJZ.

They were in New York City when the Great Depression fell upon the land in 1929. Most entertainers were quickly out of work, but The Hill Billies could still find jobs. Alderman remembered the out-of-work vaudeville friends who applied to them when they heard that The Hill Billies had scheduled three days in Brooklyn and a split weekend on Staten Island.

But home base for the group—and the musicians who floated in and out of it—was Washington, D.C., and they were the local favorites there. When Uncle "Am" Stuart died while working with the group in the late twenties, his passing was front-page news. The marriages and comings and goings of The Hill Billies were society news and grist for the mill of columnists. When the Washington press correspondents entertained President Coolidge, they chose the band to enliven the after-dinner festivities.

Their fifteen-minute film short for Vitaphone (Warner Brothers) was the first sound film to feature a professional country music act. It consisted of the band's usual vaudeville fare: fiddling, singing, skits, and Tony playing the musical saw. *The Hill Billies* was released with Al Jolson's *The Singing Fool* in August 1928. This coupling was the biggest-grossing movie event until *Gone With The Wind* was released in 1939.

On most of their recordings, The Hill Billies featured the excellent twin fiddles of Charlie Bowman and Alonzo Elvis "Tony" Alderman, the resonant voice of Al Hopkins and, at various times, the old-time banjo wizardry of John Rector (frequently confused with a second John Rector, a fiddler from the Galax area noted for his 1930s Library of Congress recordings), Jack Reedy, and Walter Bowman. Guitarists Elbert Bowman, Joe Hopkins, and Walter Hughes served time with the group, as did early slide guitarist Frank Wilson, and pioneer recording fiddler Uncle "Am" Stuart.

Other fiddlers who played with The Hill Billies were Fred Roe, "Dad" Williams, and Ed Belcher. Henry Rowe helped introduce the string bass to country music as a member of this band. Elmer and John Hopkins played harmonica and ukulele, and took part in the riotous routines that were a hallmark of the ensemble.

The band had more than its share of bad luck. John W. Rector's illnesses and business needs limited his travel. He died early in 1927. Joe Hopkins became an alcoholic and had to be dropped. Al Hopkins died in a traffic accident near Winchester, Virginia, in 1932, and the band could not continue without its singer, impresario, main comic, and sparkplug. So this group—that became famous before electric recording and before the Grand Ole Opry went on the air—ended after less than an eight-year run.

The City Barbershop site in Galax is now occupied by Barr's Fiddle Shop and still rings with music. Owner Stevie Barr has kept some of Tony Alderman's old tonsorial equipment: a fine barber chair, a long mirror and sink, and many photos of the band that named the music. "They were real," Stevie says, gesturing to photos of the young Hill Billies. "This is real history, not bumper-sticker history."

With grateful thanks to my late friends Tony Alderman and John Hopkins, and great folklorist, historian, and colleague Archie Green. For a delightful discussion of these matters, search out Archie's essay, "Hillbilly Music; Source and Symbol."

Grayson and Whitter

G. B. Grayson and Henry Whitter met in 1927 at a fiddlers' convention in Mountain City, Tennessee. During the next two years, they recorded some fifty songs and tunes, an amazing number of which became standards of country music. These include "Banks of the Ohio," "Tom Dooley," "Lee Highway Blues," "Little Maggie," "Rose Connally," "Nine Pound Hammer," "Train 45," "Ommie Wise," "Cluck Old Hen," "Old Jimmie Sutton," "Handsome Molly," and "Shout Little Lulu."

The material they chose to record was excellent, as was the quality of their performances. Indeed, the Grayson and Whitter discs are usually preferred to later recordings of many of these standards.

Both men were composers as well as avid song collectors and traders. Grayson converted the well-known banjo tune "Reuben" into his "Train 45," a melody now a favorite of bluegrass banjoists. Whitter composed "Going Down Lee Highway" in September of 1929, as his Model T chugged down U.S. Route 11 (known locally as Lee Highway) in Northeast Tennessee, on the way to a Memphis recording session. This musical

Adapted from liner notes to *The Recordings of Grayson and Whitter*, County Records, 1998. Joe Wilson wrote: "I grew up near Major Grayson's farm."

exercise soon entered the repertoire of hundreds of fiddlers as the "Lee Highway Blues."

One of Grayson's songs, "Joke and Henry" (mislabeled on the original disk as "Joking Henry"), is a close musical relative of "Frankie and Johnnie." Actually it describes the antics of two local boys who had an alcoholic party before going to sleep on a railroad track. Shortly before the train arrived they were awakened by a thrown brick. Grayson's recounting of their soiree created much laughter at my childhood home.

Grayson learned "Nine Pound Hammer" from Charlie Bowman, a fiddler from an adjoining Tennessee county who "wrote it off" a black work song. On it we have another snatch of Grayson's dry humor. "Drive her on down," he advises Henry. "Break the handle off."

"Short Life of Trouble" was recorded by both Grayson and Tom Ashley and may date from their years of playing together. "Where Are You Going, Alice?" is a Grayson composition about a local teenager who married a Civil War veteran; it relates the old soldier's dismay when she began "running around."

The Grayson and Whitter recording of "Handsome Molly," though widely copied, is still unmatched. "I've Always Been A Rambler" is a superb variation of a beloved ballad, "The Girl I Left Behind Me."

Grayson left the inimitable mark of his style on all that he recorded, ranging from the Irish stall ballad "Rose Connally," to the 1820s American ballad "Ommie Wise," to his own compositions. "Tom Dooley" was a local ballad associated with the Grayson family.

Grayson was the singer and fiddler on all their recordings, while Whitter provided guitar backup, some of the spoken comments, and a few vocal refrains such as the one offered on "Nine Pound Hammer."

Henry Whitter also wrote numerous songs, and made the first recording of "The Wreck of the Old Ninety-Seven." Whitter was a millhand from a cotton mill town: Fries, in Grayson County, Virginia, near the head of the New River Valley. That county and neighboring Carroll County produced many early string band musicians; Whitter was the first from there to record [see "Fries: Where the Music Began"].

In 1923—before he met Grayson—Whitter took his guitar and harmonica to New York and persuaded OKeh to record him, most notably "The Wreck of the Old Southern 97." In 1924, he also recorded with fiddler Jim Sutphin and banjoist John Rector as Henry Whitter's Virginia Breakdowners.

Skilled in promotion and a good showman, Whitter was living in nearby Warrensville, North Carolina, when the Grayson and Whitter recordings were made. He was plagued with poor health and died in the state hospital in Morganton, North Carolina, in 1940.

Gilliam Banmon Grayson was known to most residents of northeastern Tennessee as "Banmon." He was born in Ashe County, North Carolina, on November 11, 1887. When he was two years old, his family moved a few miles west into Johnson County, Tennessee. That county forms the northeastern tip of Tennessee. He lived there for the rest of his life.

Grayson's vision was severely damaged when he was six weeks old. His daughter Lillie said he spent a winter day staring out a window at snow glittering in bright sunlight, "took cold in his eyes," and thereafter was permanently handicapped. He was not totally blind. He could recognize people by their bulk, and tell time by holding a watch with large numbers close to his eyes.

He began playing a fretless homemade banjo as a small boy, and became locally well known for his fiddling in his early teens. Unable to farm, work in timber, or keep store, he was forced to rely upon music for the support of his wife and six children.

An itinerant musician, Grayson traveled from place to place playing his fiddle and singing at school entertainments, on store porches, street corners, or wherever coins could be earned. He did not own an automobile, and walked to jobs or waited for someone passing by to offer a ride.

At one time or another, Grayson played with most of the better musicians of the area. His daughter recalled that one of his favorites was the North Carolina banjoist, Dock Walsh. Grayson also played with Clarence "Tom" Ashley, another pioneering old-time musician from his county [see "Clarence 'Tom' Ashley"].

Ashley recalled trips with Grayson dating back to 1918, including at least two "busting trips" to the West Virginia coalfields where they performed outside pay shacks and passed Grayson's hat. They performed at the famous May 1925, Old Fiddler's Convention in Mountain City, Tennessee, a highly successful event that stimulated the creation of many similar events.

During a two-year period in the mid-1920s, Grayson lived within three miles of Ashley's home at Shouns, Tennessee, but spent most of his adult life in Laurel Bloomery, Tennessee, a tiny farming community in a beautiful valley between Damascus, Virginia, and Mountain City, Tennessee.

On August 16, 1930, Grayson visited his brother's home in nearby Virginia, on foot. Having made a bit of money from his recordings and public appearances, he seemed finally able to buy a home and had made a down payment on the homeplace where he was reared.

Neighbor Bill Millhorn stopped to offer a ride as he was returning home, but, as Millhorn's family had his one-seat roadster fully occupied, Grayson had to stand on the running board outside the car. The little brown Japanese-made fiddle he used for all his recording sessions was placed inside.

While rounding a blind curve south of the town of Damascus, Millhorn's car collided with a log truck heavily loaded with chestnut timber "extract" and driven by another neighbor, Ferd Gentry. Grayson was hurled from the running board and killed. He was forty-two.

Although poor, Grayson was a member of a prominent and respected mountain family. He was the son of Benjamin C. Grayson and a nephew of Major James W.M. Grayson of Trade, Tennessee. Years earlier, when the Civil War broke out and Tennessee seceded from the Union, Major Grayson had joined those organizing "a little rebellion within a big rebellion" against Confederate authority in northeastern Tennessee.

There is recurring speculation about Gilliam Banmon Grayson's name. In 1962, collector and musicologist Ralph Rinzler guessed that his first initial must be for "George," and put this error into print. Since then, discographers and writers have followed, sheep-like, in replicating Rinzler's error. There's a reason for Grayson's unusual actual first name, "Gilliam."

Both Grayson brothers named sons for a favorite Federal officer in the Civil War, General Alvan C. Gillem. Major Grayson's son was called by his initials, "A.G." Benjamin's son, Gilliam Banmon Grayson, was always called "Banmon," a family name from his mother's largely Scots-Irish family, the Roarks. His name was frequently misspelled—usually as "Bandman"—and the family was not correct in the spelling of "Gillem," the actual name of the officer the father wished to honor. It was a time when people were creative, and had several ways to spell names.

That his name was Gilliam Banmon Grayson is clear from Federal pension records completed by or for his mother (he was the handicapped son of a soldier), death records, and a careful recounting of these matters by his oldest daughter, Lillie Grayson Sturdivant. In 1972, Lillie carefully spelled out both names when interviewed on tape by Ken Irwin, Marian Leighton Levy, and the writer in Rising Sun, Maryland.

A root of the true vine of country music, Grayson and Whitter have been admired and emulated by other true-vine musicians for more than seventy years, among them such paragons as Bill Monroe, the Stanley Brothers, and J.E. Mainer. Their recordings demonstrate that Grayson and Whitter's rugged and stark music retains an ability to reach across generations and charm the heart.

MORE CIVIL WAR CONNECTIONS

When the Carter County Rebellion was suppressed by Confederate General Danville Leadbetter and a large army, G.B. Grayson's uncle, Major Grayson, organized one of the first groups of recruits that slipped out of the mountains to join President Lincoln's armies. Celebrated Union guide Dan Ellis led them and thousands of others from Confederate-held northeastern Tennessee along the mountaintops to Union territory in Kentucky. Major Grayson helped organize the 4th Tennessee (U.S.) Volunteer Infantry, and the 13th Regiment of the Tennessee (U.S.) Volunteer Cavalry.

G.B. Grayson's father, Benjamin C. Grayson, was a private in the ill-fated 4th Tennessee, a unit that was captured by Confederates. Benjamin's brother, James W.M. Grayson, was a lieutenant colonel in that unit, but resigned before the capture to become a major in the 13th Tennessee Cavalry, a regiment composed of Johnson and Carter County men that became the most wide-ranging unit in the Union army, fighting and raiding over more than 3,000 miles in six states. This band of former refugees killed the noted Confederate raider General John H. Morgan in one daring raid and chased Confederate President Jefferson Davis across North Carolina, South Carolina, and Georgia at the end of the war.

During the summer after the Civil War, a young stranger appeared at Major Grayson's farm at Trade, Tennessee, and asked for employment as a farm worker. He said his name was Tom Hall, his shoes were worn out, and he needed money to pay a local shoemaker to make him a pair of boots.

He worked for four days and left early the next morning on foot, wearing the boots. Late that afternoon, two deputies from Wilkes County,

North Carolina, appeared at Major Grayson's farm. They told the major that Tom Hall was actually Thomas Dula (Tom Dooley), a fugitive wanted for a sordid murder on the east side of the Blue Ridge.

Major Grayson invited them to spend the night. The next morning—July 11, 1866—Major Grayson buckled on the rimfire Deemore revolver he had carried through the Civil War and led the deputies in the direction Dula had fled.

They overtook the former Confederate at Pandora, nine miles west of Mountain City, soaking his feet in Doe Creek, seeking relief from the blisters the new boots had made. He was hanged at Statesville, North Carolina, on May 1, 1868, for the knife slaying and secret burial of Laura Foster.

The first recording of the "Tom Dooley" ballad was by Grayson and Whitter in Memphis, in 1929. A 1939 Library of Congress field recording by Frank Proffitt, of Pick Britches in Watauga County, North Carolina, led to its popularity during the 1960s folk revival. Proffitt's version seems to be derived from the Grayson recording. (Proffitt's grandfather served under Major Grayson in the 13th Tennessee Cavalry, as did Tom Ashley's great-uncle, and the writer's sixteen-year-old banjo-picking great-grandfather, Corporal Joseph T. "Lucky Joe" Wilson.)

I learned of these matters from affable and genial J. Luke Grayson, late grandson of Major Grayson and a former Attorney General of Tennessee's First Judicial District. Mister Luke's fiddling son, Frank Grayson, has been a helpful friend. The late Lillie Grayson Sturdivant was a gracious hostess and eager that errors concerning her father's name be corrected. Johnson County's wonderfully knowledgeable historian, Captain Tom Gentry, gave exact dates and details concerning the accident that took Banmon Grayson's life and was helpful with other matters. My mother, Josephine Sutherland Wilson, grew up with the children of Banmon Grayson and told me about the family. My great-grandmother, Pruda Melinda South Davis, had a stack of Grayson and Whitter 78 rpm recordings in the parlor of her house above the falls on Roaring Creek. When he lived in Fort Lee, New Jersey, Frank Mare allowed me to hear the very rare first Grayson and Whitter discs in his excellent collection. All have my gratitude.

Clarence "Tom" Ashley

• •

Tom Ashley was an entertainer before he could walk. Born in 1895, in his grandfather's boarding house in Bristol, Tennessee, he was the only child and center of attention in an extended family that included two aunts, two uncles, his mother, maternal grandparents, and an ever-changing retinue of boarders. Tom had the audience an entertainer needs, his grandfather serving as chief fan and advocate for his little boy antics. Enoch Ashley dubbed his grandson "Tom Tiddy Waddy" for a nursery rhyme. The "Tom" stuck, although Tom's real name was Clarence Earl McCurry.

His father, George McCurry, had married Rose Belle Ashley, Enoch and Mattie Ashley's fifteen-year old daughter. By the time Tom arrived, it was known that—before he took Rose Belle's hand—McCurry had not fully divested himself of an earlier wife. So this Lothario had to leave town in a hurry, and Tom's childhood knowledge of him amounted to his being "a one-eyed fiddler, hell-raiser, and big talker." When Tom's mother remarried, he remained with his grandparents in their boarding house.

Adapted from liner notes to *Greenback Dollar: The Music of Clarence "Tom" Ashley*, 1929–1933, County Records, 2001.

The Ashleys' boarding house was in Bristol, on the Virginia-Tennessee border, but the family were new residents there. Their roots were in Ashe County, North Carolina, some forty-five miles to the east. An ancestor, Methodist minister William Ashley, had arrived in Ashe County shortly after the American Revolution, settling on a branch of the North Fork of the New River. Before 1900, Enoch Ashley relocated his family from Bristol back to Ashe County. Shortly after 1900, they moved again—to Shouns, Tennessee, where Enoch and Mattie operated another boarding house.

Shouns is a crossroads near Mountain City, in Johnson County—the easternmost county in Tennessee—some thirty-seven miles east of Bristol. It is near Roundabout, the North Carolina community where the Enoch Ashley family originated. Johnson County remained Tom Ashley's legal residence for the rest of his life.

Railroads were built to haul timber from the virgin forests being cut in a Johnson County timbering boom. Brakemen, section hands, firemen, and lumber shippers resided with the Ashleys. Tom recalled that some were musicians as were all the Ashley family back to the great-grandparents. The area is rich in music, and Tom was an avid learner. Tom learned banjo playing and songs from his aunts, Airy and Daisy. His "Coo Coo Bird" came from his mother, Rose Belle.

Tom was playing banjo by age eight, and owned a guitar at twelve. In 1911, when he was sixteen, Tom joined a traveling medicine show that passed through Mountain City. He was hired as a musician and roustabout for this home-drawn caravan. Two wagons hauled tents, stage, props, and goods, while the "Doc" rode in a buggy befitting a fake professional. Trucks later replaced the wagons, and Tom traveled in such caravans for thirty-three years.

He worked most of these years with White Cloud, an "Indian" pitch-man, and with "Doctor" Hauer, a Knoxville-based herbal practitioner. Their routes followed harvest seasons, when rural people were in town and might have money. They traveled primarily in western North Carolina, eastern Tennessee, southwestern Virginia, eastern Kentucky, and southern West Virginia. Tom recalled some forays in his early years that ventured into Georgia, Alabama, Mississippi, and Louisiana. He fed and watered the horses and set up camps. During the show, Tom's main job was to draw a crowd to hear the "Doc" pitch their products. For this, he learned

the blackface comedian trade, a skill far more important than musician-
ship in a medicine show.

Blackface minstrelsy was the longest-running popular music and theatre
movement in the history of the United States. It began in New York City in
1840, and became a vessel for the nation's incipient racism and ethnocen-
trism. It percolated into folk idiom and, like other masked arts, became a
medium for speaking truths, teaching the verities, and especially for punc-
turing pomposity. [See "Minstrelsy (or Why Blacks Gave up the Banjo)"]

Tom married Hettie Osborne in 1914. They lived at Shouns. Tom was
home from the shows most of the winter, early spring, and late fall. He
and Hettie farmed tobacco, corn, and small grain, and raised a son and
daughter. In winter, Tom usually arranged one or more "entertainment"
presentations in rural schools. These involved music and a blackface minstrel act. Tom also did what he called "busting," playing for coins on street
corners and wherever else a crowd might gather. The term comes from the
older British term "busk:" to make a living on the street by entertaining.

Sometimes Tom did his "busting" with other musicians. The performer
who worked with him most—from before World War I until 1930—was
famed Johnson County fiddler and singer Gilliam Banmon Grayson [see
"Grayson and Whitter"]. They traveled to pay shacks in the West Virginia
coal camps and to the new rayon mills in Tennessee. And they performed
together at the fiddlers' conventions and contests that were suddenly popular in the mid-twenties.

It is ironic that Grayson and Ashley never recorded together. In the
mid-twenties, Grayson lived for a time within three miles of Ashley at
Shouns, a move made to facilitate their partnership. Their trio—with North
Carolina musician Ted Bare—was fondly recalled by neighbors. Other
performing partners included North Carolina banjoist Dock Walsh and
Virginia fiddler Hobart Smith, two of the finest players in Tom's region of
the Appalachians. Though not as well known, Johnson County's brilliant
long-bow fiddler Ray Dowell performed with Tom in the mid-thirties,
hugely impressing local musicians.

It was during the late twenties that recording opportunities first
came to Ashley, Grayson, and many other rural musicians. The recording
companies were seeking new markets, fearing that the new radio medium would decimate their sales. Grayson recorded first, brought to the

Gennett studios in 1927 by Henry Whitter. Whitter was a middling guitarist but a good salesman and pioneering performer. His 1922 recordings and enthusiasm for this music had helped to prove it could be sold on disc. Tom's first recordings were also for Gennett—a record label owned by the Starr Piano Company of Richmond, Indiana—and were done in February 1928. Like scores of jazz, popular, and other pioneer country musicians, Tom traveled to Indiana to audition and record in a self-appointed quest.

Famed Victor talent scout, recording engineer, and record producer Ralph Peer recorded Tom with the popular Carolina Tar Heels in 1928–1929. In 1929, Tom recorded for Columbia as a soloist, and as lead singer with Byrd Moore's Hot Shots. The Carolina Tar Heels featured Tom on guitar and lead vocals; Dock Walsh—from Wilkes County, North Carolina—played banjo; and fellow North Carolinians Gwen or Garley Foster played harmonica. The Hot Shots were directed by Norton, Virginia, barber and guitarist Byrd Moore and had Clarence Greene—from Mitchell County, North Carolina—on fiddle.

In the early thirties, Tom Ashley did additional sessions for Victor with the Haywood County Ramblers. During 1931, he recorded for the American Record Corporation with the Blue Ridge Entertainers: Gwen Foster, Clarence Greene, Will Abernathy, and Walter R. Davis. His final recordings in this era—duets for ARC in 1933—were released under the name Ashley and Foster (Tom and Gwen Foster).

Ashley was a master of theater as well as a musician. When he was making his early recordings, he was better known as a blackface comedian than as a musician. He began to specialize in comedy even more in the late thirties. Tom had taught skits and mini-plays to young medicine show artists and to the Carolina Tar Heels and the Blue Ridge Entertainers. There's a flash of Ashley humor in the ethnic-bashing early vaudeville song "Three Men Went A-Hunting," which he recorded with Byrd Moore and his Hot Shots in 1929. The song's three men come upon Moore's home town—Norton, Virginia—and it is "the end of the world; we'd better go back the other way."

Tom took to the road before radio existed and before recording companies paid any attention to traditional music. The music he brought to the studios had been honed on the street corners of the small towns of the upland South. His repertoire was rich and showed that his ears were open at home and during his travels. He sang songs and ballads from Anglo-Irish tradition such as "Coo Coo Bird," "House Carpenter," and "Rude and Rambling Man." His fine grasp of indigenous American bal-ladry is reflected in "Naomi Wise," "John Hardy," and "Frankie Silvers." Tom's unique banjo style was learned from the Ashley family, where the instrument was frequently re-tuned. His tuning for the "Coo Coo Bird" is what he called "sawmill"—gDGCD (from the fifth string to the first).

Tom's repertoire also reflected the fact that Appalachian music—usu-ally considered the most "white" of American musical forms—is in fact derived from a colonial and early American amalgamation of white and black musical ideas and instruments. There were relatively few blacks in Johnson County, but Tom's affinity for black music is reflected in "Dark Holler Blues," "Little Sadie," "Baby All Night Long," "Sadie Ray," "Drunk Man Blues," "Penitentiary Blues," "Haunted Road Blues," and "The Train's Done Left Me."

Tom helped popularize some of the nation's best-loved folk songs. His gorgeous recording of "Corinna, Corinna" was highly influential in the spread of that song. It was a beloved song, recorded during the Great Depression when few could buy recordings, so copies of the original re-cord are very rare and nearly every existing copy is "played out." Tom believed his singing of "House of the Rising Sun" at every show for thirty years, in countless towns, helped to popularize the song. He sold the lyr-ics to it and other songs—"Barbara Allen," "Frankie Silvers," and "Naomi Wise"—for a nickel. "You could sell the old kill-'em-dead songs," he said.

He recorded "House of the Rising Sun" in 1933. Roy Acuff learned the song from Ashley on a medicine show tour and recorded it in 1938. Acuff told Tom's biographer Minnie Miller that he also got his fine version of "Greenback Dollar" from Tom.

Roy Acuff was one of many young musicians who worked a season for Tom Ashley. Frank Grayson (a relative of G.B. Grayson and a Moun-tain City fiddler who worked with Tom much later) heard Acuff describe traveling with Tom in Doc Hauer's show as they worked through north-eastern Tennessee and southwestern Virginia. They lived in tents, slept on the ground, worked hard, and were paid very little. But it was Acuff's first job in music, a great learning experience, and he remained Tom's warm friend for life.

Tom's brief career—during the major-label heyday of recording traditional Americana—began when he was thirty-three and was over in five years, brought to an abrupt end by the Great Depression. He earned relatively little from it, but enough to buy seven acres and a house at Shouns. He continued with the medicine shows, but the economic climate was so difficult in the early summer of 1932 that he spent part of his time hoeing corn for a neighboring farmer, Robert M. Davis. Tom's friend Frank Grayson explains, "Times had to be very tough for Tom to run a hoe." During the Depression, he also went to West Virginia and worked for a period in the mines.

Traditional music changed dramatically during the half century Ashley was an active performer. The thirties brought the greatest change. It was the decade when electronic technology and items that could be sold—recordings, radio broadcasts, and ticketed shows—largely overtook community and street performance in defining the place of this form of traditional music. Radio hands of the late 1930s developed the still-current practice of emphasizing product sales, with the recording tail often wagging the performing dog.

The medicine show ran out of gas as a viable commercial enterprise in the thirties. There were new regulations. The U.S. Food and Drug Administration became more interested in claims made for "medicine" and what was in those bottles. States developed an interest in safety and in collecting taxes. Many towns began regulating access to the street corners. More people could read, and what they read about medicine shows was not positive. By then, Tom was in his middle years. The annual medicine show trek became a weary one, and he began to resent the unrelenting physical work of setting up staging and tents, sleeping on the ground, and the painful distances from Hettie and their son and daughter.

In 1937, Tom bought two trucks and began a general trucking business with his son J.D. as his partner. Tom hauled used furniture from eastern Pennsylvania to Mountain City. Loads of green beans were taken from Johnson County to terminal markets and canneries in Knoxville, Charlotte, and Cincinnati. Tobacco was hauled to market, coal was brought from West Virginia, and agricultural lime was delivered to farmers.

During the early forties, Tom performed with Charlie Monroe's touring show and a few years later with the Stanley Brothers. Tom's portion of these shows put him into his blackface "Rastus Jones from Georgia" role and members of the band performed with him Tom's Rastus was an upstart underdog: nimble, tricky, wonderfully bright, and happily able to theatrically thwart the big dogs that forever oppress small dogs. Most of Tom's comedy involved little content. It was timing, inflection, gesture, and facial expression. [See "The Toby Character: When Bluegrass Bands Needed Lightning Rod Salesmen"]

Though he worked as a comedian, Tom never stopped being a musician with his own band. His Tennessee Merrymakers formed in 1947 and continued into the early fifties. Tom always had an eye for talent, and the Merrymakers included the finest young musicians around Mountain City and Shouns. These included: Brownie Blankenbeckler, guitar and vocals; Lloyd Dunn, mandolin and vocals; Cart Jones, banjo and vocals; Frank Grayson, fiddle; and David Green, guitar. It was an old-time band with a fine vocal trio— perhaps the best vocal band Tom ever assembled—in front of Jones's relentless drop-thumb banjo. Tom was spokesman, comedian, and sometimes guitarist and singer on the gospel selections. The Merrymakers performed on radio in Bristol and Johnson City and toured from Kentucky to the Carolinas. They worked regularly for two land auction companies. Like Tom's other bands, they were skilled in comedy skits.

The Merrymakers broke up during 1955. Tom performed occasionally with the Stanley Brothers and drove a cab in Mountain City. By the mid-fifties, he was performing with two younger neighbors who lived near him at Shouns: Clint Howard played guitar and was a fine lead singer; Fred Price was an old-time fiddler and singer. Several old-time and bluegrass banjoists served time with them. Tom got the jobs, did comedy, and was spokesman.

On Easter Weekend of 1960, they went to the Union Grove Fiddlers' Convention in Iredell County, North Carolina. Along the way, they stopped at Deep Gap, in Watauga County, hoping to persuade Doc Watson to accompany them to the contest, but Doc was laying linoleum and felt he should finish the job. At Union Grove, they met two young New Yorkers: Ralph Rinzler and Eugene Earle. Upon hearing they were from northeastern Tennessee, Rinzler asked if they knew of a Clarence Ashley. Clint Howard recalled the moment: "Fred and me had a' knowed Tom all our lives, but we just knew him as Tom. So I said, 'No, I don't.

Do you know a Clarence Ashley, Tom?' Tom started to say, 'No,' but he had a second thought. 'Hell. I'm Clarence Ashley.'"

Rinzler and Earle knew Ashley's name and some of his early recordings from the work of eccentric collector Harry Smith. In 1951, Folkways Records had issued *Anthology of American Folk Music*, a six-LP collection Smith had compiled of late twenties and early thirties recordings by traditional musicians. Tom and his old friend Banmon Grayson were represented on Smith's *Anthology*. Some of the 1930 recordings had presented Tom as "Clarence Ashley." The record company had insisted on getting his legal name. Tom resolutely refused to use "McCurry" or "Earl" all his life, but he put the "Clarence" part down. Smith had repeated the record company error, giving Tom a name not even his close neighbors recognized.

A generation later, Rinzler explained that he and other young cultural advocates were "culture-struck by the splendor of vocal and instrumental styles" on the Smith collection. Excited by meeting one of his heroes from the collection, Rinzler arranged to return and record Ashley with Clint, Fred, and others. Tom brought Doc Watson to those Labor Day weekend sessions in 1960. These were Doc's first widely distributed recordings and his first real shot at a career in music. [See "Doc Watson: Just One of Us"]

Still in print as *Doc Watson and Clarence Ashley* in a two-CD set on Smithsonian Folkways, the forty-eight tunes and songs were lavishly annotated by Rinzler with photos, history, and backgrounds of the songs. Rinzler recalled asking the group to learn items from vintage recordings. He brought the Harry Smith collection to the session to demonstrate to Tom and the band what sounds he thought important.

Rinzler became Tom's friend and manager of the group. He took them on tour, performing in famous folk clubs in California and in New York's Carnegie Hall. Tom also took his banjo to England. And once again Tom helped to popularize a beloved song.

It was Tom, Clint, Fred, Doc, and Jean Ritchie who taught "Amazing Grace" to the American people. That "altar call" hymn had been in Southern shape-note hymnals since the 1830s, but was not listed in a 1958 study that named the nation's 100 best-known songs. Tom's rearrangement (using the first verse as a chorus) was first performed at the 1962 Chicago Folk Festival, then at the 1963 Newport Folk Festival, where it was recorded and issued by Vanguard on a live LP. Folk-pop singers Judy Collins and

Joan Baez had hits with the Ashley arrangement, as have scores of others since then. A Harris poll of 1994 found that "Amazing Grace" had become the best-known song in the nation, edging out even "The Star-Spangled Banner."

In his discussions of Ashley and Watson for their new audience, Rinzler characterized them as "rejected." Tom had "given up his music because the entertainment industry had no place for him." According to Rinzler, this happened in 1943, when Tom stopped performing in medicine shows and concentrated on trucking. Rinzler said Ashley had been retired from music since then. This minor evasion relieved Rinzler of the onerous duty of explaining to his urban audience that Tom was best known as "Rastus Jones from Georgia," but it also relegated Tom to relic status, something he never was. Blackface is a part of the still untangled history of the nation's vernacular arts. Tom Ashley was one of the last and finest blackface players, as well as a fine musician and keeper of tradition.

There was a buzz in Mountain City after the boys played Carnegie Hall, and a wish to hear them. Rinzler had gone back to New York when they played locally at the Taylor Theater. The music was good and Tom also gave the audience what he felt it needed: "Rastus Jones from Georgia" with all the trimmings. A few months before Tom's death in 1967, I asked him about the difference in performance dynamics between Carnegie Hall and a street medicine show. Tom was succinct: "At Carnegie Hall they give you the money before they sit down."

Grateful Dead guitarist Jerry Garcia told folklorist Nick Spitzer, ". . . I learned clawhammer picking or frailing—or whatever you want to call it—from listening to Clarence Ashley . . . I mean that record "Coo Coo Bird" almost set me up." Garcia said he understood what folk music really was when he heard that Ashley was a truck driver.

Driven by a passion for performance, Tom was a student and teacher of the arts of the working class. His performance hall was the streets, by far the most difficult of performance venues.

The author wishes to thank: Josephine Sutherland Wilson, Frank Grayson. Julia Olin, Nick Spitzer, Kathy James, Mickey Hart, Jake D. James [Joe Wilson's dog], Minnie Moody Miller, Charles Wolfe, Stephen Davis, and the late Ralph Rinzler.

Doc Watson

Just One of Us

● ●

Doc has smelled the hot wet feathers of the Sunday dinner chicken and blown sharp notes on the buckeye whistle. He has been to baptizings in the creek and can take either the Methodist or Baptist side of the once-in-grace-forever argument. He has felt the wrenching power of the revival meeting and knelt at the mourner's bench.

Doc's education is as good as you can get in the school of hard knocks and close listening, and if he seems a bit conservative in some matters it's because—in his experience—when things change, it may be for the worse.

Doc has picked the fiddle tunes when the fiddler didn't show and played rock 'n' roll for the drunks at the VFW because, by God, ten dollars was a lot of money and he had a family to feed and clothe.

He has fought with radios reluctant to bring in the stations playing music. He has fiddled with the knobs and pulled at the antenna stretched to the tree outside, trying to encourage that faint signal from Del Rio or Cincinnati on its way to the speaker. He has wished that he had a dollar ninety-eight to send in for that song book with the free golden cross because "this offer may not be repeated again on this station."

From *Muleskinner News*, June 1974 (Vol. 5, No. 6).

Doc has roots in a place. He lives at Deep Gap, a pass in the summit of North Carolina's Blue Ridge named by Daniel Boone two centuries ago. The morning mists last longer; the air is clean in your lungs; and you can find a quiet place to rest, think, and gaze into the hazy distances of smoky blue.

Descendants of people who followed Boone's trail still live here, raising their allotment of burley tobacco and some Hereford or Angus cattle while working full-time in one of the light industry plants or the college up the road in Boone, or the one down the mountain in North Wilkesboro.

One does not live among strangers in Deep Gap. The neighbors over the hill and up the road know you and your folks. If you are sick they will do what they can, and if you die your family won't have to pay a gravedigger, because there are strong arms here and stronger traditions.

But if one of your neighbors should find you stealing a yearling steer from his barn at midnight, he will most certainly shoot your butt off and maybe even your head too. The jury will understand his case but not yours, reasoning, by an old theory of justice, that there are some SOBs who ought to be shot but no yearling steers that ought to be stolen.

The mountains hereabouts have names like Grandfather, Beech, Stone, Long Hope, and the Peak. The nights are cold enough for a blanket even in summer. In winter, temperatures of ten to fifteen below are often as not followed by some warm days. There are ski lodges nearby and an influx of summer homebuyers.

There are no liquor stores in Watauga County. Beer isn't sold either—but it is in Wilkes County, a few miles below Doc's. A favorite watering hole used to be called "Bloody Joe's," and thirsty men came from as far as sixty miles away, across the county line, to drink beer; eat pickled eggs, pigs feet, and sausages from the jar on the counter; and survey the fly-specked bad checks tacked on the wall below the sign that advised: "This is why we don't take no checks."

At times, the sheriff's deputies wait at the county line, eager to pick off any guzzler bold enough to bring a case home with him. There have been some fast trips through Deep Gap with the law in hot pursuit. The absence of any major intersections on the twisting road helps. A favorite ploy is to round a sharp turn, switch off the lights, duck into the next secondary road, and have a 'nother one while the law screeches past.

Stock car racing is a mania here. The area's production of stock car drivers is sometimes described as an outgrowth of moonshining. Wilkes County once had more resident alcohol tax unit officers than sheriffs or policemen. But trying to get home from Bloody Joe's without a side trip to the Watauga County Jail may have produced some good drivers too.

Folklorists and song-catchers have described Watauga County as one of the richest areas for homemade music in the nation. A few miles from Doc's, Gap Creek crosses the farm that was the birthplace of the Hopkins brothers, pioneers in recorded country music [see "The Hill Billies: the Band That Named the Music"]. Folklore students of the artsy-craftsy set make pilgrimages to Beech Mountain, where they fiddle with tape reels and pester people to sing into their microphones. Books and albums have been compiled there since the thirties.

The late Frank Proffitt is the best-known musician from Beech Mountain and the surrounding communities. In the thirties, Frank sang "Tom Dooley"—a local ballad first recorded by G.B. Grayson—for a song-catcher. This led to the later financial success of the Kingston Trio, one of the burr-headed, we-got-together-on-campus groups of the late fifties.

Within fifty miles are the homes of lots of country music greats: G.B. Grayson, Tom Ashley, Jack Reedy, Dock Walsh, Garley Foster, Charlie Bowman, Frank Blevins, and Ernest Stoneman, among others. Their records—and those of the Skillet Lickers, Alfred Karnes, Charlie Poole, and lesser-known but equally good musicians—were stacked beside the old crank-up Victrolas in Watauga County parlors when Doc Watson was a boy. Uncle Dave Macon could be heard bringing down the house every Saturday night on Nashville's WSM.

But there were other influences available to a guitar picker from Deep Gap. Doc knew the music of Johnny Smith, Tal Farlow, Barney Kessel, and Django Reinhardt long before he climbed onto the Newport Folk Festival stage with Tom Ashley, Clint Howard, and Fred Price back in 1961. He'd heard Sam McGee, Frank Hutchinson, Sugarfoot Garland, and the fine flat-picking of Don Reno. Kentuckian Merle Travis's influence can still be heard in Doc's finger-picking.

Any man—especially a good musician—is far more than a collection of influences. The ability to hear and reproduce music is genetically transmitted. Some are blessed with an abundant inheritance, others with little or none. With practice and dedication, the former can become good musicians. Some of the latter go to bluegrass festivals where they holler "Rocky Top" and clap their hands, so as to drown out any good music that might be played.

I first met Doc Watson in the middle fifties. The date and location have slipped my mind, but not the song. When I walked in, Doc was singing "Groundhog" and playing a solid-body Les Paul model Gibson electric guitar.

"Playing a what?" cringe the summa-come-lately aficionados of the Herringbone Martin. Doc Watson is largely to thank for the revival of the acoustic guitar as a lead instrument; today it is hard to imagine anything else in his hands. But, in the fifties, Doc could afford just one guitar, and he played the one that brought a few dollars home. He played it on radio shows upstairs over the bus station in Boone with Frog and Carl Green, Tex Cullers, Jack Williams, and others I cannot recall. Two hundred and fifty watts winged these programs into the stratosphere. On a cloudy day, the station was inaudible just fifteen miles away.

Jack Williams put together a rock 'n' roll combo for the VFW dances at Johnson City, Tennessee, with Doc as the mainstay. VFW tastes ranged from the latest Presley hip-twister to Webb Pierce and Ernest Tubb's bar-room laments. Square dances at the Valle Crucis school featured electric country with Doc Watson, Tex Cullers, and Bryan Adams. One summer, Doc and his wife worked the pavilion at Blowing Rock. Doc played waltzes for the tourists while Rosa Lee ran the concession stand.

Even then, there was a Doc Watson cult; we all knew that he was the best musician among us. Fate had offered him limited opportunity, but he was broad-ranging in his interests, glad for any work that came his way and a good host for the musicians who came around to jam and marvel at his gifts. When Doc's turn came for an instrumental, he often chose a Merle Travis composition. He also played some Chet Atkins tunes, recognizing Chet as a fellow Travis fan. Doc named a son and Atkins named a daughter for Merle Travis.

In September 1960, Doc laid down his electric guitar and turned to the songs and tunes he had learned from his musical family and the old recordings. He laid it down for the same reason he played it: to earn a few dollars.

In his years of working in the Western North Carolina-East Tennessee area, Doc had come to the attention of Clarence "Tom" Ashley of nearby Johnson County, Tennessee. Ashley had been a rural recording pioneer of the 1920s and early 1930s [see "Clarence 'Tom' Ashley"].

In April 1960, Ashley and two Tennessee neighbors—Clint Howard and Fred Price—stopped to see Doc on the way to the Old Fiddlers' Convention at Union Grove, North Carolina. Fred entered the contest, with Clint backing him on guitar and Jack Johnson of Pilot Mountain, North Carolina, on banjo. They didn't place, but a young New Yorker approached them afterwards, told them he thought their music was excellent, and asked if they could make a tape for him. This man was Ralph Rinzler, a collector of old-time music and a musician of considerable talent.

The tape was made, and a few weeks later Rinzler wrote and asked if the group would be interested in making an album. Tom suggested that Doc be brought into the group for the record, although Clint and Fred had never played with him. Doc arrived for the session with his thin-body electric Gibson. Although suggesting that he replace it with an acoustic instrument, Rinzler, like Tom, knew a great talent when he saw one. Ashley's recording career was revived, and Doc Watson's recording career began. The two Folkways albums of *Old Time Music at Clarence Ashley's* are still in print.

Doc's first concert for a city audience was in March 1961, in New York City, with Tom, Clint, Fred, and Gaither Carlton—Doc's late father-in-law. Within two years, he was firmly launched on his career. Doc took his first solo shows because folk promoters didn't pay enough for the full group. He was instantly famous but not instantly affluent. The club dates paid very little, and Doc often returned home with only a few more dollars than he had when he left.

A relatively small group of musicians and folklorists was responsible for country music being treated respectfully on urban campuses and thus in cities. One of these, Ralph Rinzler, deeply influenced Doc Watson. Rinzler simply sent Doc back to his roots, by expressing his preference for the older tunes and styles and Doc's flat-picking, encouraging Doc to further develop these skills. He became Doc's manager, coaching him along the way in performance techniques that would reach and hold unfamiliar audiences. Rinzler also became Bill Monroe's manager, persuading Bill to relax and enjoy the honor coming to him rather than see each bluegrass band as a competitor.

Ralph Rinzler sent Doc back to the Carter Family, the Delmore Brothers, Charlie Bowman, Grayson and Whitter, Frank Hutchinson, Charlie Poole, and other old-timers that Doc had always liked. The trip has been one way for Doc. He still [1974—Doc died in 2012] looks back for much of his material and inspiration.

In 1973, Appalachian State University at Boone gave Doc an honorary degree. If such a thing had been suggested for any country musician back in the 1950s, that institution would have blown up. The cynical side of me notes that the honor came after Doc was made welcome at Princeton, Cornell, Harvard, Yale, and other prestigious places of learning. To be sure, it was students and not honors committees who opened those doors, but institutions do watch trends and follow them.

Country musicians were not accustomed to bright young Yankees who thought in terms of booking hillbillies at Harvard and treating their music with respect. The only promoters they knew were of the stripe that annually seize upon some jack-leg politician willing to sign a country music day proclamation, while grinning idiotically at a camera.

The "you like that stuff?" query is still common, and aversion to music that is country, rural, old-time, or bluegrass is so frequently encountered and strongly put that one automatically knows it doesn't have anything to do with the quality of the music. The reaction does tell us something about the pressures toward mass-spectator culture and the personal insecurity of people who say such things.

It may sound funny in 1974, but at one time we treated approval by any famous person as something of major importance—"You know, Governor Graftbagger has every record Eddy Arnold ever made!" You might say that we had a complex. A group of the bright and highly educated writing approvingly about our music and promoting it was a revelation akin to hearing an eminent headshrinker tell us that our innermost and dirtiest thoughts and dreams are both acceptable and healthy. The effect that Ralph Rinzler and his fellows had upon those who had always loved rural music was more subtle than the impact upon the urbanites, but it was equally strong.

When I last saw Doc, he told me of a meeting with Grandpa Jones and Merle Travis, two friends for whom he has the highest admiration.

WSM announcer Ralph Emery joined them and put an arm around Doc's shoulder and told him, "You know, you're just one of us." Doc liked the acceptance. He came to Nashville via a most unusual route. The road to country music stardom usually runs up Nashville's Sixteenth Avenue, going through Dallas and maybe even Shreveport or Austin before winding its way out to Bakersfield. It does not go through New York, Boston, and Philadelphia, the road Doc traveled. I wonder who the hell Emery had thought Doc was—Hugo Winterhalter, perhaps?

The road was difficult, and Doc has paid dues as great as any musician's. The music business crawls with characters who think nothing of asking a man to travel a thousand miles for five hundred bucks. When the hotel has its due, the airline its fare, and the ptomaine taverns their share for three days, what is left for wife and children? Fame? Fame, understanding, goodwill, peace, applause, and love all have their place but cannot be brought to boil in a soup pot.

Doc plays mostly college concerts now, and his schedule is a bit easier. The wolf is held at bay, and he is considered very successful by the folks around Boone. Yet any furniture dealer in Oshkosh can probably claim as much financial success.

Doc likes the college audiences and says, "You know, you can't fool these kids." But in a way he does fool them. He talks directly to them, straightforwardly, simply—perhaps too simply. Doc is a very complex man. But he is also a showman, and they pay to hear his dazzling guitar work, his honest voice and some country philosophy, some references to Charlie Poole, or perhaps about Uncle Ben Miller and the fiddle tunes Doc learned from his neighbor of long ago. The things he says are true: part of his life, his experiences and his legacy. But there are other things he holds to himself.

Doc's gifts go far beyond music. He has always been technically knowledgeable and can tell you why your stereo needs diodes, resistors, and that whole maze of circuitry. He understands matters relating to physics and chemistry and has always been an eager and avid learner, open to new and better ideas in almost any field you care to discuss.

I saw him last at Harvard's Sanders Theater. Amid marble busts of ancient philosophers, the theater was filled with Levi-chic and granny gowned de-ethnicized youth, affluent and over-optioned, self-mistrustful and in need of something that rings of authenticity. Doc had come here to lend these folks something real, perhaps just a song and a comment from his Grandma Grier. I wondered where their Grandmas were. Possibly down at the Palm Beach Golden Age Club, learning the frug and clipping investment coupons.

I have said very little about Doc's music and the changes it has undergone. Most of the changes, I'm sure, result from the fact that Doc has felt a bit freer to show some of his other sides. Also, his recording situations have changed—not always for the better. He still collects old-time records and is interested in some of the better Nashville musicians.

It is fashionable today to describe musicians and music in terms supposedly heavy with meaning. It is not enough to say that something is good or beautiful. The ultimate boast is, "It is thoroughly arranged, each note and nuance weighed and worked out like successful suicide." I cannot do this, as I find words nearly as inadequate in describing good music as music would be in describing words.

I do know that for twenty years I have found great beauty in the music of Doc Watson. I know that he is a tough and headstrong musician and that no one imposes upon Doc Watson in matters of taste. He's as much his own man as is Bill Monroe.

As we discussed the events and changes in Doc's life during the past fifteen years, I asked if any one particular thing stood out as the most important. Doc thought for a moment, smiling. His fingers begin picking a slow "Sally Goodin'." "One day I came home from a trip, sat down and wrote to the people with the State, and told them I wouldn't be needing their help anymore."

The "Sally Goodin'" he played that night was the fastest I have ever heard. It was not just any "Sally Goodin';" it was the amazing "Sally Goodin'" Fiddlin' Eck Robertson recorded for Victor in 1922, the version all others have to be measured against.

Fred Price, Old-Time Fiddler

A Remembrance

• •

The insistent buzzing of the telephone woke me at 4:00 a.m. It was Clint Howard. "Joe, we're over here at the bus station and I want you to come and get us." There was a note of urgency in his voice. He wanted me to get there as soon as possible.

The huge Port Authority Bus Terminal in New York City adjoins the 42nd Street sleaze district. In early morning, some of the strangest-looking people on earth walk through it. There are panhandlers and pimps; street-walkers and bag ladies; stone-faced cops in deep blue, walking in pairs; and wild-eyed men with sandwich boards that announce the coming of one or another form of perdition.

The bus station is a linguistic Tower of Babel: a barrage of Spanish from Puerto Rico, lilting Creole from Haiti, the metallic-toned Canton province dialect of Chinese, querulous Yiddish from Eastern Europe, and southern Italian delivered with hand motions. Even the English spoken here is strange. It is the commercial Bronx variety, high-pitched and fretful, and every third man seems to be yelling for Harry or Irving.

From *Bluegrass Unlimited* magazine, June 1998.

Few places on earth are less like Johnson County, Tennessee.

Kenneth Price and Clarence Howard had joined their fathers for this 1972 trip, and when I got to the bus station Clint and the boys were standing close together around their baggage and instruments. But Fred was standing several feet away, at a junction of hallways, engrossed in watching the people.

"Now I want you to look at that one," he said, pointing to a lanky black man who was pretending that he was dribbling and shooting an imaginary basketball into an imaginary hoop. He pretended to hit and miss, was both teams, kept score, was referee, and soon fouled himself out and ended the game.

But Fred didn't laugh or smile, and he spoke a courteous greeting to the basketball man as we walked past. His comment about him was full of compassion: "You know that poor feller must not have any other place to go, and I'll bet there's not a bit of harm in him or any of these people."

He was right. Many of the denizens of the bus station were harmless mentally ill people the city and state were then turning out of mental hospitals and dumping into the streets of Manhattan. I knew that because I'd been reading the *New York Times*. Fred knew it because he had a good heart.

The show that night was at the Folklore Center. The proprietor of that Greenwich Village landmark was Israel "Izzy" Young, a tall skinny middle-aged man with hair that reached his shoulders. Izzy was an effusive fellow and he rushed about a lot, talking non-stop and waving his arms.

Izzy was also New York's bravest musical risk-taker. If he liked the music of a group, he'd sponsor a concert. His girlfriend was half his age, but at the end of a musical evening she'd be in a state of collapse while Izzy vibrated with energy from the concert.

Izzy knew Clint and Fred from their earlier trips north, and from a visit he'd made to Johnson County with folklorist Ralph Rinzler. He spotted them as they entered the door, yelped, and rushed over and hugged both of them.

Grown men who are not related don't do much hugging in Johnson County. The boys were a bit taken aback and uneasily shook hands with Izzy. But back in the dressing rooms, they began giggling about the hugs Fred and Clint had received.

Fred soon shut them up. "He's going to hug both of you before you leave," he said. They spent much of the rest of the night backed against the wall and looking uneasy as Izzy rushed about, flapping his arms.

The next show was at the University of Massachusetts–Lowell. We had two flats on my battered Volkswagen van during the trip from New York and arrived an hour late, during the final number of the warm-up band.

Fred was standing in the stage wings, fiddle under his arm, when a worried and nearly frantic young woman who was one of the organizers rushed over. "Where on earth have you been?" she asked. Fred didn't blink. "Why I've been standing here for over an hour," he said. She was dumbfounded for a moment, then dissolved into laughter as Fred added, "Sometimes I'm hard to see."

While in the Boston area, Fred and Clint and their sons recorded an album (*The Ballad of Finley Preston*, Rounder Records) at the radio station of the Massachusetts Institute of Technology. They also performed at Harvard University's Sanders Theatre.

The audience at Sanders included graduate and undergraduate students from Harvard, Radcliffe, MIT, and Boston College. The hall is stately Victorian, with marble busts of ancient philosophers and an unmistakable aura of quality. The young men and women gathered there were the offspring of privilege, aware and very bright, Levi-chic and granny-gowned—they had come to catch a bit of American heritage in the music of a fine mountain string band, something real.

Backstage, a newspaper reporter was trying to extract a story angle from Fred before the show. "When did you play last?" he asked. "And what kind of audience did you have there?"

"Well, last week we played at a tobacco warehouse in Mountain City, Tennessee," Fred said. "We had a nice crowd."

The reporter pressed for his angle. "How would you compare that audience to this one?"

"Oh, about the same," Fred said.

The reporter was incredulous. "About the same?" he asked. "In what way?"

Fred's expression did not change. "They come in to hear some music and we play it."

As the reporter left, Fred winked at me. What he thought of Harvard University was his business.

Fred and Clint could carry a joke on longer and obtain more enjoyment from it than anyone I have known. The long-running joke for that trip concerned shirts. Clint had bought four matching shirts for the band before leaving Mountain City. Now his joke was to press Fred for repayment.

"When are you going to pay me for that shirt?" he asked.

"I'm not going to pay you," Fred responded, his face expressionless.

"But you know I bought it, and you're wearing it, and it looks good on you. It's probably the best shirt you've ever had, and I want my money," Clint said.

Fred's response was the same. "I'm not going to pay you."

The joke went on for a week, on stage and off, both enjoying it. At the Harvard show, Clint included it in his introduction of Fred.

"Now this feller with the fiddle is Fred Price, and he's a good musician and a good singer, and he's wearing a shirt that I bought for him."

"I'm not going to pay you," Fred said. "Well, all right, then," Clint said. "You can tell these folks what we're going to play next."

"The Old Account Was Settled Long Ago," Fred said, not smiling.

For once Clint was speechless. He was so tickled by Fred's wit that he had to take a little walk on the stage before he could continue. "That's a hymn and we'll do it last," he finally said. And they did.

There were other good trips. There were over 7,000 people in the Filene Center at Wolf Trap National Park, near Washington, D.C., when Clint and Fred opened the night concerts of the 41st National Folk Festival in July 1979. The lighting director hurried up before the show to suggest that Fred not wear his little hat, so that the brim would not cast a shadow and the audience could see his eyes.

"I'll wear the hat," Fred said.

Then as the lighting man opened his mouth to argue, he added, "I'll take it off when we do the hymn and anybody that wants to see my eyes can look then."

Among Fred's many gifts was his ability to communicate with children. He talked to children with a care and concern that most others reserve for adults. He listened to them, and their small affairs were important to him.

Fred performed with an early bluegrass band, the Grassy Creek Boys, during the late 1940s. He began performing with Clint Howard in 1952. Doc Watson performed in a trio with Clint and Fred for a while in the mid 1960s. There's a wonderful Vanguard double LP of that trio from a live concert in Seattle in 1966. Fred brought a Gibson banjo home from that trip and gave it to his son, Kenneth. Kenneth is now a fine banjoist, fiddler, and singer.

When I heard that Fred had died last September, I called Doc. "They don't make them like Fred anymore," Doc said softly. "I just thank the Lord I got to know him and work with him."

Fred accepted life as it came to him, and every person he met as a friend. Big or little, rich or poor, sane or troubled, child or adult, they got a smile and a handshake and some of his time, if they wanted it.

Yes, he was a fine musician. But he was more than that. He was a great person. He did not rush life. He had time for friends. He had time for his family. We can honor his memory by listening carefully to children and by being better to each other.

Doc Hopkins

Singer, Guitarist, and Banjoist, 1900–1988

● ●

Doc Hopkins died in Chicago on January 3, 1988. Born January 26, 1900, in Harlan County, Kentucky, Doc was a musician for more than eighty years. His full name was Doctor Howard Hopkins. He was the seventh son in a family of nine boys and three girls, and his name came from an old belief that the seventh son was destined to be a healer.

At age six, Doc's father made and gave him a banjo, one with a possum-hide head stretched over a square resonator. He also took him to see "Blind Burnett" whenever the traveling minstrel came to Harlan on court days.

Dick Burnett, the blind banjoist and singer, was a fine musical model for young Doc. Although he lived and traveled among small towns in a remote area, his awesome talents are far from forgotten. He wrote a long song about being blinded when shot in the face by a robber at Stearns, Kentucky, in 1907. Subjected to creative borrowing by Bob Dylan and many others, the song is known by bluegrass fans as "I Am a Man of Constant Sorrow."

Generations of singers, banjoists, and fiddlers have been instructed by the pile of 78 rpm recordings that Burnett made with Leonard Rutherford.

From *Bluegrass Unlimited* magazine, March 1988.

But Doc learned directly, watching the blind man's fingers and hearing the nuances in his voice. Doc was a stutterer but he did not stutter when he sang, and he sang the blind man's songs.

At age seventeen, Doc left Harlan, joined the Army, and served in General Pershing's American Expeditionary Forces in Europe. After World War I, he worked for a while as a railway brakeman and served a stint in the Marines.

Doc's first work as an entertainer was in Dakota Jack's Medicine Show, touring Kentucky, Tennessee, and Virginia. He had learned guitar at age nine, and his skills as a vocalist, banjoist, and guitarist were a primary asset of the show. He also sold medicine and books and acted in skits. The pay was relatively good, but the work was seasonal and Doc wanted to see other places. So he worked in the "gum woods" in Texas, barbered in Ohio, carpentered in the Navy Yard in Pensacola, and performed briefly in a touring Hawaiian band.

In 1930, Doc joined the performance staff of WLS in Chicago, a powerful radio station then owned by Sears and Roebuck—the WLS call letters were an acronym for "World's Largest Store" —and began a twenty-year stint as a professional musician. He worked solo and with such artists as Karl Davis and Hartford Connecticut (Harty) Taylor in the Cumberland Ridge Runners and with the Prairie Ramblers and the Sage Riders in personal appearances throughout the country.

Doc was a regular on *National Barn Dance* programs carried on the NBC radio network, and he recorded for Decca and the American Record Company (Banner, Melotone, Oriole, Romeo, Perfect) as well as for Broadway and Conqueror.

Like some others of his time, Doc was much more a radio and personal appearance man than a recording artist. Nowadays the recording tail has grown to such an extent that it tends to wag the entire musical dog, but it was different in Doc's heyday. The recording business had almost totally collapsed during the Great Depression, but radio still had massive audiences. It sounds almost unbelievable now, but as many as 10,000 pieces of mail a week came to the Cumberland Ridge Runners at WLS—most addressed to Doc, because he was the vocalist heard most often and a genial host when his turn came.

Yet there are some excellent recordings of Doc's music. They are part of the huge M.M. Cole Transcribed Library, a set of oversized 78 rpm discs prepared for exclusive use by radio stations. Doc is on more than 200 of the cuts, and of particular interest are those that find him in a great string band with fiddler Alan Crockett (earlier with Crockett's Mountaineers). Unfortunately, this material is out of print and it is the rare collector who has any part of it. But there is reason to hope; good material often finds its way to reissue on tape or disc.

Doc was a fine old-time banjoist and an excellent fingerpicker and backup guitarist, but his primary skill was singing. His voice was rich and resonant, and his early work on the street with Dakota Jack taught him to project his voice well and to enunciate his words with clarity.

Doc was an avid collector and keeper of fine old songs. He wrote some, rewrote many others, and made a good contribution to the repertoire of old-time and bluegrass musicians. But he was an artist rather than a businessman. Many of his songs have been recorded by people who are household names, without so much as a nickel finding its way to Doc.

The sweeping changes that came to the music business in the 1950s sent Doc to other employment, but he never stopped performing for his own enjoyment and that of his friends. When Fleming Brown sought banjo instruction, Doc was happy to oblige. In time, Fleming became a fine banjoist and teacher, and among his students was young Stephen Wade. Fleming took his star student to meet his teacher, and the young banjoist and the older man became fast friends, performing together at a pizza parlor "for fun and for the fifty bucks too."

Stephen took the skills he learned from Fleming and Doc into theater, combining banjo playing, storytelling, acting, humor, and singing. His one-man show *Banjo Dancing* was presented in theaters in Chicago, Vancouver, Cleveland, and New York before coming to an incredible ten-year run at Arena Stage in Washington, D.C., usually to a sold-out house.

Doc kept a careful eye on his students, and Stephen has a big box of letters that contain songs, stories, anecdotes, and much good advice. One begins, "Steve, I'm deaf in one ear and can't hear out of the other, but . . ." What follows is wonderfully good counsel, old showman to young showman.

Fleming preceded Doc in death, but Stephen recalls a conversation the three banjo players held over dinner in Chicago a few years ago. Each was conscious that the transmission of musical skill is most often in families. "We're a family," Fleming told them. "Family is more than blood."

Doc took a part of his family inheritance from a blind banjoist when the century was young, a blind banjoist with an emotion-laden voice and a tin cup tied to his leg. In turn, Doc had time for those who came to him for instruction, friendship, and family ties.

Carroll Best
Too Tall to Sleep in a Car

· ·

North Carolina musician Hugh Carroll Best Jr., age sixty-four, much respected by banjoists for his pioneering of melodic banjo style, died May 8, 1995. He was shot by an older brother who was consumed by jealousy.

Carroll Best was as stunning a banjo player as Earl Scruggs or Don Reno. He may seem obscure if viewed from a distance, but his performances on WLOS-TV with the Morris Brothers made him remarkably visible among musicians in the Appalachian heartland as bluegrass was taking shape.

Reared in a musical family and by parents who played banjo, Carroll took up the instrument while very young. He began performing at square dances at age ten. His mother played clawhammer style, but Carroll preferred a melodic style that had been passed down in his father's family.

During the early 1950s, Carroll performed with the Morris Brothers, who numbered Earl Scruggs and Don Reno among previous banjoists in their band. There are recordings from later in that decade which show

---

Adapted from an obituary in *Bluegrass Unlimited* magazine, July 1995, and liner notes to *Say Old Man, Can You Play the Banjo*, Copper Creek Records, 1995.

that Carroll's remarkable technique was as fully formed then as in later recordings.

In a 1976 interview, Don Reno discussed the origins of melodic banjo style. "I believe that if you'll check it out you'll find that an old boy from near Waynesville, North Carolina, named Carroll Best cracked the safe on that way of playing." [Reno and Best were distantly related.]

The Morris Brothers were on WLOS-TV in Asheville for a portion of the time that Carroll Best performed with them. Bobby Thompson was then performing on the station with Carl Story; in later years, he credited Best with inspiring his style.

In 1981, Wiley Morris recalled, " . . . he was the best banjo player I ever heard with a tune. He'd put every note in." Carroll's term for this way of playing every note was "fiddle style." He especially liked fiddle tunes such as hornpipes, where the fifth string is integrated into the melody. He performed with three fingers, and in early years used an open-back banjo and no picks. In later years he tried playing a resonator banjo with picks, but he preferred a Vega Tubaphone banjo.

Bascom Lunsford's Mountain Dance and Folk Festival in Asheville began attracting northern banjo players galore in the late fifties and early sixties. Some joined the tight circle of local players packed around the tall man playing the sparkling stream of notes. Though shy and quiet, Carroll was always glad to see other musicians. Very generous with his time, the lanky banjoist would stop and show anyone who cared exactly what he was doing. Among the awed Yankees who found their way to Carroll's place on Upper Crabtree was Bill Keith, who later developed a great melodic style. [Many people allege that this happened, including Carroll's wife; Ted Olson asked Keith about this in 2014 and he did not recall visiting Carroll.]

Carroll's ability to stand straight and unsmiling while delivering an incredible break made banjoist Glenn Potter guess " . . . he must have taken poker-face lessons from Earl Scruggs."

The life of a road musician did not wear well on Carroll Best. "I always liked playing a lot," he said of his professional years in a 1993 interview. "But after a while I figured out that I was too tall to sleep in the back seat of a car." So Carroll spent most of his life in western North Carolina with Louise and their kids. Jamming often with buddies Danny Johnson and

Mack Snodderly, among others, he went back to farming and working in a local industrial plant.

In 1990 and in 1992, Carroll was a faculty member of the Tennessee Banjo Institute. In 1993 and 1994, he was a featured performer on the national tour *Masters Of the Banjo*, organized by the National Council for the Traditional Arts. In 1994, the State of North Carolina named him a winner of its Folk Heritage Award.

Carroll can be heard on a few locally produced tapes and two CDs. Five live performances by Carroll are included on *Masters Of the Banjo,* issued by Arhoolie Records in 1994. *Say Old Man Can You Play the Banjo,* released by Copper Creek Records in 2001, includes thirty-six live and studio tracks recorded between 1974 and 1995.

A gentle and unassuming man, Carroll did not claim to have invented anything; "I learned it from my daddy." But during a gab session late one night on the banjo tour bus, three of his fellow musicians persuaded him to admit that he made some contributions. His contributions were in fact major ones, and if melodic banjo needs a father figure, he has first claim.

Memories
of Janette Carter

. . . .

Janette was not the Carter with the husky, penetrating female voice—perhaps the finest country female lead of all time. That voice belonged to her mother, Sara. She was not the lead guitarist who invented country guitar lead with its "church lick" and unrelenting emphasis of melody. That guitarist was her Aunt Maybelle. She wrote songs, but was not the greatest composer and arranger in country music history. That person was her father, A.P.

The Carter Family was a Depression-era band that broke up after a mere fourteen years, and Janette and her father returned to the Virginia mountains with considerable fame, but no cash. She never married anyone famous, and individual fame never came to her. She worked as a cook at the elementary school and raised her family.

But she promised her father to keep his legacy, and that promise was kept at The Carter Fold, a hall she financed and her brother Joe built in the style of a burley tobacco barn. There she presented the local artists

Posted to the Publore listserv for the public folklore community, January 22, 2006.

she adored and the famous who came to borrow bits of Carter magic. She kept the prices low and the quality high.

She had time for the most humble and enough love to fill the valley beside Clinch Mountain. I came to see her father at age sixteen, one of hundreds of mountain boys welcomed to his porch.

Janette had been working in the garden on a warm July day and spotted the Indian Scout motorcycle that had brought me over eighty miles of twisting mountain road. She asked for a ride, and we roared off down a gravel road to buy Pepsi. She never mentioned that ride until last year [2005] at the Carter Fold when Governor Mark Warner was seated between us and a speaker grew long-winded. During a pause, her mountain voice rang out: "Wisht you had that motorcycle and we could go for a ride."

So in my mind, the greatest Carter of all has gone for a motorcycle ride, holding on tight, the wind in her face, all promises kept.

BLUEGRASS MUSIC

Bluegrass and
Old-Time Music Defined

· ·

You'll often hear these terms used; now is a good time to check and see if you know what they mean. They are similar in some ways but also very different.

There is of course a quick and easy answer. Bluegrass is concert music, so you sit and listen and applaud when the song ends. Old-time is dance music, so you get up and dance, and applaud when the dance ends. But it is not really that simple. Old-time bands sometimes play concerts and they may have songs with instrumental breaks, just like a bluegrass band. And bluegrass bands sometimes play dances and often dip into the older repertoire of old-time.

A discussion of banjo styles often arises when the difference between bluegrass and old-time is the topic. Old-time banjo styles can be traced to 150 years ago and may be called "clawhammer," "stroke style," "two-finger," or "frailing." Bluegrass banjo is three-finger and syncopated. It arose from a North Carolina folk style that Earl Scruggs and Don Reno taught to the world at the end of World War II.

But "old-time" is also a catchall term that encompasses several different musical forms. For example, the Carter Family is often called an old-time family band. But they were in fact members of a parlor music ensemble, who utilized their own compositions as well as beautifully arranged old ballads and regional songs. They were well acquainted with the old dance music. A. P. Carter could play the fiddle, and Maybelle was a fine banjoist, but they did not play this music on their recordings.

In most cases, nowadays, an old-time band has roughly the same instrumentation as a bluegrass band: fiddle, banjo, guitar, mandolin (sometimes), and bass. But a critical difference is that, in an old-time band, the banjo is played drop-thumb, clawhammer, or two-finger, and the fiddle usually leads. This is because the music remains a historic dance-music form, one still utilizing the banjo largely for its powerful rhythms. Such bands seem to play most often at dances, although jam sessions and kitchen parties are almost as popular, especially in rural Virginia.

The term *old-time* comes from the 1920s and was a creation of the music industry. The pioneering Yankee artist and repertoire men who made the recordings thought of this music as a remnant of the old minstrel bands of the previous century. That certainly was not true of most of the mountain string bands (though many had minstrel tunes in their repertoires), yet the name stuck.

Bluegrass is a modern concert form made possible by microphone technology. It is as technologically dependent as rock 'n' roll. Since some instruments are louder than others, microphones, mixers, and speakers are necessary. These tools make it possible to "solo" acoustic string instruments and to shift the lead from one instrument to another even though there are volume differences. Of course, bluegrass is a splendid form for jamming, and technology is not needed for that. Good players learn to back off and let everyone get their sound into the mix.

Bluegrass was named for Bill Monroe's Blue Grass Boys, a pioneering band of the form. Bluegrass arose in the 1940s, a confluence of technology, some wonderfully talented groups, and a need for a new concert form in the mid-South. Introduced, of course, by radio, it was initially most important as a radio medium, with scores of daily live programs.

Virginian Ralph Stanley, one of the most noted of the founders, is not certain that his music should be called bluegrass. Ralph was playing it before the name was created, and he grew up hearing and playing old-time music. At one point, he described his music as "old-time, what you might call bluegrass," but Ralph eventually gave up on definitions. "It's mountain music," Ralph says. "We are not stingy with it. There's enough to go around."

They Changed the World

· ·

I wish you could have been with me, dear reader, in the mid-forties when it began. The weekly bath for little boys came in a Number 3 washing tub in water heated by a wood stove. Feeling very clean and smelling of the flower scent mom had put into the large white cake of home-made soap, I sat in a circle before the Crosley radio with batteries bulging from its back to listen to the Grand Ole Opry.

The crowds lifted the rafters of the Ryman Auditorium with their roaring approval of a young banjoist named Scruggs who never said a word. His sparkling sound went into thousands of hollows like ours, and it sparkles still and speaks to the soul.

This is a collection of biographical material about musicians who changed the world they inherited. They changed it suddenly and dramatically, and their creations are still evolving and reaching into the future.

Many of them are from a time, a time after a great war had ended, when their nation felt free to create a new and better world. They are

---

Foreword to *The Bluegrass Hall of Fame: Inductee Biographies 1991–2014*, by Fred Bartenstein, Gary Reid, and others, Copyright: International Bluegrass Music Museum, Holland Brown Books, 2014.

from the ascending side of progress, and felt free to adjust and improve, to reach for greater quality, to assert their sound.

They were all born in the United States, and the art form they made reflects American history and values, yet their creations have been adopted and adapted by people in scores of distant places. Millions turn to that sparkling stream of sound, knowing instantly that it speaks to their souls. Nothing created on our shores is more instantly recognized as "American" than this music called bluegrass.

Working people invented this music, using concepts, songs, and instruments borrowed from earlier styles of music. Many had walked behind horses and mules on upland farms. They had mined coal and tended cotton-weaving machines. They had moved to Detroit to build cars, and to Maryland and Pennsylvania to pick mushrooms, build dams, and fix anything that needed fixing. Most are from the Southern mountains, a place that has long produced more sons and daughters than it had places at the table. After the war, they left in a steady stream, a greater outpouring than that of the Dust Bowl. Their sparkling new music became a favorite sound in the honky-tonks, bars, and construction-worker dives in Dayton, Cincinnati, Baltimore, and Washington, D.C.

It was a commercial music from its outset. One paid an admission fee and sat down to hear a concert. It involved the lost loves of ancient balladry, dead mother stories from Victorian parlors, hot "breaks" from several instruments, and vocal harmonies that could wring the heart. It also involved the microphone, an innovation of the early twentieth century that enabled the amplification necessary for bluegrass's subtle mix of solo voice, harmonies, instrumental leads and turnarounds, as well as the rhythmic "chop" and other backup timekeeping.

The larger 50,000-watt stations, such as Nashville's WSM, let millions hear bluegrass. The pivotal first band—Bill Monroe, Earl Scruggs, Lester Flatt, Chubby Wise, and Howard Watts—debuted on WSM's Grand Ole Opry. But local radio was even more important. Local daily "live" shows by scores of bands became part of daily life. Few of these artists were paid by their stations, but they could promote paying gigs at an endless series of schoolhouses and small halls: the aptly named "kerosene circuit."

Bluegrass often benefited from accidental juxtapositions. Ola Belle Reed built her New River Ranch performance park in Maryland, 400 miles north of her birthplace on Grassy Creek, a stream that tumbles into the New River on the Virginia-North Carolina Blue Ridge. Her little park, and Sunset Park at Oxford, Pennsylvania, put mountain-born bluegrass and old-time music performers within easy driving distance of New York and Washington's folk music circles. They yearned for roots, these urban seekers who had sat at the feet of Richard Dyer-Bennett, Alan Lomax, and Pete Seeger. Ola Belle welcomed them with open arms.

Poverty is the father of bluegrass. Even in its halcyon early years, the founders barely made ends meet. The foot soldiers of bluegrass, these men and women who attempted to make a living performing it, often starved out. The "day jobs" they accepted to save body and soul ranged across the employment landscape. Carl Sauceman told of a fiddler who sidelined as a safecracker. It fed on passion, on love, on roots that run deep, and a yearning to improve the musical future.

Throughout his long career, Bill Monroe carried on a killing pace of touring, an endless series of one-nighters. Time away from loved ones and very poor pay led to major turnover in his band. But in time this turnover was understood as a blessing. Monroe chose fine artists, schooled them in his reach for perfection at a furious pace, and many of them soon had fine bands of their own, adding to the reach of the music.

Even Monroe had to be told that bluegrass had been invented. Among those who informed him was Don Reno. When Earl Scruggs left the Blue Grass Boys, Monroe brought in Jackie Phelps to play electric steel guitar. Nothing was said about the absence of the banjo at the next Grand Ole Opry broadcast. Listening in North Carolina, Reno realized what had happened and immediately left for Nashville. Arriving there, Reno was told that Monroe and his band had left for a performance in North Carolina. So the intrepid Reno reversed his direction on US Highway 70, returned to North Carolina, and there he found Monroe. The band was already on stage, so Reno uncased his banjo, tuned for seconds, and walked unannounced onto the stage. Monroe strode over to the bold young veteran of war on the Burma Road. "You're Don Reno, aren't you?" Monroe inquired. "I've been thinking about calling you."

Ozark musicians, such as Vern Williams and Ray Park and a talented band called the Dillards, drifted westward and took the sparkling new sound to California, Oregon, and Washington State. The Lilly Brothers and Don Stover left the coal-mining region of the Cumberland Mountains in West Virginia and carried their exciting brand of bluegrass to a dive in a low-rent part of Boston.

The industrial heartland of Ohio, Indiana, Illinois, and Michigan made rich contributions to bluegrass. Many of the great performers who worked there are in the Hall of Fame, but please do not assume that all who made bluegrass are listed here. Nothing could be farther from the truth. Many thousands from across the nation have been steeped in this burst of creativity, including brilliant artists who did not care for the poor pay, living in motels, and riding every day. Moreover, it is still being made and, though I obviously care for the early inventors, who am I to doubt that some of the best contributions are still to be made?

When I hear a Japanese, Czech, or Russian bluegrass band, I know a very kind compliment is being paid to the working people of our nation, and it makes me smile.

The converts made by the missionaries who went north, west, and overseas were initially attracted to the instrumental sounds rather than to the lyrics of bluegrass songs. Most had not left a home in a hollow or ever owned even one good coon dog. So the finest of the new urban bluegrass bands sang compositions reflecting the pain and angst their stuck-on-the-beltway urbane fans would better understand.

Journalists, folklorists, and musicologists still struggle to explain bluegrass. They often compare it to jazz, pointing to the virtuosity inherent in both forms, and say bluegrass borrowed its soloing of instruments from jazz. This is dubious, as some of the earliest country groups to go on radio—such as the immensely popular Hill Billies in 1925—featured solos on guitar, banjo, fiddle, and uke on many of their songs. Some assume the knife-edged coal-mining ridges and hellfire religion of southwestern Virginia inspired the brooding homeplace-obsessed music of the Stanley Brothers. Yet Jim and Jesse McReynolds, another set of bluegrass brothers from another mountain farm just over a few ridges and miles to the south from the Stanleys, gave sad songs a happy turn and helped inspire the musical generosity of the Grateful Dead. So we should ask those who write about bluegrass to assume very little, and to be careful. The creativity of the masters listed here is as complicated as that of other great masters.

As bluegrass music was still getting started, a half dozen bands called "The Country Cousins" arose across the nation. One of them, performing in 1955 on WATA in Boone, North Carolina, had a theme song with a wry twist that echoes the humble beginnings and the out-beyond-the-stars cosmic reach of this music from the people:

Where did he come from?
Where did he go?
Where did he come from?
     Cotton-eyed Joe?
From over the Blue Mountains,
Near the land of Nod,
Digging taters, seeking God.

Bristol's WCYB

Early Bluegrass Turf

• •

B ristol has two of everything: two mayors, two police chiefs, two post offices, two city councils, two large high schools. The middle of State Street—the main street for the city—is the Tennessee-Virginia border, and lane-swapping drivers can enter and leave a state with a twitch of the wheel.

The two-of-everything consistency of Bristol holds even for part of the musical history of the city. It was on the Tennessee side of State Street forty-five years ago that pioneer recording engineer Ralph Peer made the first recordings of two of the greatest acts of old-time music, a few days apart: Jimmie Rodgers and the Carter Family.

A short distance away, on the Virginia side of State Street, is another site of importance in musical history. There's not much to see there, but this was the site of WCYB. During the late 1940s and 1950s, many bluegrass and old-time musicians gathered at the WCYB microphones. Some of the best of those who are still playing can trace their professional beginnings to this spot.

From *Muleskinner News*, October 1972 (Vol. 3, No. 8)

Lester Flatt and Earl Scruggs came to WCYB after leaving Bill Monroe, and the *Farm and Fun Time* announcer usually introduced Flatt with a line so bad that I can still remember it: "Here's the man with the hat, Lester Flatt." Listeners of the daily program supported and sustained Flatt and Scruggs and other early groups during the formative years of the sound, before the term "bluegrass" was known. In turn, Flatt and Scruggs were the most influential band to play there, and they set the stage for much that happened there later.

Mac Wiseman came to the station at least twice. He had a band of his own there in 1947 and returned in 1948 to do some memorable singing with Lester Flatt, Earl Scruggs and the Foggy Mountain Boys. He stayed briefly, then drifted on. Everett Lilly also joined Flatt and Scruggs for a short stint there.

The Stanley Brothers certainly equaled and may have even surpassed Flatt and Scruggs in local popularity. With daily programs over what was at best an area within a hundred miles of the station and with limited distribution of a few records, they enjoyed an artistic and financial success that would be enviable today.

I once saw the Stanleys fill to capacity an auditorium that would seat 450 people twice in a single Saturday night (I know the capacity because it was the auditorium of the high school I attended). This was in a town of 1,200, in a county of 10,000. Forced to leave after the first show so that people outside could get in for the second show, I examined the shiny new Cadillac they had parked near a rear door. Then I joined others who had gathered at the open windows to hear more good bluegrass until the second show ended and they emerged, still dripping sweat, and signed the song and picture books they had sold.

From the beginning, the Stanley Brothers combined the graceful vocal harmonies of a "brother" act with hard-driving instrumentation to produce music of power and depth. I thought then that it was the best music I'd heard, and time has had very little effect on that opinion.

The Stanleys were at WCYB early, beginning about 1948 for a stint of two or three years, and then returned later in the fifties. They were one group that could make frequent re-appearances in the towns of that area. Even their comedy was good—far better than the "rube" comedy used by most groups at that time. At one point they featured old-time musician Clarence "Tom" Ashley doing portions of his act "Rastus Jones From Georgia." The old timer had perfected his wildly funny routines in thousands of medicine show stage appearances, and Carter Stanley was a convincing actor in his parts. [See "Clarence 'Tom' Ashley"]

Bill and Earl Bolick—the Blue Sky Boys—were at WCYB shortly before they ended their career. Like the Monroe Brothers, they influenced other "brother" acts of the area. One of the best of these, and one that was surely influenced by the Bolicks, later came to WCYB. Even then they called themselves "The Virginia Boys," but Jim and Jesse McReynolds were a mandolin-guitar duo then, and unless my memory is playing tricks with me, Jesse played fiddle on some numbers.

Most of WCYB's live programming of bluegrass and old time music was confined to the two-hour daily *Farm and Fun Time* show, beginning at 12:00 noon, Monday through Saturday. An exception was the hymn programs that a few bands had on Sunday mornings at various times in the history of the station. Usually only one band had a Sunday morning "hymn time," and it was early, beginning at 7:00 or 8:00 a.m.

I recall hearing Carl Story first on "hymn time" programs, though he was also a *Farm and Fun Time* regular. At the time, Story called his band the "Rambling Rumbling Mountaineers." He featured the mandolin "turn-arounds" between verses that have since become common in bluegrass gospel singing. I'm sure that Bill Monroe started this, but Story's band adapted it and has in turn been widely imitated by others. I seem to recall that "Little Red" Rector was behind the mandolin, but since it has been twenty-odd years, and I was ten or eleven at the time, I'm inclined not to trust my memory about specifics of that sort.

Bob Osborne was another mandolin player found in front of the WCYB microphones for a brief period. He came there with Jimmy Martin in the early fifties. Still another mandolinist who served time there was Curly Seckler.

From the early days with Earl Scruggs and Ralph Stanley until live programming ended in the late fifties, there were good five-string men at the station. I first heard Larry Richardson and Porter Church on WCYB.

Naming all of the fiddlers who played there would be almost as difficult as naming all of the fiddlers who drink hard liquor, but I can recall a few: Leslie Keith, Chubby Anthony, Art Wooten, and Lester Woodie with the Stanleys. Ralph Mayo, Charlie Cline, Curly Ray Cline, and Bob Slone were also there. Yes, the same Bob Slone who later played bass with J.D. Crowe. He was a teenager at the time and billed as an "upside-down" (left-handed) fiddler in a band that Buster Pack fronted at WCYB.

Remembering "Fiddlin' Ralph" Mayo and Porter Church there brings to mind one of the good unsung bands that played at WCYB. This group was called the Southern Mountain Boys and was fronted by Mayo, from Kingsport, Tennessee. There were personnel changes over a period of two or three years (Mayo stayed longer than most), but among the best musicians were Church and blind guitarist Jack Cassidy. Cassidy provided a piercing tenor lead and joined Mayo in tasteful duets. Mayo took the lead at times and had a pleasing voice of unusual timbre, especially in gospel singing. The group was always paced by a driving banjo, and Mayo's droning fiddle lent an archaic flavor that was very appealing to me. Although Mayo recorded cuts with the Stanley Brothers, and also made a few 78s using the Southern Mountain Boys name, I've yet to hear a recording that captured this band at its best.

Bonnie Lou and Buster Moore had a long run at the station, with Lloyd Bell. Buster played mandolin and frailed the banjo, and the group toured with the "cowboy" act of Homer Harris for a part of their stay. Bonnie Lou, Buster, and Lloyd were a trio throughout their WCYB stay and had an old-time flavor. They didn't add steel guitar and other electric instruments until they moved to WJHL-TV in Johnson City, Tennessee, in the early fifties.

A few novelty acts toured at times with WCYB musicians. "Suicide" Jones worked ballparks and other outdoor shows with Mayo's group. The "suicide" act consisted of Jones climbing into a plywood "coffin," placing a stick of dynamite a few inches from his head, and detonating the charge. For these festivities, "Suicide" very judiciously donned a football helmet and placed a thick sheet of steel between his head and the charge. Mayo also carried a "hell driver" automobile act with him at one point.

But of all the novel acts that passed by the WCYB microphones, bass player "Lindy" Clear of Hansonville, Virginia, was one of the most unique. Lindy's forte was rural sound effects; his ability to vocally recreate complex sequences of sound was amazing. He reproduced the starting of a wheezy Model T from the first spin of the crank and futile hiss of the motor, through several false starts, until he finally sent the weary farmer backfiring and spluttering over a hill. His "dog meeting a dog" contained all of the growls, sniffings, and explorations of two tough mutts meeting for the first time, as well as the inevitable dogfight that followed. His ear-splitting mule bray punctured many instrumentals, and even a long-legged jarhead calling for some hay had to be in good voice and enthusiastic in order to match it.

On the air, WCYB musicians sold feed for farm animals, rat poison, flour, soft drinks, laxatives, headache powders, chewing tobacco, snuff, fertilizer, insecticides, menstrual tension remedies, baking powder, "over-halls," used cars, chain saws, farm tools, and you name it. Recently a friend asked what song was most associated with Charlie Monroe. I remembered his Wildroot Cream Oil jingle first and "Rose Connolly" second. This is just an example of how effective some of the radio selling was.

Many also sold song and picture books on the air. But these musicians we're selling themselves as much—or more—than they were the products that sponsored them. Very few were paid by sponsors, and none by the station. The idea was to advertise show dates and the talents of the group, and to attract audiences for personal appearances.

Almost all of the musicians were teenagers or in their early twenties when they came to WCYB. They played at the schoolhouses of the area with the local sponsorship of PTAs, volunteer fire departments, civic clubs, and others that could obtain an auditorium, nail up a few posters, and hopefully sell a few tickets. The pitch for show dates went something like this: "If you'd like to have the *** Brothers appear in your neighborhood or at your school, just have your club or organization drop us a line here at WCYB, Bristol, Virginia, telling us what dates are best for you and we'll get in touch with you. It's good clean, family entertainment." Most groups soon "played out" the area, and the turnover in groups was fantastic.

WCYB was called "The Five-State Station" and the show was heard in portions of Kentucky, North Carolina, and West Virginia, in addition to Tennessee and Virginia. The lunch hour timing of *Farm and Fun Time* was one reason for its success. Returning from the fields, tobacco grading, or other work on the farm, I automatically switched the radio on. Judging from the popularity of the show, many thousands of mountain people did the same. The difficulty of persuading me to return to work at

1:00 p.m.—rather than 2:00 p.m. when the show ended—was a source of considerable friction in my family for years.

The intensity of the *Farm and Fun Time* impact surpassed that of any program I have known since then on radio or television. Flatt and Scruggs, the Stanley Brothers, and Bonnie Lou and Buster were discussed by listeners with the familiarity usually reserved for close friends and members of the family. Television performers—including bluegrass musicians who perform on TV—have not built the audience affinity or identification that approaches that of early radio.

Why did WCYB become the bluegrass station of the 1940s and 1950s? There were, of course, dozens of other live country shows on radio stations across the South and Southwest and even a few in the North. Radio had been the primary medium for the dissemination of country music since the early 1930s.

One explanation that I have heard points to the "purity of taste" of the mountain people. I don't agree. The people 100 miles north and 100 miles south of that area surely had equal "purity of taste" (whatever that may mean). In my view, it happened there because Flatt and Scruggs came and with the Stanley Brothers built an audience for the music. It could have happened elsewhere, but it seems fitting that the town which saw Jimmie Rodgers and the Carter Family begin their career also made a home for bluegrass and *its* developing years.

How "The Old Prospector"
Met Ralph Stanley

● ●

with Walt Saunders

WALT SAUNDERS: The Stanley Brothers had disbanded in 1951, something they did several times. Ralph apparently was weary of the road,
but Carter wanted to continue in music and called Bill Monroe. Shortly
thereafter, Monroe hired him when Jimmy Martin left (something Jimmy
did several times).

While Carter was working with Monroe, banjoist Rudy Lyle was
drafted into the military. Bill asked Carter to call Ralph to see if he would
fill in. Carter did, and Ralph filled in for several shows. One—in August
of 1951—was in Dunn, North Carolina. Pee Wee Lambert accompanied
Ralph when they drove to North Carolina.

Following the show, Ralph and Pee Wee started back to Bristol, Virginia. When they stopped for gas, Pee Wee took over driving and Ralph—
being very tired—fell asleep. As I recall Ralph telling me, they had gotten
up in the mountains. They were taking U.S. 421 out of Boone, North Carolina. Around Shouns, Tennessee, in the early morning, they went around

Personal correspondence with Fred Bartenstein, October 4, 2005. Virginian Walt Saunders
writes the column "Notes & Queries" for *Bluegrass Unlimited* magazine. *The Old Prospector*,
a 1938 short film based on a Bruce Kiscadden poem, depicts an old man who never made a
strike revisiting old ghost towns with his mule.

a mountain curve and met head-on a truck full of day laborers, which had swerved to avoid a driver in a jeep who had shorted the curve. It was a bad wreck and Ralph was injured seriously enough to spend some time in the Bristol hospital. While Ralph was recovering from his injuries, Carter visited Ralph several times and the brothers decided to get back together.

JOE WILSON: The accident was on old U.S. 421, a short distance north of the Shouns crossroads. There's a sharp blind curve there. A World War II surplus jeep had strayed across the centerline, and in avoiding a head-on collision, Pee Wee Lambert and Ralph Stanley's car swerved left, turned over, and ended up in a cornfield beside the road.

My home is about six miles south of the accident spot, and everyone around there knew a man we called "The Old Prospector." He was a crazed fellow who believed there was gold on Long Hope Mountain, and traveled there from his home in Damascus, Virginia, six days a week to hunt for it. Never mind that the gold, if found, would belong to the Vicks Chemical Company, which then owned the mountain.

Even in high summer, his jeep would chug up the road past our place every morning, shortly after daybreak. (I think the accident was around dawn, and that would be consistent with driving from east-central North Carolina in those pre-interstate years when the roads were two-lane and went through every little town, half of them speed traps.) He'd come back down around 3:00 p.m., and if I was at the road—work done and hitching a ride to town—he'd stop and offer a ride. I'd climb in, and he'd say, "Goin' to town, son?"

"Yessir."

"Well, I guess we'll make it—if we don't run into the Stanley Brothers."

I told Ralph about that and he said, "You know, that old bastard nearly killed me."

A new 421 was built a quarter mile west of the accident spot and was open by 1953. But the old road is still there, and you can see where Ralph nearly bought the farm.

Ralph is a great traveling companion, gets up feeling good every morning, and likes a joke with breakfast. He will be at our 67th National Folk Festival in Richmond, Virginia, next weekend [2005], and I get to do a workshop with him. I'm going to tell him you boys are discussing the time when he got his ass busted by "The Old Prospector."

Everett Lilly, Don Stover, and Tex Logan at Loy Beaver's, 1969

· ·

It was all wonderfully improbable. Here, a few miles west and north of the George Washington Bridge, was this basement zoo of New York and Jersey music geeks, all hard-core fans of the most hard-core Appalachian music. One guy was a stock analyst and another was a postman. One night, I asked a regular—a fireman—how his face had turned so brown, and he told me about crawling up the steps of a burning Manhattan tower, face close to the stairs to keep below the smoke. "That must be the worst," I opined. "Nah," he said. "The worst is the citizens who are leaving: the rats, the cockroaches—they walk up your face as they go down."

Loy Beaver owned the house above the basement, and he was improbable. He owned one of the finest hillbilly record collections on earth, and he was from Ducktown, in the Tennessee mountains where the trailing end of the Great Smokies touch Georgia. Loy had been in New York for a while, working as an undertaker for an Orthodox Jewish funeral home. A guy who can speak Yiddish with a hillbilly accent can only happen in real life; fiction never reaches that far into the improbabilities of America.

March 2004 liner notes for a CD that was never released. The concert described took place on November 26, 1969.

Most of the band members drove down from Boston, made the common error of misjudging weekend megalopolis traffic, and were late, but that was okay. The friends who gathered had much to talk about. This group of a hundred or less was largely organized by Dave Freeman, who—six years earlier—had founded County Records and County Sales, then and now the best source of Appalachian music. Rich Nevins had not yet founded Shanachie Records, but he was there, along with Larry MacBride, who founded the Merrimac label. Another world-class collector of vintage recordings, Frank Mare of Fort Lee (now of Georgia), was always there, along with guerilla radio hostess Kathy Kaplan.

Many performed for Loy's basement series: Bill Monroe, Ralph Stanley, Ted Lundy, Curly Seckler, the Bailey Brothers, and others. Clark Kessinger and Gene Meade stood us up. Keith Whitley, there as a teenager with Ralph Stanley, said he'd never before had people applaud his syncopated Shuffler-picking on guitar.

The band members who arrived that night were a study in contrasts. Tex Logan was tall and courtly in wide-brimmed hat, shotgun pants, cowboy boots, gambler's shirt, and preacherly coat. He looked like a rainmaker, or perhaps a Methodist circuit rider of yore. He spoke like a professor—well-informed, wonderfully genteel—while looking his listener straight in the eye. His fiddling was clearly from Texas, he pronounced "Jordan" as "Jerden" (which is correct) but he had a decidedly un-Texas physical wiggle when he performed. That he was from Big Spring, Texas, and MIT made perfect sense. Where else?

Everett Lilly also had a Stetson hat, but it was of the white Open Road variety. His pants and shirt were wonderfully mismatched, and he spoke in exuberant tones of Jesus, full gospel salvation, and going back to West Virginia one of these days. His playing and singing were animated and joyous. He had cloned Bill Monroe's mandolin style from his pre-bluegrass Monroe Brothers days, and even improved it with a great rhythm snap at the end of phrases. He was clearly a force of nature, one of the greatest of the unsung heroes of the music that was becoming known as bluegrass.

Don Stover lived at the edge of laughter, and his irrepressible humor and brilliant banjo style were a revelation that night. Once, Everett launched into an interminable version of "Barbara Allen" and Stover came close to killing my pal Bill Vernon and me, enlivening it by inserting Chuck

Berry licks and making them fit. Everett sang on, unaware. Stover's harmony vocals with Everett and his sons were perfect, and every turnaround he played that night sparkled with originality. Bill and I decided that he must be one of the finest banjo players to ever walk the face of the earth.

They'd been performing in Boston's "Combat Zone" [an adult entertainment district, since redeveloped] for eighteen years, arriving in the early fifties to accompany Logan, a graduate student at MIT. Really. Could I invent anything that improbable? The dive they enhanced was frequently the scene of fisticuffs and thrown bottles, but it seemed to have had little effect upon them. They were country friendly and genteel, open to all who loved music. Everett had a huge store of ancient ballads and sentimental Victorian songs, and he had become a New England influence. Among his acolytes was an Italian kid from Boston's North End, Joe Valiante, a typewriter repairman by day. Logan dubbed him Joe Val. Like Everett, he became an unsung hero of bluegrass, founding his own New England Blue Grass Boys.

Stover inspired a bevy of the Yankee banjo pickers—most notably Bill Keith—and the West Virginia banjoist lives on in their affections and performance.

Those who adore the music of the sweat-stained sometimes erect pedestals and name musicians to stand on top of them. This is appropriate; we need heroes to honor, and who better to honor than those who make us happy? But the figures atop the pedestals at times appear lonely to me, and we know they traveled in good company. So whenever I catch sight of a lonely hero of bluegrass, twisting on his pedestal, I summon up a vision of Don Stover, with a gleam of humor in his eye, to stand just in back of him and to festoon an empty place in whatever is happening with a Chuck Berry lick, or perhaps a surf music arpeggio. He'd say: "You got that, didn't you? Heh, heh, heh."

So this was the night that I met one of my favorite bands of all time. I'd grown up in the shadow of the Stanley Brothers, a friend since their first broadcast on WCYB in Bristol. I'd worked a year at the Grand Ole Opry, always attending Bill Monroe's rehearsal of the Blue Grass Boys in the little room adjacent to the Tootsie's side of the Ryman before their broadcast. But I'd never heard anything like this band. They were keepers of the tradition in a wonderfully unselfconscious way, and they infused their music with an instrumental inventiveness and brilliance that inspired awe.

They were delivered by Fred Bartenstein—then a fresh-faced under-graduate at Harvard—earnest and much aware that he was traveling with giants. I am grateful to him for making this possible, as I am to all of the musicians.

Life abounds with odd opportunities. Vermin may walk up your face one night, but the next night you can stand inches from the giants of a musical form. That concert lasted less than three hours, but it will be with me forever.

Bluegrass Breakdown
The Making of the Old Southern Sound
Robert Cantwell

● ●

In his preface, Robert Cantwell calls bluegrass a representation of traditional Appalachian music in its social form, one drawn from Afro-American and European sources that are largely Celtic. This familiar theory follows the scenario created by folksong revival writers who have been defining bluegrass in print for thirty-five years. Cantwell's subtitle, "The Making of the Old Southern Sound," has two sources. First, Bill Monroe, "the acknowledged 'Father of Bluegrass,'" believes his music is "the old Southern sound." Second, Cantwell finds in it links to the minstrel stages of the nineteenth century and believes it is a continuation of Celtic folklife handed through the generations and best preserved in Appalachia.

Much of this book is about Monroe and his creations. The social context of his youth is discussed, along with the milieu of country music during his career, the rise of bluegrass to popularity, African and Appalachian

(Urbana and Chicago: University of Illinois Press, 1984)

Excerpted from the published review in Journal of Country Music, Volume 10, Number 1, 1985 and re-edited to Joe Wilson's original text.

antecedents of his music, other notable bluegrass creators, folk revivalism, the imagery and rituals of his music, and its evocative powers. Cantwell demonstrates an analytical grasp of musicology in his descriptions of bluegrass and comparisons with other forms. He includes a bibliography and excellent notes.

Cantwell is a literary critic who writes with verve and eloquence, addressing a dizzying range of matters he feels impinged upon bluegrass at one time or another. He hopes some bluegrass musicians will read it, but says his book is addressed, "with great assiduousness and constancy," to a former academic colleague who told him that he should not write about bluegrass if he wished to advance in academia. The hoped-for bluegrass reader will be able to understand Cantwell's concepts but may have difficulty with his examples. For instance, the figure of Falstaff would be understood if his recent reincarnation as Junior Samples were mentioned, but Cantwell does not subject his former colleague to the strain of reaching that far outside the classics.

He has a keen sense of humor. Jeannie Seeley's band members "surround her with a sort of proprietary zeal, as if they had just won her from a gumball machine." There's no point in trying to talk to Monroe when he is resting on his bus before a show; "one might as well address a gardenia." Monroe and Seeley have a conversation and "the Blue Grass Boys, like pastured cows, look on impassively."

Cantwell comes from that school of literary criticism where it is traditional to assume that every thought and emotion of the author is of interest to the reader. This, and a tendency to reach for a globality of understanding even when the subject at hand seems small, creates a mind-clogging intensity. The reader's senses become overexposed and, like film, darken and cease to register. This is a book to be taken in very small doses; a chapter per sitting is plenty.

There are a few errors of fact. For example, Jimmie Rodgers did not introduce the Hawaiian guitar to country music. Tom Ashley lived in Tennessee, not North Carolina. There are some incomprehensible generalizations. For example, few students of older country music would agree that old-time string bands had "a mechanical quality."

In concept, this work is an intellectually agile and highly detailed restatement of the folkie history of bluegrass, the accepted one that has been gathering steam since Alan Lomax wrote his "folk music in overdrive" piece for *Esquire* in 1959. It is a far more erudite statement than most, but it follows the familiar folkie pattern of simplified sociology and romanticized history to support building the pedestal upon which the hero will perch. The initial folkie hero was Earl Scruggs, but during the 1960s Ralph Rinzler supplied a course correction. Since then, Bill Monroe has been the Christopher Columbus of bluegrass—and he deserves enormous credit, of course.

Cantwell offers no evidence to support his thesis that bluegrass is primarily a social form of Appalachian art. No one ever has. Bluegrass was assigned to Appalachia at its moment of creation. No member of Monroe's classic band was a native of the Southern mountains; all were flatlanders. But their new creation sounded old when compared to other modern country musics, so it was assigned to Appalachia. It was from the first as technologically dependent as any other form of modern country music; the taking of breaks on various acoustic instruments from a stage was impossible before the advent of microphone technology. But the instruments were not plugged directly into electricity, so an illusion of purity was preserved—a musical form of technical virginity. And bluegrass soon became popular in the mountains, as it did everywhere in the Southeast.

Cantwell's favorite sociologist seems to be Claudia Lewis, a daring Manhattan schoolmarm who came to the wilds of Tennessee during the 1940s and found the natives speaking—surprise, surprise—what was almost a dialect of Elizabethan English. Cantwell guesses that Monroe's childhood in Kentucky, a generation earlier, was similarly rustic. The romanticized isolation theory of Appalachian history that the antiquarian folkies borrowed from the late nineteenth-century local-color writers recurs in quotes: Peter Kennedy's silly supposition that fiddles and banjos were hidden when the word went up the hollow that Professor Sharp was coming and the Lomax comment that mountain singing is more "British" than British singing. Cantwell buys even the common fiction that mountain people are largely Scots-Irish in ancestry; he went to Scotland and he detected in bluegrass "the imprint of the Celtic imagination." He finds bluegrass "restrained and severe," and its Nashville cousin "irrepressibly ostentatious and vulgar," and between them "a yawning moral gulf."

That he is repelled by the audience and performers of Nashville music and, to a lesser extent, the performers and indigenous audiences of bluegrass, is also clear in repeated gibes about dress and physiognomy. The distance that the romantic and scholarly vision allows is preferred. Up close, he realizes that even Monroe "is only a hayseed after all; yet he retains the power to fascinate, this strong and handsome father figure who says so little in words and so much with his music."

There's nothing new about the fictional attribution of musical innovation to specific regions or to people viewed as having greater authenticity. A nineteenth-century example is minstrel music, largely a popular Yankee creation but attributed to Southern plantation slaves. Thus the "old Southern sound" in Cantwell's title is really an old Yankee sound. But Cantwell believes the hoary claims made by the burnt-cork performers about Southern fieldwork: " . . . the minstrel show extracted the comedic elements of black folk music, subjecting it to theatrical laws . . ." From this, you'd think Emmett, Rice, and Christy were the nineteenth-century counterparts of the New Lost City Ramblers, socially acceptable performers of the music of socially unacceptable people.

Those who build pedestals for heroes seldom make room for more than one. Given the quality of his early associates, Monroe's perch seems especially lonely.

[In an April 10, 1987, letter of apology to author Robert Cantwell, Joe Wilson wrote:

Dear Bob:

I have just finished reading your book again. And that sent me into the old computer, seeking a hard copy of that book review that did not please you. How'd it read the second time? Well, dammit, though normally numbered among the saints and angels, I may have erred. Lest there be a stain on the white robe that I wear to the great singing up Yonder, I offer this apology.

It was not fair to use a review of your book as a vehicle to give you hell for not having my concepts of where and how this music came about. (Now there's a dense sentence. Pray over it. Have a glass of wine and a slice of cheese. But bear in mind that, nowadays, consumer choice determines identity. One slice of Velveeta makes you a hick, and a cracker load of brie announces that a new man of substance is about. You've had both? There's no hope.)

The review was poorly edited by [someone] who did not think it important to check his changes with me. . . . I'm enclosing a copy of what I sent out. You won't like it any better, but I'm a proponent of accuracy in dislikes.

I feel it is OK for a reviewer to second-guess and disagree, but methinks I went too far. It is better to prick you and make you jump than to skewer you. Of course, I still see these matters from a very different perspective. But, should I ever review your work again, I shall announce my perspective whenever it intrudes, rather than pretending that it is The Truth or obvious. Perhaps like this: "I have a view of these phenomena from where I sit on the highest hill, a view unobstructed by clouds of any kind. My vision is 20/20 and my conceptual powers are at their zenith. Meanwhile, poor Cantwell has his head thrust into an orifice anatomically impossible and is able to see only through the use of mirrors and communicates through the use of sign language."

See, I knew you'd like it better.

Best regards. Call before you come to town and I'll think of something good to do.

Joe]

The Seldom Scene
Creators of Urban Bluegrass

● ●

If someone had made a list of bluegrass garage and basement bands least likely to change the direction of that music in 1972, the Seldom Scene would surely have topped the list. When would they have time to practice or play?

Lead singer and guitarist John Starling was a surgeon specializing, as waggish bandmate John Duffey put it, "in ear, nose, throat, and wallet."

Banjoist Ben Eldridge was a mathematician creating technical applications for a corporation and, as Duffey put it, "penetrating the impenetrable, and getting little squirts through the impermeable."

Trio baritone singer and resophonic guitarist Mike Auldridge was a graphic artist for the *Washington Star*. Duffey saluted him for creating ads " . . . that get you to buy stuff you don't want or need, and would be better off without."

Bassist and sometimes singer Tom Gray was a cartographer for the National Geographic Society, and was thus honored by Duffey as " . . . the only one of us who always knows exactly where he is."

Liner notes to *The Seldom Scene: Creators of Urban Bluegrass*, Cracker Barrel Records, 2002.

Duffey was mandolinist, sometime lead singer, and the creator of many of the band's best arrangements. He made and repaired fretted musical instruments, tended his garden, and was fiercely devoted to his bowling and softball teams—to the point of declining an invitation to perform at the White House because it interfered with a softball game.

Duffey's father had been a Metropolitan Opera singer, but John denied that bluegrass was part of his adolescent rebellion. "The old man was happy about anything that got me off the couch and out of the house."

Duffey was the only one of the five who had been a full-time professional musician, and he had quit because he despised the travel imposed by that occupation. In 1957, he'd been a founding member of the Country Gentlemen, the first urban bluegrass band to deserve and get national attention.

He humorously adapted the Scene's name from a comment by Charlie Waller, a former bandmate in the Country Gentlemen. Told that Duffey was performing in a new band, Waller opined that they'd be "seldom seen."

They were not the first bluegrass band composed of young urban professionals. That distinction seems to belong to another nonprofessional group with a great sense of humor, The Dismembered Tennesseans, formed in Chattanooga in 1947. But the Scene was the first urban-bred group to bring major innovation to the genre and to influence and hugely enlarge the acceptability of the form.

It is no accident that they were formed in suburban Washington, D.C. That city, along with adjacent Baltimore, had—and still has—the greatest percentage of residents who are migrants from Appalachian counties. Yes, an even greater percentage than Dayton, Cleveland, or Detroit.

So members of the Scene were reared with the sounds of the Stanley Brothers in their ears. But, as their repertoire shows, their ears were also open to a wide range of musical composition—progressive country, rock, singer-songwriter creations, blues, and ancient balladry.

They began, Duffey said, " . . . like a poker game for boys," meeting every Thursday night in a basement. Resophonic wizard Auldridge said they wanted to be free to play anything from bluegrass standards " . . . to James Taylor and the Grateful Dead."

But, like other basement and garage bands, they soon developed the desire for an audience. No one intended to become famous or influential; they simply needed some giggles at their gibes, and for someone to notice their harmony and arrangements.

Their first gig was at the Rabbit's Foot, a downtown D.C. bistro. Those shows abruptly ended when a person in charge there demonstrated a stunning lack of bar management foresight by refusing to turn off a TV football game for the Scene's performance.

They retreated for beer and discussion to the Red Fox Inn, a beer joint in nearby Bethesda, Maryland. Owner Walt Broderick invited them to bring their Thursday night sessions to his place.

Lightning struck. The Fox was instantly packed to the rafters while disappointed would-be patrons waited outside, hoping someone would leave and make a seat or standing room available. It seemed that the reputation of this new band went across the nation at the speed of light.

Four LPs were released on the Rebel label during the Seldom Scene's Red Fox years, before their move across the river to the Birchmere, in Alexandria, Virginia, a showplace where they played for twenty years. They were first recorded, of course, in a basement studio. Those early recordings offer a hint of the power, joy, and genre-bending insouciance the band brought to bluegrass.

Many of the heroes of rock and country found their way to their D.C.-area performances, and those that the band respected were invited to climb onstage and sing. Emmylou Harris showed up often, and one of their favorite devotees was Linda Ronstadt, who occasionally guested on their recordings.

Eldridge and Auldridge were top instrumentalists and became models for younger players all over the nation. Auldridge helped make the resophonic guitar (sometimes called a Dobro, after a famous maker) a fully accepted part of bluegrass. Eldridge dared even to play the banjo slowly.

But the Scene became popular largely because of the strength of its singing and its powerful vocal arrangements. John Starling had a voice with the stylistic authority of a Johnny Cash and the melodic sensibility of a Marty Robbins. John Duffey was among the finest tenor singers to ever grace a genre that prizes great tenor singers, and he was also a great lead singer. Mike Auldridge owned a pleasing baritone, and sang with Starling and Duffey in the Scene's trio.

Like most basement and bar bands, they eventually went separate ways. Eldridge is the only original member in the current edition of the Scene [he retired in 2016], and he still loves the music and plays it with verve and great skill.

The Scene's founder, John Duffey, died in 1996. One of his fans, Congressman Dave Obey, put a eulogy in the *Congressional Record* that reflected the feelings of many who had followed Duffey: "He was a remarkable singer of bluegrass, possessed of a powerful vocal instrument, one that could soar to impossibly high notes or become the soul of harmony and touch the heart. He was a good performer with mandolin and guitar, and he was the prince of wit and laughter."

In the decades since its founding, the Scene has become the most imitated band in its genre. Scene-like trios are prized everywhere, and one does not need to wear string ties or sit on bales of hay to play this still-developing form of American roots music.

The contribution of the Seldom Scene, simply put, is that it took a music that was largely rural and Southern in its themes and audience, and made it accessible and delightful to millions of others.

Doyle Lawson

Standing on the Rock

· ·

The religious revivals that swept the nation during the second "Great Awakening" began in 1800 on the frontier, then in Kentucky. They spread eastward across our new nation, sweeping away the old religious authority and its forms. This new religious practice brought with it shape note hymnody. The term "shape note" refers to the older tune books' use of the shape of the note rather than its position on the staff to tell its pitch.

Taught by itinerant "singing school" teachers in two-week evening classes, this form of circuit-riding musical literacy left an indelible imprint upon the music of the nation, which continues to this day.

This legacy of music came to Doyle Lawson in rural schoolhouse musical gatherings, at church, and local live radio broadcasts of religious singers and string bands that could be heard weekly and even daily, in some cases.

Doyle was reared amid the mountains of northeastern Tennessee in a tiny rural farming community called Fordtown. Though small, Fordtown

Liner notes to *Doyle Lawson: Standing on the Rock,* Cracker Barrel Records, 2004.

has produced other notable musicians, including Tennessee Ernie Ford and the brilliant 1920s recording fiddler, Charlie Bowman.

Doyle's father, mother, and sister sang in a cappella trios and quartets in area churches and schools, and Doyle began playing the mandolin at the age of eleven.

Doyle still lives between the Clinch Mountain range and the western slopes of the Blue Ridge, where shape-note religious song traditions and string band traditions powerfully coexist even today.

In his childhood, microphone technology and its ability to "solo" instruments enabled the new bluegrass style to develop as a new concert style, growing out of the earlier dance music. Like many other younger mountain musicians, Lawson eagerly embraced the new concert form. But, unlike others, he retained affection for the earlier vocal styles and a tendency to experiment with them in the new format.

His skills put him in several groundbreaking bluegrass bands: Jimmy Martin's, J.D. Crowe's, and the Country Gentlemen. In these bands, he became known for leading brilliant four-part harmony gospel arrangements with string band accompaniment. Quicksilver, the band he has led since 1979, continued this practice and became noted for it.

There had been well-known groups combining string band sounds and shape note hymnody before Lawson—among them the Brown's Ferry Four, the Chuck Wagon Gang, Ernest Phipps's Holiness Quartet, and James and Martha Carson.

Bill Monroe's early bluegrass bands often ended concerts and broadcasts with a gospel song in four-part harmony with mandolin and guitar. Others followed, most notably Flatt and Scruggs, the Stanley Brothers, Carl Story, and the Lewis Family. Lawson heard and learned from all of them, and he also developed affection for African-American gospel singing.

Lawson's bands have been the greatest force in string band gospel for a quarter century. Yet Lawson has never restricted himself to gospel; he also makes secular recordings. Without making any speeches, he tends to be balanced and genial in his approach to music and life.

So what are his contributions? Simply put, he has pushed this art to a new and higher level. There is a razor's edge of excellence in all that he does. His singing is so good that it inspires; his arrangements infuse songs with movement and a richness of feeling; his harmonies soar and touch the spirit; and his timing borders on being perfect. So many graduates of his band have gone on to fame that it is jokingly said that Lawson "runs" the farm team for great singers. Today, Doyle Lawson and Quicksilver still tour the nation, and we hope you have the opportunity to see them perform.

Farewell to Kenny Baker, 1926–2011

Today we say farewell to Kenny Baker, brilliant and influential fiddler and a National Heritage Fellow. His wake is tonight in Jenkins, Kentucky, in the coalfields, near where he was reared. He will be buried tomorrow close to his father and grandfather, both also notable fiddlers.

In tours of *Masters of the Folk Violin,* which the NCTA had on the road for portions of three years, legendary [African-American] jazz fiddler Claude Williams would startle jazz and country audiences by putting his arm around this former coal miner and saying, "This is my good friend, Kenny. He invented tone."

Some of you will recall Kenny as the poker-faced lean fiddler in tightly rolled cowboy hat standing near Bill Monroe for some thirty years, framing his every sound, helping to invent classic bluegrass. Yet Kenny never thought of himself as a bluegrass fiddler. "I was supposed to be a swing fiddler when I played for Don Gibson," he told me in an interview, "but I was always a coal miner on parole."

Posted to the Publore listserv for the public folklore community, July 11, 2011.

He had an infectious sense of humor. He thought it very funny that his partner, Dobroist Josh Graves—a veteran of the Lester Flatt and Earl Scruggs bluegrass band—would speak to Claude Williams about "Lester," never realizing that Claude had no idea of who "Lester" was.

Then Claude spoke to Josh about "Ella," not realizing that Josh did not know about Ella Fitzgerald or Claude's one-time partner, Charlie Christian, or that he had been a member of the Nat King Cole Trio.

In proposing a toast to Josh and Claude, Kenny observed, "What these guys have in common is that they would starve to death in a coal camp."

Kenny was passionate about seeking the company of a dwindling group of fiddlers that he thought were the very best of the old-timers. I met the legendary "Blind Dick" (Richard Burnett) through Kenny, and he was also a fast friend of Tommy Jarrell and Herb Combs.

Kenny left many fine fiddle recordings, but there's also a fingerpicked guitar CD [*Kenny Baker & Josh Graves: The Puritan Sessions*, Rebel Records, 1989] that is a memorial to Ernest Johnson. He was a black man who sold peanuts and played guitar on the streets of Jenkins when Kenny was a boy. Kenny's take on his style is sparkling, wonderfully melodic, genial, and utterly distinct. Kenny explained, "Well, he let me watch him and I thought his style should not die with him."

The other famous fiddlers on those NCTA tours—Cajun, Cape Breton, Irish, even an age-sixteen Alison Krauss—loved each other, but they were awed by Kenny Baker. Yes, it was that nearly unbelievable tone. But it was also his richly textured approach to a tune, with variations that gave one chills. It was also his approachability. Kenny mixed being extraordinary with being humble, and that is rare.

MODERN COUNTRY MUSIC

When Willie Came
to Town

· ·

Okie pointed out the window at Willie Nelson, who was walking toward the door of Linebaugh's restaurant in Nashville. "That's him!"
Willie was young and armed with a friendly grin. This was several years
before his Nehru jacket costume, and half a generation before his uniform
became a mixture of hippie and cowboy grunge.

Okie [Otho Jones] had worked with Willie on the *Big D Jamboree* in
Dallas. He was certain that this young Texan with limpid eyes and relentless grin was the world's best salesman. That was because Willie could put
on slacks and jacket, assume the aura of a seminary student, and go door-
to-door down any residential street and sell a set of *Encyclopedia Britannica*.

Unpublished. Joe Wilson wrote: "I wrote this potty-mouthed account of Willie Nelson's first
night in Nashville in the nineties. I sent a copy of an earlier draft to a country music rag then
getting started in Nashville. A dude responded and said I needed to 'clean it up.' I had no
interest in that. I wish you could have been with us that night and had juicy pork barbeque
on a white flint cornbread hoecake with an Oertle's 92 draft out on Tennessee Highway
100." After Joe's death, the editor called Okie Jones, who confirmed some of Joe's facts and
corrected others. The events appear to have occurred late in 1960, but time and substances
consumed on the night in question may have dimmed the witnesses' testimony.

The commission was huge for a sale of that monument to parental guilt. In two hours, he'd earn enough to feed his songwriting habit for a week. I was impressed. Many of Nashville's best cab drivers and bellhops were feeding songwriting habits, but they had to work far longer hours.

Willie was also a songwriting loser, a breed of victim we respected. He'd composed a song—"Family Bible"—and sold it for fifty dollars. Claude Gray's recording of Willie's song was a huge hit and on the charts for thirteen weeks in 1960. Okie figured Gray earned a pile on his fifty-dollar investment.

There were then no superstar songwriters among Nashville crooners. But there were superstar song buyers. We knew who really wrote most hits, and we admired writers more than singers. It was important to us to know who actually wrote the good songs. Among our heroes was Arthur Q. Smith, a Knoxville songwriting genius and drunk who never sold a song for more than $100. Some of Nashville's biggest reputations were bought from Arthur. We heard that his enduring standard, "Wedding Bells," went for 20 bucks and a quart of Dago Red.

Linebaugh's was a musician's hangout located on lower Broadway, and it never closed. It was near the Ernest Tubb Record Shop and across Broadway from Tootsie's Orchid Lounge, a beer joint with a back door that led to the Ryman Auditorium and the Grand Ole Opry. On Saturday nights, Roy Acuff sat at a table distant from the Linebaugh jukebox and spent an hour drinking coffee and eating a slice of cherry pie. Maniacal songwriter and brother-singer Ira Louvin held court to a passing scene of young women. Sidemen and stars ate Linebaugh's excellent beef stew, and some topped their meal with hot blackberry cobbler and ice cream.

It was not proper to speak to Jim Reeves or Ray Price if they wandered in. You could nod and smile, but those with their names painted on buses were never hassled when they ate at Linebaugh's. The regular patrons were vigilant enforcers of that rule. The nervous tourist approaching Acuff with an autograph book was advised, "Not in here."

Among the regulars at Linebaugh's during the early morning hours was Sucking Susie, a retired hooker who now earned her keep by babysitting and as the chief supplier of good quality dope to songwriters and musicians. She earned more from the dope than the babysitting, but the latter work enabled a relationship with the better young sidemen that she adored. At one time, she babysat during afternoons for steel guitarist Jimmy Day, while keeping Tootsie's mom during the early evening hours. Susie usually arrived at Linebaugh's shortly after midnight.

This was before Leary and Alpert popularized marijuana at Harvard and everywhere else, and we'd sometimes stroll down lower Broadway smoking a joint, knowing it was unlikely to be recognized. Susie grew weed to a height of ten feet in a yard behind Tootsie's house and dealt only in top leaf. We despised the Harvard professors who made weed a scandal and called the new urban users "schoolboy dope fiends."

But pills were Susie's main business. Ten-grain bennies cost a dime each and she had a graduate student delivering a new crate of them every Friday. Two of these gems would enable a touring musician a wonderfully pleasant wide-awake drive from Nashville to either of the Portlands. When downed with beer, they created visions of babbling brooks, desert sunsets, and first love.

When Nashville cops busted Susie, the *Nashville Banner* pulled out of reserve a giant-size headline type it had saved to announce the Second Coming. The *Banner* estimated a half-million dollar street price for her little crate of bennies and twelve pounds of weed.

She assured the investigators these goods were for her own use. One asked, "Susie, how long did you intend to stay high?" Her response to that half-humorous, half-officious query was classic Susie: "How LONG is long, man?"

Due to a defective search warrant, she was back in her usual booth at Linebaugh's within six weeks. She had suffered a brain hemorrhage while in jail, but a guard noticed her distress and rushed her to a nearby hospital. She raised her eyes and hands to heaven and proclaimed to the Linebaugh regulars, "They saved my life, children! Jail is sometimes the right place to be. I'd have died if I had been at altar call in the First Baptist Church, or in bed with the mayor."

Susie was always beautifully dressed and carried herself with a graceful elegance that led the uninitiated to suspect she was an aristocrat from someplace important. She often carried a copy of *Elbert Hubbard's Scrap Book*, and read poetry from it when an audience could be cornered.

I've always believed her "Sucking Susie" title was derived from a nervous speaking peculiarity. Before she spoke, she'd pop her lips and inhale sharply, creating an audible "fuhh shoo." Others thought it derived from aspects of her regular work, but had no proof.

She was reading poetry from *Hubbard's Scrap Book* to two young acolytes one night, during the wee hours, when Faron Young wobbled in. Then at his performing and recording peak and nicknamed "The Young Sheriff" for his role in the 1956 B-movie *Hidden Guns*, Faron had been engaged in a wrestling match with the wares of Jack Daniel, and his speech was slurred.

He addressed a request to the elegant one that made the room grow quiet. "Susie, I'd like to have a little pussy."

Susie fixed one the greatest crooners of the decade with a gently discerning eye and slight smile. "So would I, Faron. Mine's big as a horse collar."

The laughter bounced off the kitchen wall and went on until Young wobbled over to the old hooker and gave her a hug. She hugged him back and returned to her reading.

Like Willie, Okie was a country music loser. But his loss was as a performer. In the fifties he'd appeared several times on Arlene Francis's nationally distributed TV show. Handsome and effervescent and a favorite of the hostess, his most popular record was, "Send Me a Penny Postcard."

Singers with hit songs were supposed to go out and feverishly work the nation, and hopefully save enough money to get beyond the dry spell that often follows hit songs. But Okie's manager thought he should go into real estate and invest in starting a new performance venue. So they went to Spruce Pine, North Carolina, and bought into the *Carolina Barn Dance*. The song was spent and Okie was flat broke ten months later when he drove out of Spruce Pine.

He went to Dallas and other country music towns before coming to Nashville. He was a guest on the Opry several times, and Paul Cohen recorded him for a venture label, but the old magic never returned. He had enjoyed driving his bus, and one day in frustration told his friend Marty Robbins that he was sick of beating his head on industry walls and asked if he could become his bus driver.

But Okie kept his songwriting skills, and one of his songs—"Father's Table Grace"—became a hit for bluegrass singer Lester Flatt. Like many other country songs, it related an actual experience, a gripping story about Okie's father using a table grace to speak to enduring values and recognizing his son was departing the family hearth and entering into manhood and its dangers.

Okie was working for Robbins when I wandered into Linebaugh's and met Pete Drake—then steel guitarist in the band—and Robbins's manager and bodyguard, Lee Emerson. Emerson (who would later write "Ruby Ann," a 1963 number one hit for Marty Robbins) asked if I knew how to type and be nice to people, and I got my first paying job in the music business.

Sometimes the work was not musical. At one point in this frenetic period, Robbins had the band and staff at Smyrna, Tennessee, building a micro-midget race track—musicians and paper wranglers learning to operate rented bulldozers, graders, water rollers, and other earth-moving equipment. Robbins backed a bulldozer over a fence we'd finished building moments earlier, and there were other mishaps. It was a scene that could have been created for a Laurel and Hardy movie.

Robbins had a congenital heart defect and needed protection from the country bullyboys that sometimes came backstage, intent on fisticuffs with him. And why would anyone wish to commit mayhem upon this genial singer who sparkled with good humor? It was always jealousy. The sullen fellow's girlfriend liked Marty, and, even though the singer had never laid eyes on the lady, he was to be thrashed.

Bellicose boyfriends were handled gently, offered understanding and a clutch of tickets to the show. But if they persisted, Lee Emerson was the staff member who most often took up the case. Lee was arguably the best barroom brawler to ever uncork a haymaker. The bellicose swain was shortly flat on his back, and often missing a portion of his eating apparatus.

As friendly as a wet puppy and with the looks of a matinee idol, Emerson was a Nashville contradiction. The composer of the gently ethereal ballad, "I Thought I Heard You Calling My Name," he was also famous in our world as the Big Papa of bust-ass street fighters.

He was shot and killed a dozen years later by Sgt. Barry Sadler, the self-appointed hero who composed and recorded the Vietnam-era song, "Ballad of the Green Beret." Both Sadler and Emerson were interested in the same lady, and Emerson told Sadler he was coming by her digs and intended to alter his appearance should he be on the premises. The fearful hero shot Emerson when he drove up, even though Emerson was unarmed.

A country bullyboy who receives a well-deserved haymaker often goes whimpering to a lawyer in the aftermath, seeking solicitude and cash. So Emerson had a lengthy "record" that Sadler's defense attorney waved at the Nashville court. That and Sadler's ersatz hero status was enough in a Nashville then blinded by even a hint of celebrity; Sadler got away with murder.

But there was vengeance. Shortly the strutting hero went off to Guatemala to be an "action hero" like those in his paperback novels. In Guatemala City, a robber shot him between the eyes, turning him into a vegetable. Some of us thought Jesus may have used that robber and recalled rants by gangling loose-jointed preachers telling of the unorthodox but direct ways of the Lord.

But we need to get back to poor Willie. We've left that lad sitting in a Linebaugh booth on his first night in town, and need to tell of the wonders that almost instantly came to beguile his career and light his night.

His high-mileage Oldsmobile had a prize under the front seat: a small brown paper bag of ready-roll joints, each wonderfully fat with top weed. I had enough cash to buy us a six-pack. Susie had blessed us with a tiny supply of white pills. We were fully fortified and able to take on the Nashville night, and Okie always had a recreation plan.

First stop was to be the *Opry Star Spotlight*, the WSM late evening and early morning radio show then blanketing Dixie with truck-driving songs. Mouthpiece Ralph Emery was then perched on this cricket box of sound, taking phone calls, interviewing an occasional celebrity, and letting his drip-dry opinions be heard. The signal was 50,000 watts clear-channel, reaching more than half the nation, so touring musicians usually listened and it was a good way to make it known—to those looking for good songs—that Willie had relocated.

Getting to Emery's emporium required traversing a holy place, the WSM radio lobby once shot to smithereens by Ernest Tubb. We stopped for a few minutes to peek at a ricochet mark. Tubb was one of our heroes, and this was a rare site where a composer and singer had prevailed.

Jim Denny had been manager of the Opry when Tubb came to town from Texas, and he also had a management agency. If a singer wanted good placement on the Grand Ole Opry, he needed to have Jim as his manager. Good placement required being on at least one show before 9:00

p.m., when the huge farm audience went to bed. But Tubb was loyal to his agent and irritated at this blatant conflict of interest.

Tubb was old Texas and one evening, in his cups, he called Denny and proposed that they meet at WSM and shoot it out. Denny agreed, but rolled over and returned to his sleep. Tubb loaded his six-shooter, got into his new baby blue Cadillac, and drove himself to WSM.

This auspicious building was in the shadow of the Tennessee Capitol building, near the War Memorial Building, and across the street from the grand hotels. It was beige marble, testimony to the huge sums early radio once earned. The lobby where Tubb waited in vain for Denny was spacious. We never heard who challenged him in that place, but that he shot it up was legend.

Of course they fired him [WSM was owned at the time by the National Life and Accident Insurance Company]. Nashville was then the "Athens of the South," had seventeen colleges and universities, and the Southern Baptist printing and songbook industry. The gentlemen who operated the major interests of that place could never put up with rude behavior, not even from one in a glitter-cut western suit and his name painted on a bus. So what if hundreds of thousands adored him?

Only a few years earlier, they'd canned the Bailes Brothers at the apogee of their career, when the brothers' great song "Remember Me" topped the charts. The infraction had been lesser; a well-married, beautiful young society lady from Shelbyville had lost her mind over Johnnie Bailes, an easy-on-the-eyes brother given to great harmonizing and easy virtue. Some said Johnnie would screw a rafter if he thought a cockroach was under it.

So the lovely one followed Johnnie to his hotel on Nashville's lower Broad and a room he shared with a stunning bandmate and singer, Evelyn Thomas. A discussion between the ladies ended with the society lady leaping through a third-floor window, breaking her pelvis and anonymity and making the newspapers. The Bailes Brothers were soon heard on Shreveport's *Louisiana Hayride*, and their career waned.

But the money men quickly learned that Tubb was not easy to fire. His affection for his fans was obvious and returned in full measure. The policyholders objected, as did some shareholders. Tubb was good for business and he survived. Of course, he was "talked to"—even "dressed down"—and took it like a man.

It was the first glimmer of big influence from a hillbilly and—told that this very genial sweetheart of a man could also be a bad boy—no one ever came backstage intent on fisticuffs with Tubb. "He's my best friend," the night guard told as we looked at the ricochet mark. "If I got into trouble, he'd be the first person I'd call."

But upstairs, our greeting was less effusive. Anyone associated with Robbins was welcome but expected to be quiet. We were not in a quiet mood and found Ralph-the-mouthpiece dour, reminiscent of a deacon with a boil on his ass. We decided to abandon him and take our talent to WLAC.

That station was yet another insurance-funded 50,000-watt cover-the-South wonder, one with two delightfully different audiences. Did I say different? A difference this great could only happen in real life—fiction as outrageous would not be tolerated.

The first audience was rural blacks, farm folk in a wide arc that extended from the Carolina and Georgia coasts to the Gulf, and over to Texas. Everyone in the Mississippi and Arkansas Delta listened, and this station owned full allegiance from black folk in Memphis. The signal hit the Midwest almost as hard, and there were urban listeners in Chicago, Indianapolis, and Cleveland.

It was a time when many rural people, and especially farm families, did their meager buying in the mom and pop stores still dotting the back country South, selling laxatives, headache powders, and Clabber Girl baking powder. The chewing tobacco extolled on the station was plug, and the snuff was made in Memphis and dusty. Flour came in twenty-five-pound bags, corn meal was self-rising, and brown-bag sugar came from Louisiana.

But WLAC was the richest source for Delta blues in the nation, a musical mecca, a non-stop pipeline for the rising sounds of Jimmy Reed, Otis Redding, Howling Wolf, and Muddy Waters. New songs were heard here first, and one could buy them from Nashville mail-order record shops. This was a musical cult with a passion that bordered on religious ecstasy.

WLAC deejays were relentless in inviting listeners to come see them: "We're in the tallest building in Nashville, the Life and Casualty Tower.

Find that building and the elevator on its side—it only goes to the top—and that is where we is!"

The second huge Southern audience for the WLAC signal was white college and high school students who called Delta blues "lower-your-drawers music" and loved it with as much passion as its black creators.

Though the products were largely aimed at black farm folk, the dee-jays often took side aim at the white kids. Gene Nobles praised a hair-straightening pomade with a double entendre: "You boys been getting some bee-hind in your dating, need some of this White Rose Petroleum Jelly—make things easier for you."

The recordings sold through mail-order record shops went largely to white kids who could afford them, while cheap food, beauty, and tobacco items were sold to blacks in tiny stores. Were they aware of each other? Perhaps, but only dimly.

But it was not the zen of mutual incomprehension that brought Willie, Okie, and me to the top floor of Life and Casualty. We went there to see the black listeners and the white deejays take stock of each other.

The big joke was that the deejays were all white men cultivating black accents. Most of the white kids thought they were black, and marveled at the things blacks could say on radio and get away with as part of their commerce. Blacks adored the music, and wanted to put faces with these familiar voices.

Willie, Okie, and I were devoted to shock. There were no visitors when we arrived, so we sat on a wall bench like three starlings on a tele-phone wire, watching pudgy white men mark copy with yellow pencils then read it in black voices.

An extended family of rural blacks arrived, positioning in genteel order on a bench opposite us. The men wore khaki pants with shirts of solid colors, their shoes well polished. The women wore hats, colorful cotton dresses, and carried white purses.

A pudgy white man began a pitchman's colloquy in black voice with one of his fellows about Brown Mule Chewing Tobacco. "Now, Charley, I knows you chews tobacco . . ."

As the pitch continued, a look of palpable shock overtook the visitors. Not a word was said, and they rose as one and quickly exited. We waited until they were gone and then fell, flailing the floor in silent hysteria. Why? I'm not sure. It is called dope for a reason.

We were still there when Bob Jennings, the early morning farm dee-jay, came in to turn the station's sound to country for the hundreds of thousands of farm families that arose and switched their radio on at 4:00 a.m. He invited us to go on the radio with him and tell road stories, and we had some, though of limited intellectual reach. One involved a South Texas lad we'd squeezed until he was free of BS, enabling us to bury him in a matchbox.

Jennings was also a singer who recorded for Gene Autry's Hollywood-based Republic label, and we learned he had a session coming up. Willie had no dubs of his songs, but I'd seen a disc-cutting recorder in a room down the hall and could operate it. Jennings had a Martin guitar, Willie wrote out the words and Okie held them as Willie played open chords and sang.

We recorded three songs with the disc cutter as the sun lifted, showing fog drifting from the Cumberland River. Within weeks, Jennings had one on a Republic single. ["That's What Children Are For," released in November of 1960.] It may have been the first song Willie got recorded in Nashville under his own name.

The demos were not his best songs, but as we trudged toward the high-mileage Oldsmobile, we knew it had been a good night's work, exactly what country boys were supposed to do in big cities.

Nashville Cats

*On the Road with Cowboy Copas
and Grandpa Jones*

• •

Out on the road, up near Calgary, a hotel clerk peered across steel-rim glasses at Cowboy Copas and Grandpa Jones. Cope and Pa were pals and always roomed together on package tours. Both were old-style country musicians adapting to Nashville.

Cope was from Blue Creek, Ohio, but he looked like a man from Oklahoma—long and lean, boots, striped shotgun pants, tooled belt, cowboy shirt with pearl snaps, and a wide-brim Stetson with a rakish roll perched on his angular head. His old Martin guitar case had a missing handle, so he sometimes carried it on his shoulder. His name was Lloyd Copas, but everyone called him "Cowboy" or "Cope."

Cope had had some dry years since his first hit, "Filipino Baby," after World War II. The King label had dropped him, but during the winter of 1959 he'd flatpicked and sung "Alabam" to fill out a Starday LP of his radio songs to sell on the road. He'd changed the racist lyric from the n-word of minstrelsy to "tramp," thus obtaining full composer's credit. It had become an improbable country hit, and every wheat farmer's wife in western Canada was now humming a Cowboy Copas song.

Unpublished, undated. "Alabam" entered *Billboard*'s country charts in July of 1960. So these events must have occurred between then and Copas's death, in March of 1963.

Package tours allowed five or six "name" artists to tour in one bus with a single band—more star power to draw audiences, but lower expenses. Cope and Pa were "names," but barely.

Pa Jones's nasal vocal style and patrician phrasing on country radio had earned his "Grandpa" moniker a generation earlier, when he was barely out of his teens in Kentucky. He had a large store of Anglo-American ballads from the mountains of eastern Kentucky and was perpetually puzzled that country audiences preferred coon dog songs to "Fair Ellender."

The packed bus had left a trail of blue diesel smoke as it roared across almost 400 miles of Canadian prairie before the show. A sold-out crowd was in the hall before the sound check ended. The promoter had hustled, and there had been a two-thirds house for a second show at 10:00 p.m. Cope and Pa had a 30-minute break between shows and had spent it selling records and pictures.

The autograph line after the second show was long, and Cope and Pa sat in folding chairs and talked and shook hands until the last red-faced wheat farmer and his floral-dressed wife trudged off toward their pickup truck.

It was 2:10 a.m., and Pa was still wearing his stage costume of logging boots, gray twill pants, red and black checked shirt, suspenders, and battered crushed hat as he stared balefully at the harried hotel man in his three-piece suit and steel rims. Suddenly, the clerk found in the register the names he'd been seeking.

"Ah," he said, with the aura of Edison explaining incandescence. "Here it is, Cowboy Jones and Grandpa Copas."

"That'll do," said Pa. "Gimme the key."

Out on the prairie, the wheat farmer's battered truck grumbled down a dirt road, stirring dust in the night. His wife held the pictures of the Grand Ole Opry stars with both hands in her lap. She knew exactly where she'd place them.

They'd go on the wall with the two pictures of her parents in oversize plaster frames, near her grandchildren's school pictures in metal frames. That would place them opposite the window facing south and the pictures of Pope Pius, Jesus, and the Blessed Virgin.

The inscription, "With thanks to Clementine Askew from her friend, Cowboy Copas," would show well in that light.

Nashville Babylon

The Uncensored Truth and Private Lives
of Country Music's Stars

• •

Here's how you become successful in country music: you spend ten years advertising yourself every day in every way that you can. It is a deal with the devil. If you're a big winner, the devil gets your privacy. You spend the rest of your life in a goldfish bowl, your nether regions and most intimate transactions exposed to the gaze, gibes, cheers, and giggling of the populace.

It is an old problem. Among the treasures found in the Valley of the Kings in Egypt is a fresco that shows one or another of the Ramses clan watching a parade of prisoners, the spoils of war. The gimlet eye of the chief sun-god worshipper is fixed upon the well-rounded derriere of a female captive. This royal indiscretion, from a time before Moses parted the waters, was not recorded for history by a royal hand. No, this clay was molded by the grubby hand of a commoner, and probably that of a slave.

Randall Riese. (New York: Congdon & Weede, 1988.)

An abridged version of the review that appeared in *Journal of Country Music*, vol. 12, no. 3, 1989. p. 50–52.

Randall Riese brings to this hoary tradition a sensibility honed in Hollywood, that least culturally conscious place in our great republic. In his book, country musicians are devoted to racism, sexism, guns, dope snorting, alcoholism, child abuse, wife abuse, bed-hopping, felonious assault, murder, fag-bashing, pedophilia, and "The Old Rugged Cross." One longs to ask Riese, "When do they squeeze in some time for music?"

There's a maddening lack of conceptual consistency in Riese's book that leaves one wondering just what in hell he is laying bare. It can't be Nashville as a place, since the difficulties of people who have always lived at great distance from Nashville are discussed. For example, he says the 1961 murder of Ella Cooley by her husband is "the scandal Nashville would like to forget." I was in Nashville that year and can assure Riese that Nashville didn't notice.

Spade Cooley never lived, worked, or recorded in Nashville. He performed a music, created in Texas and Oklahoma from southwestern and Harlem Renaissance elements, that soon shifted its base to California. He had quit music and become a wealthy real estate developer. It would be as logical to associate him with Harlem or Donald Trump as with Nashville.

In this book, Bakersfield, Austin, Shreveport, Chicago, LA, Provo, Cullman, and Bogalusa become part of greater Nashville. Moreover, the lives being laid bare are often not from country music. Wearing a Stetson, keeping a straw in the teeth, and performing in a Hollywood sitcom about a small town are enough to make one a resident of this newly enlarged Nashville. Which raises a question: is the author a half bubble off plumb, or does he imagine the audience for his book to be awfully stupid? You think both? You would.

There's a tone in this writing—a mental state, a level of information—that needs a name. We'll call it "conventional contemporary bubbleheadism" (CCB). The guiding tenet of CCB is that appearances are vitally important and stereotypes are the foundation of all life. Gospel singer Christy Lane is here due to her husband spending some time in the slammer. CCB holds that only black gospel is gospel, so Christy is a country music singer whether or not she realizes it.

Bubbleheadism's reliance upon overstated regional stereotype and superficiality jars most when applied to place and history. In this book, Nashville is southern stereotype, racist, and redneck mean. It is, "buried deep in the muck of the Bible Belt, far from being the most liberal-minded metropolis."

Riese is outraged that not one black person has been elected to the Country Music Hall of Fame. He does not complain about the absence of whites from the roster of really good blues singers. He does not seem concerned about the division of other popular arts into black and white genres.

He notes that the Ku Klux Klan was formed in Pulaski, Tennessee, which through a miracle of geography is now a suburb "just south of the city" [it is 75 miles from Nashville]. He says that country music was terribly racist in its treatment of black Opry pioneer DeFord Bailey. The only country music singer who gets whole-hearted approval and is found to be totally free of defects is, of course, Charley Pride. Poor Charley. He's always avoided the bubblehead embrace.

Bubbleheadism travels in its own cocoon. Riese probably visited Nashville, but he never knew where he was. That it really is among the most progressive and liberal cities in the nation must not have seemed possible. Why? Well, he'd seen the Easy Riders shot off their bikes west of New Orleans. And he didn't dig far enough into the clippings to find DeFord's dictum: "Don't worry so much about the colored and white of it, son. The bad arguments are always about money."

Riese spoons carefully through the manure pile of drug, alcohol, and adultery problems. Sleaze is mixed with accounts of the random accidents and murders that stalk modern life.

We again visit the sites of plane crashes and car wrecks. Here's a photo of Patsy's hairspray and bra in the leaves. Here are photos of the crumpled corpses of Stringbean and Estelle. Why? Well, bubbleheadism holds that it is as scandalous to die by accident or murder as it is from snorting idiot dust. So never mind that String and Estelle lived lives of great dignity and decency; never mind that this reviewer's fishing friend died fighting back with great courage; show the gore, make a buck.

There's nothing remarkable about country music sleaze. Randall would find the same stuff in any middle-class suburb if he mined divorce court and DWI records and told the uncensored truth about accountants, store managers, professors, lawyers, teachers, and business people.

Gentle reader, by now you're probably saying, "okay, okay, but isn't there a lot of juicy stuff about stars here that I'd enjoy?" Not very much. Nashville's best stories are missed.

When this book arrived I looked first for the Songbird Murder. A national war-hero singer-songwriter shot another great songwriter dead in a dispute over a groupie. He then faked a gun battle to mislead the police into thinking that his shot had scared the songwriter into shooting himself by accident. Really! Could I invent such a detail?

There's some terrible half-telling of stories here. That Ernest Tubb shot up the WSM lobby is told, but not why. The poor reader is left to surmise that E.T. may have been a bit erratic when he'd had a few drinks. Nothing could be farther from the truth. E.T. took his six shooter down there because it was the right thing to do, an epic attempt at public service, a cowboy hunting a businessman, offering a you-go-first shoot-it-out to an adversary he thought a sleazeball.

While detailing the habits of Nashville, this book leaves one subject taboo: male homosexuality. It hints that Dolly's girlfriend might be more than a friend (as half-baked an idea as I've ever seen in print), but there's a careful tiptoeing around what the boys may or may not do. Riese knows about it, he says, but does not wish to do any harm to careers. It is an odd sentiment for an author who has raked the manure pile very low on virtually every other subject and has been especially attentive to heterosexual hanky-panky.

It is also another misconception. Nashville has always ignored lifestyle choices. When "queer" jokes were at a zenith in New York and Hollywood, none were told from the Opry stage. Old-style southerners have always left bedroom matters in the bedroom. In the late 1950s, Nashville's most admired manager-agent was matter-of-fact gay. He was admired because his artists made lots of money and because he brought an affable gentility to the business and community. Everyone knew. No one thought it remarkable.

There are great stories in Nashville: funny ones, crazy ones, amazing stories about those who would climb the greased pole that is country music. But those stories await a better teller, a teller with heart, with humor, with enough understanding to deal with the layered complexity that is Nashville.

Kentucky Thumbpicking

· ·

That folk communities may keep and burnish creativity from earlier times is well known to folklorists. Yet the first collectors to write about vernacular guitar styles in the United States seemed to have little information about the recent history of the guitar and some relied upon vivid imaginations for a considerable amount of misinformation [see "Men and Kings: A Mini-History of the Guitar"].

The cowboy, some guessed, got his guitar from Mexican vaqueros. The blues, others guessed, had leapt from West Africa to the Delta in a single great and impossible bound across almost 400 years of history.

The first descriptions of what local residents in western Kentucky call "thumbpicking" were equally misguided. Hearing the thumb keep the beat while the fingers picked out the melody, these early scribes noted a similarity to the style of such contemporary black players as Mississippi John Hurt. Ergo, the style must have black sources—but where? One informant recalled that some black men who had helped build a railroad

Adapted from liner notes to *Eddie Pennington Walks the Strings . . . and Even Sings*, Smithsonian Folkways Records, 2004. The CD credits Eddie's arrangement of "Duncan and Brady" to "music fan Jake D. James," actually Joe's schnauzer/poodle two generations earlier had had a guitar, so anonymous "black railroad workers" were duly appointed as the first players in this style.

That black players from the Delta and western Kentucky coal miners might have had a common source—a white, middle-class Aunt Minnie playing in her parlor—is a concept too outlandish for popular acceptance in a nation where stereotypes still rule perception. One has to wonder if the feminine roots of this style may have escaped even careful researchers. How could these very male coal miners and Wild Sam, the hard-drinking skirt-chasing bluesman, have been influenced by sweet Aunt Minnie, picking in her parlor? Good heavens! Is nothing sacred?

Yet it is clear that the influence of Aunt Minnie and multitudes of her musical sisters reached far beyond their parlors. A huge number of young middle-class women throughout the nation took up the guitar in the post-Civil War period, and the result was a seismic shift in the direction of American vernacular music. Moreover, most of the parlor-influenced players who took the thumbpicker style on a fifty-year creative ride were still around and performing when the erroneous assumptions about the source of this strand of music were being made.

The thumbpicking style developed among a handful of players in a single rural county—Muhlenberg—in the coal-mining region of western Kentucky. One player: Merle Travis, a native of Muhlenberg County, brought it to national attention. He began performing on regional radio in 1937 and, during World War II, took his skills to Hollywood and other show-business capitals. He spent forty-five years as a professional performer, and many guitarists still call this way of playing "Travis style."

Thousands of younger players heard Travis and took up the style. Notable among them was Chet Atkins, a Tennessean who eventually became better known than his idol. Atkins often turned compliments aside, pointing to Travis: "But for that man, I'd have spent my life looking at the world over the back end of a mule."

And Travis told anyone who would listen that Muhlenberg County coal miner Mose Rager was *his* teacher, his friend, and his guitar hero. Much of what is known about the early history of thumbpicking comes from genial Mose Rager, a brilliant and highly creative guitarist and beloved teacher of many of the finest players in the style.

Travis said he once tried to persuade Rager to fly to California for one of his recording sessions. "He was not feeling well, so I told him he would not have to play. I knew if he was sitting with me I'd play better. He could lift you up."

Mose talked about how guitar playing fitted into a miner's life. Whatever the weather or work situation, miners had to go to the company gathering place for two or three hours. If there was no work that day, they'd pass a guitar around. Their songs and tunes had humor, and the more accomplished players developed show-off pieces.

But who were the very earliest players, the original plant stock that was refined and developed by this artistic process? Mose knew one source. He spoke with gratitude and affection of Kennedy Jones, a former miner and fine guitarist, born in 1900. He and other local players learned their rudiments from Kennedy Jones before the older miner moved away to find more rewarding work.

And Rager knew where Jones had gotten *his* instruction. Most of it had come from his mother, Alice DeArmond Jones. Born in 1863 at nearby Dunmore, Kentucky, she had been a young woman when the parlor movement swept the nation. She had kept her guitar and the parlor methods of playing it and had instructed her son and his friends. Mose had no doubt that the roots of the style had come to Kennedy from his mother.

Kennedy Jones had also performed informally with Arnold Shultz, an itinerant black guitarist and singer who occasionally passed though the area until his death in 1930. Some collectors, still digging for the elusive origins of what they assumed to be a "black sound," guessed that the rudiments of the style may have been taught by Shultz. Jones lived until his ninetieth year (1990) and spoke often about his mother and the origins of the style. He was irritated by suggestions that he had been taught by Shultz. He said he had played with the traveling musician a few times and liked him, but this was after he was grown and had his own style.

The supposition that Shultz invented the style puzzled Bill Monroe, a founder of bluegrass music, who grew up occasionally playing with Shultz for country dancing. Told in 1986 that some music fans assumed the style Travis had made familiar actually came from his old friend Shultz, Monroe gave an emphatic and terse response: "That's not right."

Mose Rager said that, during his teenage years, if one saw a circle of men, Kennedy Jones would be inside that circle. A cult of local pickers followed Jones, and Mose's friend Ike Everly (father of the Everly Brothers) is recalled as one of the most devoted members. Mrs. Everly tells a humorous story about Ike's fascination with Kennedy Jones. Once Ike came home with a cane. Asked why, he said that Kennedy Jones had one. (A few days later, he learned that Jones was using the cane because he had been hurt in the mines.) Mose recalled Ike saying that if he could be President Roosevelt—a hero of the miners—or Kennedy Jones, he'd be Kennedy Jones.

The first person to attempt to earn a living with Kentucky thumbpicking was Kennedy Jones. He organized a group of local boys into a band to play bars in Chicago during the Depression. Jones recalled that the wife of one of them showed up one night before the show with a message: "Kennedy, Charlie can't play tonight," she said; "he's dead." Jones later moved to Cincinnati, and music became a part-time activity.

Mose Rager also quit the mines. After World War II, he worked on the road with banjoist and comic singer Louis M. (Grandpa) Jones, fiddler Curly Fox, and on tour with Grand Ole Opry pioneer Uncle Dave Macon. But the endless travel did not please Mose, and he became in turn a barber, country storekeeper, and barbecue chef. One of his last jobs was at a giant steam plant, the one with such a voracious appetite for strip-mined coal that it inspired caustic commentary in John Prine's song, "Paradise." Finally, asked by Chet Atkins if he was still working, Mose said, "Naw, I done throwed a rock at it."

Mose Rager saw any kid who wanted to learn guitar as a blessing, and the brilliant kid who stayed longest and came most often was Eddie Pennington. Mose was forty years older than Eddie, but the kid inside Mose was well preserved, eager to trade licks, and learn as he taught. No money ever changed hands. This was friendship, and Mose had a proverb: "You can keep it if you give it away."

Eddie Pennington is the son of a musical coal miner, and was reared at Nortonville, Kentucky, some twenty miles from Mose's Drakesboro home. Beginning in May 1974, a teenaged Eddie became a frequent visitor and devoted student of the Drakesboro guitar sage. While a student at Western Kentucky University, Eddie detoured by Mose's house coming from and going home on weekends. One semester he had no classes on Wednesdays after 9:00 a.m., so he visited Mose most of those days. His visits continued until Mose died in 1986. Eddie reveres Rager's memory, and can turn a bit misty-eyed when he speaks of his friend. The years of instruction served him well, and Rager's tunes are a favorite part of his repertoire.

Eddie preserves more than the dazzling technique of the founders of the style. He also has their sense of place, irrepressible sense of humor, and optimism. Like many of them, he is physically built for heavy lifting, but the music that emanates from his guitar is wonderfully delicate, as if scores of great-grandmothers had sent their intricate music to his flying hands.

Eddie is like the earlier great players, in that he is making his own notable contributions to the style. They amount to a passion for tone, a sense of timing akin to that of an atomic clock, and a delightful sophistication in phrasing. His ever-present sense of humor and genial presentation make him the most accessible and best showman among modern thumbpickers.

Nowadays, there are thumbpicker clubs and organizations throughout the world, and Eddie and other top players visit them often. Eddie toured the nation twice as a member of the *Masters of the Steel String Guitar* tour. He has performed at the Library of Congress, the Kennedy Center, at festivals and events in every part of the United States, and in Western Europe. Yet he—like Mose Rager—feels most at home in western Kentucky.

In 2001, the National Endowment for the Arts honored Eddie with a National Heritage Fellowship, the nation's highest honor for a traditional artist. Broad-shouldered and imposing, he took to the stage in a glitter suit and brought down the house with a question, "Can you see me okay?" The music that followed was a startling contrast, as delicate and beautifully worked as gold filigree.

Eddie's innovations and dedication to tradition have also been honored at home. In 2003, Western Kentucky University awarded him an honorary doctorate for his jubilant keeping of the music of his family, dear friends, and region.

The departed founders of the style are alive in his thoughts as well as in his playing, and he speaks with great respect of thumbpickers Odell Martin (and his mother, Mrs. Ellis Shanklin Martin, who played in parlor style), Bob Barber, and Paul Yandell. He's especially proud of his son, Alonzo Pennington, and feels that he is developing into the best player yet.

He had a request: "Be sure to tell everybody that the thumbpickers have a hall of fame, a list of people we owe. It has all the names you'd expect: Kennedy Jones, Mose Rager, Merle Travis, Chet Atkins, Ike Everly. And it has a lot of other names as well, and I'm proud to say that Mrs. Alice DeArmond Jones and Mrs. Ellis Shanklin Martin are among them."

THE BLUES

The Birth of the Blues

One hundred years ago, a new musical form gained popularity in the South. The plaintive songs had bent, "blue" notes and roots in black gospel and work songs. I first heard the blues on a hot June afternoon in 1943, in the Tennessee Blue Ridge. I was five years old and had been following my grandma along a dusty gravel road that led us past Brushy Mountain Prison Camp Number Three. [See: "Blues and Bluegrass: Tough Arts of the Underclass".]

An unusual experience? Not for a Southerner of my generation. As I got older, Nashville's radio station WLAC programmed the blues and pitched products for rural black folk with a signal so powerful it reached every nook and cranny of the South. My college classmates listened to nothing else. We naively wondered if the 1954 Supreme Court ruling outlawing school segregation meant we would soon be able to visit the better blues joints.

This [1998] seems like a good year to declare a blues centennial. Historians and musicologists agree that this American musical style began in

Adapted from *The Old Farmer's Almanac*, Southern Edition, 1998, Dublin, New Hampshire.

the 1890s. They are unwilling to assign a specific year, but should the blues be denied a centenary celebration because the creators were too engrossed with work to leave a paper trail? They had mules to shoe, fields to plow, cotton to chop, turpentine to distill, barges to load, and wood to cut. The blues were first made by the sweat-stained black folk of the rural South, many of them children of former slaves.

Historians are equally vague about where the blues began. It was somewhere in that vast stretch between the Atlantic coast and Central Texas, and south of Illinois. Blues were reported in New Orleans, St. Louis, and Shreveport before the turn of the twentieth century, and in rural areas of Oklahoma, Missouri, Mississippi, and Georgia. Blues scholars are fond of finding blues antecedents in Africa. The West African storyteller musicians called *griots* are often viewed as proto-bluesmen and their instrumental techniques compared to blues guitarists.

The great blues artist Son House (born around 1900) recalled, "When I was a boy, we was always singing in the fields. . . . We made up songs about what was happening to us . . . and I think that's how the blues started." Blues singer Ma Rainey told folklorist John W. Work about first hearing the blues in a small Missouri town, before the turn of the century. A broken-hearted girl sang for Rainey a poignant song about a man who had left her.

Some early bluesmen earned a hardscrabble living as traveling musicians. Collecting songs in Mississippi and Georgia from 1905 to 1908, sociologist Howard W. Odum heard blues from migratory workers on levees and in lumber camps.

The bluesman was a free spirit who loved women, booze, gambling, and good times. Peetie Wheatstraw called himself "the Devil's Son-in-Law." Many spent portions of their life in jail and more than a few died young; among the latter was Robert Johnson, the most legendary of players. Some of the most famous bluesmen have been blind: Blind Blake, Blind Lemon Jefferson, Blind Willie McTell, Blind Willie Johnson, Blind Boy Fuller, Blind Gary Davis, Blind Joe Taggart, Blind Jimmy Strothers, and Blind Sonny Terry. Other great players had lost a limb: among them Furry Lewis, Peg Leg Howell, and Peg Leg Sam Jackson.

Songs were often common property, in the beginning. Older ballads were adapted to the new blues form. Some songs reflected the influence of the "holler," a top-of-the-range rural yell intended to communicate over long distances. Others showed evidence of work calls, the rhythmic call-and-response music that coordinated generations of corn shucking, net lifting, tobacco stripping, cotton pressing, wood chopping, and track laying.

The classic blues form amounts to a three-line verse in twelve measures of four-four time, with an AAB rhyme pattern and a line length usually measured by five stressed syllables. Blues verse has a unique storytelling character, due to repeating lines and the use of verses to build the theme.

In rural areas, the primary blues instrument was the guitar, which had recently been improved by American designers [see "Men and Kings: A Mini-History of the Guitar"]. A worldwide fad for parlor guitars among upper-class women spread the instrument and characteristic playing styles to the South in the decades after the Civil War. A blues guitar technique of keeping time with the thumb while the fingers pick a lead is adapted from parlor guitar style. New methods of mass manufacturing and the Sears Roebuck catalog soon made the guitar available everywhere at modest cost.

The rural makers of the blues created and transferred their music by ear and in person rather than by notation. When their rural sound was transcribed and published by professional musicians in the South and Midwest, the sheet music was sold largely to a white market outside the South.

The first piece was published in 1912: Hart Wand's "The Dallas Blues." An Oklahoma City bandleader, Wand said he got the melody from a black porter who had moved up from Texas. A few months later, W.C. Handy published "The Memphis Blues." This composition borrowed from Wand's tune but was largely a rearrangement of "Mister Crump," an earlier song that praised the Memphis political boss—Edward H. Crump—who had commissioned the song.

Born in Florence, Alabama, W.C. Handy (1873–1958) was a professional musician. In 1903, he had been "tank-towning" the South with bands for a decade when he met with a lanky Tutwiler, Mississippi slide guitarist who sang a plaintive Delta blues. Handy recalled it in his autobiography, *Father of the Blues*, as "the weirdest music I ever heard."

Handy's publisher apparently had no faith in the appeal of the new blues form, as the sheet music cover for "The Memphis Blues" promoted the song as three things it was not. Ragtime was popular, so it was described as "A Southern Rag." Sousa's military bands were popular, so a military band was depicted, with a resplendent leader. Minstrelsy still had an audience, so the cover also sported a blackface caricature.

In 1913, Handy's now-independent music company published "Jogo Blues," a composition either written or arranged by a local pianist. It was not a commercial success, but a year later Handy added two strains and published it as the "St. Louis Blues." The song became a giant international hit, the first in the classic blues form. Handy's sheet music introduced the blues to whites and to many northern blacks.

A genteel man with finely honed self-promotion skills, Handy became a popular-music fixture who assiduously followed the trends through the 1930s and 1940s while laying claim to his "Father of the Blues" title. (Knoxville street musician Crippled John questioned Handy's title. "Starvation is the father of the blues," John said. "I know him well.")

After sheet music came recording sales. The blues were largely an underground genre until the advent of electrical recording, which led to radio play and increased performance opportunities. Recording companies found their way to folk blues performers from the rural South in the early 1920s. Their recordings are filled with intensity, urgency, and conviction. Here was a music of raw emotion and few frills. The new product was sold mainly to black Southerners and black Southern migrants in the North.

Female singers were accepted before men by the major labels. Mamie Smith's 1920 "Crazy Blues" was the first blues recording released, and its success created a market for female vocals. Other notable female vocalists were Sippie Wallace, Alberta Hunter, Ma Rainey, Victoria Spivey, and Lucille Bogen. Sister Rosetta Tharpe and Memphis Minnie were outstanding guitarists.

Chattanooga's Bessie Smith—a veteran of black "chitlin' circuit" touring—was rejected by several recording impresarios for her deep southern accent. Among those who spurned Bessie for being a mush-mouth was Thomas A. Edison, inventor of the phonograph, who noted "voice n.g." on her audition file. Bessie's 1923 "Down Hearted Blues" sold an astounding 800,000 copies for Columbia after artist-and-repertoire man Frank Walker gave the irrepressible singer a break. Later, when Bessie was the foremost blues singer and one of the highest paid entertainers in America, she had a railroad car outfitted in red velvet for her travels. A jar of pickled pig's feet perched at one end of the car. "They remind me of where I came from," Bessie said. "And besides, I like 'em."

Bluesmen recorded in the 1920s and 1930s still attract the admiration of fans. Notable among them are Charlie Patton, Son House, Blind Lemon Jefferson, Robert Wilkins, and Sleepy John Estes. The most admired player is Robert Johnson, a brilliant guitarist who made twenty-nine recordings in 1936 and 1937. His songs are a roller coaster of passion: brooding desperation, a sense of futility, a fear that a very real Devil is waiting and watching.

Poisoned by a jealous husband, Robert Johnson died in 1938 at age twenty-seven, near Greenwood, Mississippi. He had been scheduled to perform on John Hammond's "Spirituals to Swing" concert held later that year at Carnegie Hall, a cutting-edge event that would surely have brought him to national attention. In 1991, a box set of all Johnson's recordings—including outtakes—became an unlikely international bestseller, remaining on the popular-music charts for most of a year.

No other folk creation comes from closer to the heart of the people than the poignant blues tunes of the South. Virginia bluesman John Cephas [see "Cephas and Wiggins"] says the blues are a text from working people, one largely free of the distortions of interpretation. "They allow people to tell the truth, because you don't have to put in the details; the feelings are enough. When Blind Willie Johnson sang, 'If I had my way, I'd tear this building down,' you know he meant every word of it."

Cephas and Wiggins
Masters of the Piedmont Blues

● ●

John Cephas and Phil Wiggins perform Piedmont blues, the oldest form of the blues, with repertoire and performance links to the black string bands that began in colonial America. Slave musicians in those early string bands combined the wood and gourd African banjo with the European violin to create ensemble forms that are at the root of much of popular American music.

Many songs from the black string bands survive in Piedmont blues, but the main survival is a passionate and richly melodic performance style that remains acoustic a half-century after other blues turned electric. Also called "East Coast" and "Tidewater," this older style can still be heard among folk blues players from the eastern shore of Maryland to the Gulf Coast.

This regional American music takes its name from the Piedmont: the foothills region of Virginia, South Carolina, North Carolina, Georgia, and

Adapted from the *Echoes of Africa* tour booklet, National Council for the Traditional Arts, 1994, and liner notes to *Masters of the Steel String Guitar*, Arhoolie Records, 2000; *Cephas and Wiggins: Masters of the Piedmont Blues*, Cracker Barrel Records, 2002; and *Cephas and Wiggins: Somebody Told the Truth*, Alligator Records, 2002.

Florida. Some important early Piedmont blues musicians were Blind Boy Fuller, Reverend Gary Davis, and Sonny Terry; their influence can be heard in the repertoire and technique of John and Phil. John Cephas also cites Blind Lemon Jefferson and Tampa Red, as well as music of the ragtime era, as influences on his playing style.

In 1987 and 1989, Cephas and Wiggins won the coveted W.C. Handy Award of the Memphis-based Blues Foundation for the year's best traditional blues recording. Also in 1989, Cephas was awarded a National Heritage Fellowship from the National Endowment for the Arts for his exemplary keeping of a historic and treasured music.

Cephas is the primary singer in the duo, with younger partner Phil Wiggins sometimes singing a chorus and taking an occasional vocal lead. But Wiggins is present mainly to perform on the harmonica, and he is a world-class player on his humble instrument.

John Cephas was born in the Foggy Bottom ghetto of Washington, D.C., near where the U.S. Department of State now stands. His father was a minister in that community, and gospel music was the first that John heard. It remains a favorite, and John usually mixes some gospel numbers into his performances.

John's mother was from "down in the country" in the Tidewater region's Caroline County, northwest of Richmond, Virginia, and very much in the "Piedmont belt." Her family has lived there for generations. Little John was sent there every summer to stay with Grandpa John Dudley and learn the survival skills of country people.

There was much to learn. Aunt Lillian taught him guitar chords, and Cousin David took him to house parties and country breakdowns (so named because the vigorous dancing sometimes caused cabin floors to collapse). Playing the guitar and singing full-throated blues were competitive pastimes there every weekend for young men; John absorbed from local players the complex alternating thumb-and-finger-picking that characterizes the Piedmont blues style. He loved Caroline County, and decided to move there as soon as he could.

John served in the infantry during the Korean War. He was a bass singer in a traveling gospel quartet. He worked on fishing boats off the Atlantic coast. He became a highly skilled finish carpenter and lead carpenter in a large crew. But he was always a bluesman. Musical skills first learned from

Aunt Lillian and Cousin David went with Cephas to Korea, the boats, and the construction sites. There were always weekend and evening blues jobs, and there finally came a time when blues became John's only task.

Phil Wiggins grew up in Washington, but his family is from Alabama and they brought Deep South skills and sensibilities with them to the big city. His fascination with the harmonica began in childhood; it was honed on street corners and in jam sessions of all kinds. Among the musicians who welcomed the kid with the harmonica was slide guitarist Flora Molton, who wailed gospel songs on the streets of downtown Washington for two generations. He performed in clubs with Mother Scott, a veteran blues singer who had her first job with the Rabbit Foot Minstrels when Bessie Smith was in the troupe. And Wiggins jammed with D.C.-area Piedmont masters such as John Jackson [see "John Jackson: Front Porch Blues"] and Archie Edwards.

Wiggins began composing melodies and songs when he was very young. His material has been recorded by an array of musicians in several genres. Some of the best songs in contemporary blues are from his pen.

Phil provides a boundless stream of harmonica pyrotechnics, which he weaves through, behind, and between the singing and playing of his partner. It seems impossible that so much music can be coming from one man. Wiggins is passionately devoted to his little instrument, as both a teacher and a student. He has taught hundreds to play it and he admires and keeps track of a fascinating array of other harmonica players, living and deceased. He has taught performance skills at some of the nation's finest universities, to high-risk youth in Washington's more troubled neighborhoods, and to classes of inmates at Lorton Prison. "You get full attendance and good attention there," he says.

John and Phil first performed together in 1976, as members of Wilber "Big Chief" Ellis's band at the 38th National Folk Festival. Since then, they have worked in clubs and at festivals throughout the nation and have performed three times at the White House. They work in Europe almost as much as the United States and have toured in Asia, Latin America, the Caribbean, China, Russia, Africa, and Australia.

John was the lead actor in the Kennedy Center play *Blind Man Blues,* which toured internationally. In 2002, they were featured in the long-running Arena Stage production of Zora Neale Hurston's play, *Polk County.*

They and two friends—pianist Daryl Davis and trombonist-percussionist "Little Butch" Miller—were the onstage band effusively praised by *The New York Times* in a rave review of the play [see "Little Butch (Norvus Miller, Jr.) Memorial"].

The music they perform reflects some of their urban and firmly grounded rural complexity. There are items that John first heard "down in the country" many years ago, and thoughts from Phil about our time. They are living and laughing at the foibles of life today, but with an abiding respect and affection for those who taught them. As Cephas reminds us, "This is music from the heart; it tells the truth."

John Jackson
Front Porch Blues

● ●

John Jackson was born and reared in Woodville, Rappahannock County, Virginia, where the green rolling hills of the Piedmont join the smoky vistas of the northern Blue Ridge. There, the Rappahannock River begins a tumbling meander to the great bay of the Chesapeake, where some of the older residents have a polysyllabic musical lilt in their speech.

John Jackson's family lived there before the Civil War. His father, Suttee Jackson, was a musical tenant farmer who performed on a $4.98 guitar and on mandolin, homemade fife, and banjo. His mother, Hattie Roberta Haney, was a singer with a strong, clear voice. John learned songs from both parents, but not much guitar from his father. "He was left-handed, played upside down and backwards."

Suttee Jackson and his brothers had a dance band that performed in the ancient black string band style on fiddle, banjo, and two guitars. This is a musical form much older than the blues, one that can be traced in Virginia to the early colonial period, when the African banjo and European fiddle combined to create the first American musical ensemble. John recalls

Liner notes, Alligator Records, 1999.

the rhythmic force of that band as his father and uncles performed such tunes as "Walk Down the Devil's Stairs" at country dances.

Two of John's older brothers and a sister learned to play the blues on Suttee Jackson's guitar. Jack and Dick performed in and around Woodville, and Alice—two years older than John—enjoyed playing guitar for her little brother. Another family string band, composed of his mother's cousins, was the house band at the famous Panorama Hotel at the summit of the Blue Ridge.

John became serious about music at age five, after his sister Mary "Tee" Jackson made enough money "taking in washing" to buy him a $3.75 mail-order guitar. That guitar came to a bad end a few years later when brother Jack borrowed it for a house party job and—when a brawl erupted—had to use it to defend himself. Left without an instrument, John went visiting to his mother's sister, who had married a banjo-picking Indian in nearby Flint Hill. John still plays some banjo tunes learned during that portion of his childhood.

A chain gang trusty and waterboy named Happy taught John open tunings for the guitar during visits to the Jackson family spring. On the family Victrola, John heard the 78 rpm recordings of Blind Lemon Jefferson, Barbecue Bob, Jimmie Rodgers, The Carter Family, and his favorites: Blind Blake and Blind Boy Fuller.

At age twenty-five, John moved his young family to Fairfax County, Virginia, near the growing suburbs of Washington, D.C. He took a job on a dairy farm and built a house for his family with his own hands, working evenings and weekends. He dug graves with a pick and shovel and worked as a handyman, eventually creating the small business which he still operates with his son James, who is also a blues singer.

John was holding forth on his guitar at a Fairfax Amoco station in 1964 when guitarist and noted folklorist Dr. Charles L. "Chuck" Perdue stopped by. The Jackson and Perdue families became instant friends. Chuck and Nan Perdue introduced John to the thriving blues revival of the sixties and the Ontario Club in Washington, D.C., where the heroes of the blues performed.

Mississippi John Hurt and Skip James literally lived at the Ontario for a time. John became friends with them and also met and performed with Reverend Gary Davis, Victoria Spivey, Son House, Furry Lewis, and Big Joe

Williams. Sam Chatmon and Buddy Moss stayed with the Jacksons when performing in the area. John enjoyed the good company, but he continued to play in the style he had developed as a boy in Rappahannock County.

A favorite of President and Mrs. Carter, John performed a memorable concert for them on the White House lawn. He was the bluesman on the tour of *Southern Music USA*, a globe-trotting event that set a distance record for international touring (47,000 miles in 8 weeks). He has performed for the royal family in Thailand and in many of the great halls in Europe and North and South America. In 1986, the National Endowment for the Arts gave John its National Heritage Fellowship, a "living treasure" award and the highest honor the nation offers a traditional artist.

The most gentle and good-hearted of men, John tends to become embarrassed when paid a compliment. He loves children and talks to them with an unwavering attention and focus that lead them to instantly accept him as a friend who should be taken into their confidence. He remembers names, hugs friends, and is a careful listener. A lifetime of hard work has made him physically powerful, and his handshake has vigor and strength. His eyes turn misty if a departed friend or family member is mentioned.

Music, work, family, and friends are inseparable in John's world. They give pleasure, sustenance, and a sense of place. John has traveled far, but his values reflect a Woodville of long ago and music kept in the generations of a family.

Little Butch
(Norvus Miller Jr.)
Memorial

● ●

T he exuberance that marked the life of Little Butch (Norvus Miller, Jr.) was a joy to many who knew him as the ultimate trombone player and lead singer in shout bands based in the Washington, D.C., area. I knew him from childhood, and he always had the ability to lift any audience—church or secular. He moved easily and sweetly between audiences.

When the Barbican Centre opened in London with an amazing run of American arts of all kinds, the organizers feared the effect of long lines on ticket sales. So the bright lad in charge thought it would be good to hire a New Orleans street band to walk up and down the lines, playing favorites from the Crescent City. He found a fine band, but matters did not go well as the dates in London grew near. The price kept increasing, and key players dropped out and were replaced by lesser artists. Ten days out, there was an explosion of wills, and the deal came to an end. The voice from London was wan, "Ah cahn't think of a marching group that

Posted to Publore, a listserv for the public folklore community. Norvus Miller Jr. died March 24, 2015.

might do this. Can you?" So of course I thought of Little Butch, and others we called "The Miller Band."

The day of their first performance to the lines, London was on the telephone. "Ah am having a terrible time with the band you sent over," he said. "What on earth is wrong?" I asked. "Ah cahn't get the people in the lines to go inside and listen to Herbie Hancock," he said. So we laughed and laughed, and knew it was a blessed day when Little Butch was born.

When Zora Neale Hurston's great work, *Polk County*, was presented as a play at Arena Stage, Little Butch was in a stunning blues and hotshot band with John Cephas, Phil Wiggins, and Daryl Davis [see "Cephas and Wiggins: Masters of the Piedmont Blues"]. Little Butch provided rhythm on a wooden slap box, and his bubbling intensity lifted the band to a performing height that left audiences agog and garnered that rarest of accolades for non-Broadway plays, a rave review from *The New York Times*.

Little Butch brought his power to enchant to a fundraiser I helped organize for Dave Obey, then a member of Congress and chairman of the House Appropriations Committee. Rosa Parks was then working for a Detroit congressman, and she sat in her usual spot and was enraptured by Little Butch. "Who is that young fellow?" she asked. I told her he was brought up in the House of Prayer for All People and was the son of Butch Miller, one of the great teachers who helped spread brass band music in their churches near and far. After the show, I brought Little Butch over, and he and Mrs. Parks talked. Before he left, Little Butch kissed her cheek and said with uplifted arms, "Thank you!" in tones only he commanded.

I just read online a vision a friend experienced of Little Butch entering heaven a few days ago. I know he is right in saying the trombones blared, the tubas grunted, the trumpet soared, and the drum was dead on. Yes, of course, the welcoming committee was headed by one of the finest men ever, Butch Miller, Sr., and musicians stood in lines to be hugged. But also on the welcoming committee was a well-tailored little lady who so loved her people that she refused to have them ride forever on the back of the bus.

Blues and Bluegrass
Tough Arts of the Underclass

• •

Blues and bluegrass are arts of the underclass that are prospering despite the inattention of New York, Hollywood, Nashville and Washington. Yes, I know it is jarring to speak of an American underclass. We like to pretend that we have only one socioeconomic group ("middle"), structured like ancient Egypt, with upper and lower parts. This odd egalitarian myopia distorts our artistic perception and confuses understanding of why our popular culture is so strong.

The recent success of blues and bluegrass fascinates because these musical forms are modern branches of an ancient tree of American culture, one that has grafted European and African forms since colonial times. As in other folk arts of the American underclass, blues and bluegrass fuel our popular culture. Concepts that came to North America long ago from Africa and Europe continually jostle, blend and re-blend: minstrelsy, cakewalk, ragtime, jazz, country, rock, rap, hip-hop. Some of these sounds reflect our national experience and our highest and lowest yearnings: cakewalk

From Chapter 6 of *The Changing Faces of Tradition: A Report on the Folk and Traditional Arts in the United States*, written, edited and compiled by Elizabeth Peterson, Research Division Report #38, National Endowment for the Arts, 1996.

music grew from a fundraising tool for 19th century country schools, jazz from the background music in New Orleans dance halls and brothels.

The South has been the place where Africa and Europe jostled and blended most. It is an especially interesting place today, as Europeans and a stream of Japanese engage in what has been dubbed "cultural tourism." At Ole Miss in 1994, I met a vanload of young German tourists, blond, rich in accents, generous with beer, and eager to talk the blues. They'd been trekking the torpid and featureless Delta in a rented minivan, visiting sites associated with blues master Robert Johnson. Mysteriously poisoned in 1938, the youthful Johnson was laid in an unmarked grave. Any search for artifacts associated with him is invariably fruitless, but still tourists come. One earnest European pleaded, "Tell me how you discover the blues?" in the soul-searching manner of a zealot inquiring after a conversion experience. He told of having his life changed by hearing Hound Dog Taylor in a Chicago blues joint where fistfights were almost as common as third beers. I told about a long walk on the western slope of the Blue Ridge in Tennessee's easternmost county fifty years earlier and meeting a musician wearing horizontal stripes. They listened with rapt attention.

I first heard the blues on a hot June afternoon in 1943. I was five years old and following my grandma along a gravel road that led past Brushy Mountain Prison Camp Number 3. The inmate barracks were long rows of A-roofed whitewashed frame buildings. The prisoners were all black, and most were from five hundred miles to the west in Memphis ("the real capital of Mississippi"), chain gang members who repaired roads and bridges. White guards in porkpie hats and bib overalls with 30-30 caliber lever-action carbines in shoulder slings watched from rickety towers perched outside a high barbed wire fence.

Grandma and I were walking from Mom and Dad's little farm on Bulldog Creek to her home above the high falls on Roaring Creek. It was ten dusty miles, and we'd walked six before we came to the prison camp. Grandma thought it would be good to rest her young charge and drink some water at the springhouse of the Bryant home, across the road from the camp entrance. One of the Bryant children explained stripes to me. Vertical stripes meant they'd be released some day. Horizontal meant they'd be in prison until they died.

A huddle of prisoners had gathered at a twelve-inch square opening in the fence. Through it, they sold hand-tooled leather wallets and belts. A big man with fierce countenance and horizontal stripes was playing a booming Sears and Roebuck guitar and singing with a heartfelt passion that enchanted me. My new friend whispered that he was Booger Bear, lead trusty on the bridge crew. He said he only looked scary, that he was actually very nice. My grandma had to take my hand and pull me away from his intense and euphoric performance.

After that, I saw Booger Bear many times. A showman, his powerful hands could bend in half a steel bridge rivet. Guitar players visited Booger's bridge crew, seeking instruction in his fluid fingerpicked guitar style. There was a lore about him: he'd caught his wife in the arms of another man and strangled both. His songs were the blues classics of the Mississippi Delta: "I Want to Die Easy Lord," "My Dough Roller Is Gone," "Walking Blues," "The Easy Rider," and the oft-requested "Wish I Could Bring 'Em Back," a song we believed to be his autobiography. Nickels and dimes earned with his music bought his supply of Prince Albert smoking tobacco, but most went into "Booger's bucket." This container was emptied each December to buy hams for the camp Christmas dinner.

Three years after hearing Booger Bear, I discovered bluegrass during its earliest defining moments. Electric power had not yet found its way to our part of the Blue Ridge, but my family had a battery-powered radio and we sat in a warm glow of yellow kerosene light as we listened to the Grand Ole Opry on Saturday nights.

We were present at the radio in 1946 when youthful North Carolina Piedmont banjoist Earl Scruggs joined Bill Monroe's band, the Blue Grass Boys. It seemed that the entire South tuned in during the weeks that followed. Scruggs offered effervescent banjo "breaks," and Monroe's mandolin stuttered and soared, while Southern long bow fiddler Chubby Wise tied ribbons of rich phrases around their sound. No band in the history of American music has spawned as many instant imitators.

First performed for live audiences in country schoolhouses on the Southern backwoods "kerosene circuit," this new sound soon moved north with Southern migrants. When I arrived in Washington, D.C., in 1956, it blared in tough hillbilly bars and on a Virginia radio station advertising used cars and cheap furniture. The station offering blues was just one notch to the right of the bluegrass station on the AM dial. But by the time I arrived in Nashville to work in the recording business in 1959, interest had waned. The music business anticipates fads, invests early, and gets out. No one in the business believed that blues or bluegrass had a future.

The industry could hardly have been more wrong. There was a revival of these arts in the '60s among young Yankees protesting the war and their own—shades of Egypt—upper middle class origins. Blues and bluegrass were adopted by a small educated elite, in a process that was at least as political as it was musical. But revivals and adoptions are puny processes when compared to True Belief.

During the '50s and '60s, migrants from the Delta made Chicago blues an urban music performed in clubs with dance floors. The music became electric in order to compete in noisy barrooms. There was a corresponding growth in bluegrass, in beer joints and clubs but also in rural country music parks and, later, outdoor festivals. The audiences for these forms are carefully focused. In fact, "audience" is not a word that serves well. Here it is not easy to separate sellers and buyers. Tickets and other products are purchased by persons who are sometimes performers themselves, and absolutely certain they own this art.

Over a period of twenty-five years, networks of organized support developed. The cliched term "grassroots" is often applied to this support from mom and pop businesses, independent record labels, and voluntary associations. There's a welter of statistics which shows that small businesses and voluntary groups have engendered growth and stability in these art forms. Eight recording companies issued most blues recordings in 1960. In 1995, there were 233 companies releasing blues recordings, most of them issuing *only* blues recordings.[1] This proliferation of small independent record labels renders major recording companies largely irrelevant to new recordings of blues and bluegrass (and, for that matter, other forms of traditional music).

Chicago-based Alligator Records is now a premier blues label, one that has a worldwide following. It had its genesis at a concert by blues performer Mississippi Fred McDowell. In the audience was college student Bruce Iglauer, who recalls, "It was as if he reached out and grabbed me by the collar, shook me, and spoke directly to me." Iglauer immersed himself in the blues, hosted a blues program on the college radio station, and took a job as a shipping clerk for a small Chicago blues label. He used a $2,500 inheritance to start Alligator in 1971.

The Sugar Hill label specializes in bluegrass and contemporary folk music. Located in Durham, North Carolina, it was the 1978 creation of Barry Poss, then a James B. Duke fellow at Duke University. In mid-thesis, Poss abandoned a budding academic career to start a shoestring label. Sugar Hill now issues best-selling bluegrass recordings and is a frequent recipient of record industry awards.

Much of this is obviously a triumph of niche marketing. It reflects the use of cutting-edge technology and communication skills to weld new audiences that support and expand the audiences for older folk art forms. But there's a critically important factor not to miss: Iglauer, Poss and other businessmen who created a new wave of successful recording companies in the past twenty-five years were inspired by the artists and art forms, not by business schools. They are as much in thrall of great artistry as any other group of arts leaders.

In 1995, there were 127 local blues societies and 289 local bluegrass societies in the US—almost all created during the preceding 20 years and virtually all volunteer-run organizations.[2] They range in size from a hundred members to thousands. Most have newsletters and sponsor summer festivals and concert series supported by ticket sales. An example is Washington's D.C. Blues Society; it began in 1988 with a meeting of eight fans in a barbershop. A year and a half later, it had grown to a thousand dues-paying members.

In 1965, the first multi-day bluegrass festival was held in Virginia. In 1996, 516 bluegrass festivals will be held in an amazing array of locations, including five on winter cruise ships.[3] These are in the USA and Canada, but other nations have them as well. The largest outdoor music festival in the Czech Republic is a bluegrass festival. Today, more than 300 bluegrass bands are active in Tokyo, Japan.

What speaks to these audiences? Many audience members seem to share the Iglauer moment: grabbed by the collar, shaken, and given a message. The blues are as much religious experience as art form. They enable the sharing of a sublime joy or a whisper from the abyss. Bluegrass seems to speak internationally to working people; one of the finest young contemporary bands is Russian.

The statistics are impressive, but attendance figures, record sales, and audience demographics are not the critical measure of any art form. A far more important measure is concerned with elasticity. Is there room for growth? There seems to be plenty in these forms. Blues and bluegrass continue to evolve, and good ideas are welcome. These two modern branches of the old-growth Southern string band tree tell us that a secret of longevity is innovation; one keeps the old by keeping it new.

But surely the best kept secret is that ownership enables continuity. Blues and bluegrass are two of the more marginalized American art forms, supported sporadically and often ignored by philanthropic and commercial entities. Yet they are surviving and thriving. This is because they are like other great art forms in having the power to speak to the soul. And these tough arts of the underclass offer up a lesson for everyone: art is kept in the heart of believers or not at all.

NOTES

1. *Living Blues 1995 Blues Directory* (Oxford, MS: University of Mississippi, 1995). Totals are based on the author's tabulations.

2. Ibid.

3. Source of information is the International Bluegrass Music Association.

COWBOY MUSIC
AND POETRY

The Cowboy Tour

· ·

During the summers of 1983 and 1984, nine cowboys representing different cattle-raising traditions traveled to cowtowns across the west, ranging from the Texas border to the Dakotas, and from the Montana badlands to the lush uplands of Hawaii's Big Island. They recited cowboy poems offering a glimpse into their lives and times; told jokes and big windy stories; sang in English, Spanish, and Hawaiian; and performed on fiddle, guitar, ukulele, and harmonica.

They attracted attention even in towns where half the citizens wore boots and Stetsons. "Who are these guys?" was the question put to those traveling with them. "Real cowboys," we said. Some went home to get cameras. A North Dakota waitress told them she was going to treat them all to peach cobbler at her expense, "because I loved my grandpa and you remind me of him," she said, wiping a tear.

They stopped at all Western museums, halls of fame, and similar establishments. They questioned the motivations and intellectual acuity of the creators of these institutions with a verbal analysis and running

Liner notes to *The Cowboy Tour: A National Tour of Cowboy Songs, Poetry, Big Windy Stories, Humor, and Fiddling*, Rounder Records, 2000.

commentary that was always very funny. They approved of Judge Roy Bean's restored Jersey Lilly Saloon in Langtry, Texas, and had their picture made on the porch. They liked a tiny local museum in South Dakota that was unattended but had a barbed wire exhibit and the hats of local old-timers encircling the wall. They did a fundraiser in Sun Valley, Idaho, for the Western Folklife Center in Elko, Nevada, then in planning stages.

They traveled over 7,000 miles in the interior West. Their favorite towns were Medora, North Dakota; Fort Stockton, Texas; Hamilton, Montana; Elko, Nevada; and Waimea and Makawao, Hawaii. Lead cowboy van driver Glenn Ohrlin made a rule that interstate highways were not to be used if a two-lane road was available. Also, a road should not be used twice if there was a reasonable alternative. We giggled as we watched Glenn discover that there was just one road in and out of Oakley, Idaho. He retaliated with a stream of comments reflecting on our ancestry which turned the morning air blue.

In the years since the tour, four of these cowboys have been honored by the National Endowment for the Arts with National Heritage Fellowships, the highest honor that our nation can offer a traditional artist. These are Brownie Ford, Glenn Ohrlin, Duff Severe, and Kindy Sproat. Also, a booming regional interest has developed in cowboys, their poetry, tack, and regional history. There's even a growing awareness of the contributions of Hawaii, where cowboying began in 1830, before most of the West was settled.

The last tour performances were in Hawaii and were memorable. In Waimea, on the Big Island, *paniolos* [Hawaiian cowboys] and their families packed the hall. The huge Parker Ranch, surrounding that place, then had more than 500 working cowboys. They hooted and yelped and would not let the show end. In Makawao, Maui—a tiny cow town perched halfway up the towering Heleakala volcano—the tour performed for the last time at the rodeo grounds. The cowboys then strolled over to Club Rodeo, a bar.

In bars across the West, local folk had pulled the cowboys aside and shared with them a favorite poem or song. Here at 2:00 a.m., two great keepers of Hawaiian tradition, Manu and Ipo Kahaialii pulled Kindy Sproat to a corner, where Manu and Kindy sang together. Then Manu and Ipo sang the last song of the tour, accompanied by Manu's driving gut-string guitar. Trusty tour sound technician Ceil Mueller was there to capture the moment on her recorder.

This tour was organized by the National Council for the Traditional Arts (NCTA), a private nonprofit arts agency in Silver Spring, Maryland, that has presented the arts of cowboys and other working Americans since its inception in 1933. There's a list of credits for the tour, but one good agency deserves major credit. That agency is the National Endowment for the Arts. The genial and brilliant former director of the NEA's Folk Arts Program, Mrs. Bess Hawes, encouraged this work and provided critical funding. More than a century ago, her father, John A. Lomax, was the first to collect and treat respectfully the songs and poems of cowboys. I know Mrs. Hawes and all the cowboys would want me to also thank every taxpayer as well. The NEA is supported by your dollars. Thank you very much for helping with this.

Brownie Ford
The Clown Who Taught Courage

• •

Howard Sacks, Brownie Ford, and I were ready to leave Brownie's ru-ral store and home near Monroe, Louisiana, and cross Texas to San Antonio on the two-lane roads. Brownie had insisted on two-lane roads. "We might as well see what progress the citizens are making in screw-ing up the goddamn country," he said. "Might see an old pony or two, or maybe a cow-meat operation."

Brownie's wife, Miss Cody, called me back into the store while Brownie and Howard filled the van with fuel and checked the oil. "You sons-of-bitches are going to take care of Brownie, aren't you?" she asked, a plea in her voice. I promised her we would.

Born at Gum Springs in the Indian Territory in 1904, Brownie was half Comanche. He'd not been accepted at the Indian or white schools. "Kids can be awful mean," he said, a glimmer of old pain still in his voice. He joined Pawnee Bill's Wild West show at age twelve. He caught wild horses for Uncle Sam during World War I.

Unpublished. Joe Wilson wrote: "This was written in 1985, after our cowboy tours. I'd hoped to place it in the Monroe, Louisiana daily, but don't recall that happening."

Brownie worked in early rodeos. He rode broncs and helped develop the rodeo clown business, learning ways to protect thrown riders from irate bulls and bucking horses and doing comedy in a funny suit with a well-trained long-legged red mule named Fred.

After a show in Fort Stockton, Texas, an old cowboy from Brownie's rodeo years told me about encountering him on a Texas road during the Great Depression. Brownie's friend had quit rodeoing and taken a job driving a gravel truck for the county. Driving down the road a year later, he saw Brownie, perched on a road bank with his gear and tall mule.

He learned that Brownie had developed employment problems, knocked hell out of the boss, and quit between towns. They talked awhile and decided to go into town for a few drinks. The gravel truck had a tiny metal bed set over its high wheels, with short walls to hold rocks. "We had a hell of a time getting that mule up there," he said. "We had to back up to the bank and talk sweet to him. But Lord, I wish I had a picture of that now. We'd not had a shave in a month—ragged and dirty—two damned old cowboys riding into town in a jalopy gravel truck with a mule on top of it."

I wish I had a picture of them with Fred, the mule, too.

An aging Texas rodeo historian assured me that the Brownie Ford listed on our poster could not be the original Brownie Ford. "I saw him killed in Dallas," he said. "I was working on that rodeo." I argued a bit, but the man was adamant. Back at the motel, Brownie told me I should apologize to the old-timer. "A horse fell on me, and they took me out of there in an ambulance. I was in the hospital a long time, and they moved on. Yeah, a lot of people thought I was dead after that—but I was home, drinking coffee and letting some bones knit."

Too young to help General John J. Pershing chase Pancho Villa on the border or to serve in World War I, Brownie was too bone-crushed and battered to serve in World War II. So he drove a tractor-trailer truck, specializing in high-speed delivery anywhere in the United States. Among his souvenirs was a ticket from the Baltimore City Police, who said they had timed Ford's big truck "exceeding 70 mph on Route 40" in downtown Baltimore at 2:31 a.m.

After years as a ranch boss in West Texas, Brownie found his way to Louisiana, punching cows on grassy hammocks in swampland, sometimes wearing spurs over gumboots. "Hell, anybody can punch cows on dry land," he said. During one of my visits, Brownie and a neighbor lad had caught a giant snapping turtle in the swamp near the store, and were attempting to drag it out, using ropes and a VW Bug. Brownie gestured toward the nearby ghetto, "Some of my neighbors are good at butchering turtles, and this one has a lot of good meat."

Brownie talked about a Texas spread he'd run for "the old Colonel." I thought this gentleman was part of history until the night Brownie told me the old Colonel and his daughter should be added to the show guest list. This gentleman turned out to be only slightly more ancient than Brownie and looked appropriately "colonel" with his white suit, white hat, string tie, goatee, white Lincoln Continental, and blonde daughter.

Across the West, old cowboys—former bull and bronco riders who had been saved by him from slashing horns and stomping hooves—gathered after shows to talk to Brownie. They were diffident, respectful, and grateful.

One old cowboy, now a preacher, quoted the Bible, a phrase about the greatest love inspiring men to lay down their lives for a friend. "I didn't love you a goddamn bit, " responded Brownie, his arm around the preacher. "But that dang Brahma was about to turn you into a grease spot, and I was in charge of cleaning up."

Children of the old cowboys had heard for years about the fearless clown. They stood back in the circle, feeling his presence. Brownie doffed his Stetson and gave wives a Southern gentleman's bow: "I'm honored to meet you, madam."

Brownie had a wonderfully deep, expressive voice and a rich repertoire of songs, many of them from an Anglo grandmother. He was awarded a National Heritage Fellowship by the National Endowment for the Arts when he was in his eighties.

It seems ironic that the half-Indian kid the white kids would not accept became one of the best carriers of the Anglo ballad tradition that ever came down the pike. Of the music he loved, Brownie said, "Without tragedy, anxiety, and a little bit of happiness every now and then, there wouldn't be songs like these."

Grizzly Ropers and Bald Grazers
A Mini-History of Cattle Ranching and Cowboying

••••••••••••••••••••••••••••

Christopher Columbus introduced horses and cattle to the New World during his second voyage, landing the first near Cap-Haïtien, Haiti, in 1494. Hernán Cortez brought horses to the mainland at Vera Cruz, Mexico in 1519, and the next year Gregorio de Villalolos landed calves near the present-day city of Tempico. Though now famous as a gold-seeker, Cortez was more interested in ranching and became the first large-scale rancher in North America.

Cattle raising spread rapidly in the area stretching from Veracruz to Mexico City. Nineteen years after the first stock was imported, Francisco Vasquez de Coronado departed with 500 head of cattle on the famous expedition that took him to Arizona, Texas, Oklahoma, and Kansas. Some cattle probably reached what is now the United States, but they were eaten. Some thirty years later, Jean de Onate brought 7,000 head of livestock to what is now New Mexico.

This rapid growth in stock raising gave rise to a new occupation, the vaquero. These men were at the bottom of the social totem pole, owning

Adapted from *The Old Puncher's Reunion* tour program book, National Council for the Traditional Arts, 1983.

little more than the clothes on their backs. But their innovations in tools and skills still mark cowboying. The modern stock saddle is not much changed from ones they made, nor are skills with the rope. To the vaqueros we owe boots, hat, bandana, and much more.

Cattle spread north to Texas and northwest to California. Meat became so cheap that cattle were slaughtered just for their hides and tallow. Grizzly bears fed on the discarded meat, giving rise to a grizzly population explosion. In California, vaqueros team-roped grizzlies; one caught the throat, another the feet. One traveler tells of seeing vaqueros kill forty grizzlies this way in a single day.

Thousands of land-seeking Americans came to Texas after 1825, enticed by the new Mexican nation's generous offering of land grants. It was a time of financial distress in the United States. Land cost $1.25 an acre, and the settler had to buy at least 80 acres. It sounds virtually free today, but then it was beyond the means of many. The Mexicans offered free land—277 acres for farmers and 4,338 for those intending to raise stock. Most settlers said they would do both and got 4,615 acres.

The Americans who came west to Texas and elsewhere were well acquainted with cattle raising. The frontier moved, and land grants and large purchases had always assured room for grazing. There were large natural meadows in some areas, especially at the tops of the Appalachian mountains. When the frontier was there, Piedmont stockmen drove herds west to the "balds" for grazing. There's evidence there of the traditional nature of cattle raising as an occupation. One Appalachian family has grazed balds since 1783 and has cattle-raising relatives in six Western states.

Ranch owners tended to be nearly as poor as their vaqueros until after the Civil War, when technology made it possible to market beef in distant places. Important technological developments included canning and refrigeration, but most important was the extension of railroads. Trail drives from Texas to Kansas railhead towns created new fortunes and led to the expansion of large-scale cattle raising to the Northern Plains and elsewhere in the West.

Much has been written about the end of the free range and conflicts between cattlemen and homesteaders in the 1880s and 1890s, but these writings tend to mask a more complex situation. Such conflicts began generations before in the East. Grazing began as soon as hunters and others had pushed out large predators and Indians. But the arrival of more settlers led to conflicts, some of which were settled by violence. This situation was familiar to Thomas Jefferson, who in his 1781 book *Notes on the State of Virginia* contrasted settled farmers and free grazers. He also noted that farm-raised steers had been slaughtered "that weighed 2,500, 2,200, and 2,100 lb. nett. and those of 1,800 lb. have been frequent." It seems that steers have improved slowly if at all.

HAWAIIAN RANCHING

Cattle came to Hawaii with early European explorers, and ranching has a history perhaps even more colorful there than on the mainland. The first settlers had no knowledge of cattle or horses. Polynesian voyagers came to Hawaii 1,500 years ago, mainly from the Marquesas Islands, more than 2,000 miles to the south. There were subsequent immigrations from Tahiti, and when the British explorer Captain James Cook sailed to Hawaii in 1778, he found a population of 300,000.

To redress conflicts with the islanders during Cook's explorations, the British sent navigator George Vancouver to the Islands in 1792 with a diplomatic gift of two shiploads of cattle. The recipient of this largesse was Kamehameha, premier chieftain or king. Kamehameha had great *mana*, a potency derived from the gods and genealogically inherited, and he made cattle *kapu* (taboo) so that they would not be eaten or disturbed. Wild herds increased rapidly in this excellent cattle country. Within a generation, they were eroding forests and sometimes endangering the population.

The years following 1800 were a period of rapid change in Hawaii. The people were receptive to outsiders, including the traders who poured into the previously isolated Islands. In 1832, Kamehameha III decided to enter the cattle business. Faced with the difficulty of handling herds of the size and nature of those on the Islands without horses or horsemen, the premier chief sent to Mexico for assistance. Three vaqueros came, and their influence is still evident in the language, equipment, and skills of the *paniolos* [Hawaiian cowboys].

Getting cattle to the Honolulu slaughterhouses was not easy. That city is on the island of Oahu, and ranches are on the islands of Maui and Hawaii (the "Big Island"). The Hawaiian old-timers' methods were direct and of the kind that cowboys anywhere would appreciate. A steer was roped; a hitch was taken around the saddlehorn; and the animal was dragged into the Pacific surf, lashed to the gunwale of a longboat with other animals, and rowed or towed to a cattle ship waiting offshore.

Although this work began a generation before the Texas cattle drives to Kansas, Hawaiian cowboying has remained obscure in the rest of the United States. Distance from the mainland is a factor, as is the ranches' remoteness even from Honolulu. Also, the imaginations of those who created the popular image of cowboying in the mass media seemed to rebel when confronted with the Hawaiian cowboy. In this world of stereotypes, a Hawaiian could be a jolly fellow who wears a layer of leis, but a cowboy? Never.

Yet, Hawaiian cowboys are serious competitors wherever mainland and Island skills are tested. A *paniolo* won the world championship in rodeo steer roping as early as 1908. In the 1970s, Karin Haleamau and other cowboys on the Huehue Ranch were catching "uncontrolled cattle" from a herd of 500 that had never seen men—work akin to that on the Texas range a hundred years earlier.

The largest individually owned ranches in the United States are in Hawaii. The cowboys on these ranches work hard, like cowboys everywhere, and Island cattle ranches are strongholds of Hawaiian ethnicity. On ranches one can still hear the language of Hawaii and experience the receptivity, neighborliness, and *aloha* spirit of a remarkable people.

THE ENTERTAINMENT COWBOY

When one seeks the origins of the Hollywood cowboy, one is led to Horace Mann, the leading proponent of free public education in the United States. By 1860, a majority of the states had public school systems, and half of the nation's children were getting some formal education. The years of formal education were few, however, and new readers were not satisfied with the mixture of editorialized news and social gossip in the newspapers of the time.

During the 1830s, melodramatic stories began appearing in what were called "mammoth weeklies." Their covers enclosed tearful narratives—usually fiction but often related as fact, poetry, anecdotes, and curiosity items. In the 1850s, they were replaced by the "story weeklies," which were smaller and better edited. During the same decade, the popular magazine arose. After the Civil War, the illustrated magazines and newspapers were joined by the famous dime novel, as the flood of fictionalized local color and purple prose became a tidal wave.

The Texas cowboys who trailed cattle into Kansas towns came to the attention of these writers almost as soon as they arrived at the railheads. Some early accounts of these men were relatively unadorned; apparently their garb, occupation, arms, and Spanish-influenced vocabulary were fantastic enough to interest mass-circulation readers. Cowboys were instantly famous and popular with readers, and the hunger for more colorful characters, heroes, and praiseworthy deeds led authors to much embellishment.

People back East were eager to see cowboys. Interest sparked by the publishing industry created another industry: the Wild West show. William F. ("Buffalo Bill") Cody had been a popular character in publishing. Like several other early characters, he was a real person and one with a gift for show business. In 1883, Cody and W. F. Carver took the first show of this kind on the road. It was a sensation, and similar shows soon followed. Rodeos, which had started a dozen years earlier as local events, eventually incorporated much of the content of the Wild West shows.

Since then, cowboying as entertainment has spread to other mass-market media, often at their earliest stages of development. The first film depicting cowboys was shot by the Edison Company in 1898. The first movie "Western" with a discernible plot was *The Great Train Robbery*, shot thirty miles west of Manhattan on the tracks of the Erie-Lackawanna near Dover, New Jersey. A few working cowboys have become entertainment cowboys, but most often as bit players. In general, the breeds are as separable as sheep and cattle. Stetson-wearing Hollywood actors have at times been described as the Americans who are most widely recognized in foreign lands, but film industry market tests show that Mickey Mouse has a recognizability ratio that beats any of these fellows four to one. Surely there's a message in that.

COWBOY POETRY

Strange as it may seem, cowboys appear to be the only occupational group in the United States with a high percentage of members who write and recite poetry. Those who know cowboys best say a fondness for poetry marks the breed. Glenn Ohrlin recalls poetry as an interest of older co-workers who were on the Nevada ranges where he began buckarooing in 1943, at age sixteen. "Most of the oldtimers didn't play guitar or even sing, but they knew songs. They'd recite songs just like they did poetry. Some had poems that were theirs. After a while you knew them, but they were personal, so you'd never recite a man's poem without asking if you could."

It probably isn't fair to ask why cowboys write poetry. A better question is, why did everybody else stop? A century ago it seemed that this ancient tradition would go on forever. Newspapers that emerged across the country (a result of increased literacy) contained much poetry. A well-known folk melody or popular tune was often cited along with the poem, so these were technically songs. But much more than Victorian custom was involved. American newspapers had contained such material since before 1800, and "broadside" ballads had been sold on the streets of London, Dublin, and other cities for generations before that. No artistic custom of the English-speaking people seemed more embedded; among literate people, life's triumphs and passages were celebrated in verse.

The subject matter of folk poetry was what moved people: the deeds of Captain Kidd; the grim visage of the London hangman, Derrick; or perhaps a wondrous victory in battle, such as the one that inspired Francis Scott Key to write the "Star Spangled Banner" and flute player Christopher Durang to set Key's poem to music [see "Durang's Dance and Hoffmaster's Tune"].

Like generations of versifying predecessors, cowboys wrote about national events and deeply personal matters. There are poems that celebrate Mrs. O'Leary's cow (she kicked over the lantern that ignited the fire that burned Chicago) and many that reflect upon the home far away.

But why did cowboys continue to write poetry after others had stopped? One answer is that they have deep respect for the habits and skills of old-timers in their profession. Another is that their verse is good and they enjoy it.

Among noted cowboy poets was D.J. O'Malley, born in 1868 at San Angelo, Texas. While working as a cowpuncher in western Montana from 1881 until 1901, O'Malley contributed poems to *The Stock Grower's Journal*, a weekly newspaper published at Miles City, Montana.

An early O'Malley effort entitled "After the Roundup," published October 6, 1883, quickly entered oral tradition as "When the Work's All Done This Fall," and cowboys spread it through the West. Today it is among the best known cowboy compositions. Almost an archetype of the Victorian poem, it casts the puncher as the prodigal son, killed in the stampede before he can get home to plead for his mother's forgiveness and the bed of shucks.

Twenty-five years later, O'Malley's verse had matured, and he was no longer punching cattle. But his 1908 poem, "The Cowboy's Kick," contains a common theme of cowboy poetry:

Where once we could ride miles on horseback
Across the prairie so fine,
We now have to zig-zag along a road
Laid out on a section line.
We used to move 'round on a bronco,
Urged on by a spur of steel,
But now we are forty years back of the times
If we don't ride an automobile.
No more rides the cowboy on roundup,
No more the sheep herder and dogs,
All you see is the dry farmer's homestead
And four or five-million hogs.
The buffalo, Indian, and cowboy
Or horse chaser no more you'll find.
They have all found a hole up near the North Pole,
Crawled in and closed it behind.

Seventy-five years after O'Malley bid farewell to the old punchers, some are still around and writing poems that echo the sentiments he expressed.

LYING AS AN ART

Like their poetry, the "big windy" storytelling of the cowboys reflects influences from the nineteenth century, when verbal skills were prized. From 1800 until the 1890s, the colorful teller of windy stories from a specific locale was a fixture of both written and oral literature. This character appeared shortly after 1800 in New England as Brother Jonathan [see "The

Toby Character: When Bluegrass Bands Needed Lightning Rod Salesmen"]
and continued with Davy Crockett in the 1840s, along with many similar
localized figures. This body of material greatly influenced Mark Twain and
other notables of nineteenth-century humor.

Among early "big windy" stories from cattlemen is one by colorful
Texas cattleman and trail driver Shanghai Pierce, who described an 1852
cattle drive to New Orleans. His account begins as a seemingly factual
description of the difficulties of getting his herd through the Louisiana
swamps. Soon, however, Pierce has longhorns balancing on loops and
swinging by their horns from wisteria vines like monkeys in order to get
across, and the sight makes his horse laugh. It is a story that might still be
told by an old-time cowboy.

COWBOY MUSIC

Cowboy music is many musics: bouncy norteño polkas played on harmonica or accordion; an a cappella account of death in a stampede that
is half spoken and half sung; breakdown fiddle tunes played for dancing;
the rippling instrumentals of Hawaiian slack-key guitar; or a narrative
ballad sung with understated guitar accompaniment. It is all these things
and more—all traditional, but traditional to different places and people of
different origins, and flavored by regional style.

Like other living traditional forms, cowboy music is subject to change
over time. The song and much of the style may be handed through the
generations, but the singer may choose to change a line, a verse, or the
tune. New material may be written, and if the group accepts it as an item
of the group, it is traditional.

Newspaper and magazine accounts of cowboys from the nineteenth
century mention music only infrequently. But there are a few good descriptions, and one important scholar—John A. Lomax—began collecting
cowboy music before 1900. He was the first to proclaim that the arts of
working Americans expressed a national purpose, and he was the first to
record those arts. From his collections we know that much of this music has long been solo, and that a passion for words has marked Anglo-
American cowboy music in the mainland West. No other group has con-

structed verses with more care or treated them with greater respect. The material comes first; no singer interferes with it.

Early accounts mention the voice, harmonica, and fiddle more often than other instruments. Not much is known about harmonica styles among cowboys, but fiddle styles are known. The most complex is the long-bow Texas style, the source of western "contest" fiddling. The guitar became common after 1900; two non-musicians—Mr. Sears and Mr. Roebuck—appear to be largely responsible for its availability. By 1920, it was clearly the instrument of choice among cowboys. Some probably received it from vaqueros, but documentation is virtually nonexistent.

The favorite instrument of the vaqueros employed on the huge King Ranch in south Texas during the 1920s and 1930s was the accordion, often accompanied by the bajo sexto, a large-bodied, twelve-string guitar. The accordion came to their music shortly after 1900, slowly pushing out the violin. Though the vaqueros performed a variety of musics, the polka, waltz, and corrido (narrative ballad) were especially popular.

The *paniolos* of Hawaii perform on several instruments, but the one that surprises musically inclined mainlanders most is slack-key guitar. An otherwise conventional guitar is tuned in an open chord, with perhaps one or more strings dropped lower or tuned higher in order to have as many unfretted notes as possible for a specific melody. Once that is performed, the player may "slack" the keys and retune for another piece.

But, with all this complexity, how can one be sure that a song or tune is cowboy in origin? Perhaps the final word on this was spoken by Glenn Ohrlin: "If I learned a song from a cowboy, and he did too, it's a cowboy song."

OTHER VERNACULAR
MUSICAL STYLES

The Chestnut Grove Quartet
"We Come from a Place . . ."

• •

A mong the many innovations that came to bluegrass in the 1970s is the a cappella singing of gospel songs. Most of the founders of bluegrass grew up in small country churches that could not afford musical instruments, and they certainly knew such singing before the 1970s. But where did the recent wave of post-modern, old-style singing come from? I believe I know, and it is a pleasure to introduce the Chestnut Grove Quartet to those who have enjoyed the trend they initiated.

More people have heard about this group from the mountains of Southwest Virginia than have actually heard them. Singing religious songs without accompaniment on a small-town radio station, they influenced the development of a cappella singing in many distant places.

The Chestnut Grove Quartet was created in the years following World War II. No one recalls a date. The original members had sung together since childhood. They evolved as a musical group during the ten years after they came home from the war and began rearing families.

From *Bluegrass Unlimited* magazine, July, 1995. Joe Wilson wrote: "In 2000 Virginia's 9th district congressman, Rick Boucher, honored the Chestnut Grove Quartet with a breakfast, inviting over 100 friends. As a teenager, Rick had served as the announcer for the Quartet's broadcasts on Abingdon radio. He asked me to tell the citizens who they were."

Original Chestnut Grove members Bill and Jim Nunley and their uncle, Archie Reynolds, started performing in the mid-1930s as members of a vocal group with string band accompaniment, the Moccasin Gap Ramblers. There were three other Ramblers: brother Manuel Nunley, cousin Gilbert Reynolds, and a friend, Danny Harmon.

They performed at home and at school functions in the Moccasin Gap community in Washington County, Virginia. "We had to make our own music," Bill Nunley says of the times. "Some folks around here were good at that." The members of the original Carter Family were reared nearby, as were Jim and Jesse McReynolds; their fiddling grandfather, Charlie McReynolds; and the Stanley Brothers, who had a musical mom.

In 1937, they began performing on Saturday matinee jamboree programs on radio station WOPI in Bristol. Their announcer was Ernie Ford, later famous as "Tennessee Ernie." Bill played guitar, Danny the banjo, and Archie the harmonica. Older brother Jim was usually the lead singer, and Bill owned a soaring tenor with an emotional edge. It is a quality that, in these parts, is called having "heart."

They had their own style. Bill recalls that they loved and sometimes learned songs by the Blue Sky Boys and by Wade Mainer and Zeke Morris, but any good song was fair game. They learned Gene Autry's "Silver Haired Daddy," and they knew some old ballads. But even as a string band, most of their songs were religious.

They attended the Chestnut Grove Methodist Church in their community. Built in 1890, the church was then a wood-frame structure, painted white, without a steeple, and on a gravel road—like hundreds of others in the rural South. Most members of the Chestnut Grove Methodist Church were named Nunley or Reynolds and were descended from families who settled in this remote area near the time of the American Revolution. There was no piano or organ; music was created only by the human voice.

It was at Chestnut Grove, while they were all very young, that Bill, Jim, and Archie met and became close friends with Gale Webb, the fourth member of the original quartet. Gale's dad was Ed Webb, a singer who knew shape notes and was respected for his vocal powers. The Webb family lived in the Brumley Gap section of Washington County, six miles from Moccasin Gap.

Both communities are west of Abingdon, in southwestern Virginia, and named for gaps in the Clinch Mountain that for a hundred miles forms the first towering barrier of the Allegheny range. Moccasin Gap is still a very small community, but it is famous among those who know about Daniel Boone and his early travels and fights with Indians.

These four had learned shape notes in the one- and two-week singing school evening sessions taught annually at Chestnut Grove and other local churches. Many were held in early fall, before evangelical revival meetings. Instruction was by itinerant local teachers, whose primary qualifications were that they were fine singers and could teach the rudiments of shape notes in two weeks or less.

New paperback shape-note hymnals were bought by the church every year or two, mostly from the Stamps-Baxter Publishing Company or from the James D. Vaughan Company. These usually contained "Amazing Grace" and similarly familiar old works of Southern hymnody, but they also had new songs. It was a boom period for such wonderfully prolific composers as Albert Brumley, who wrote "I'll Fly Away," "Cabin In Gloryland," "Rank Strangers To Me," and many other songs during the 1930s.

World War II halted the musical activities of the four friends who became the Chestnut Grove Quartet. It was especially disruptive to the lives of the three Nunley brothers. Jim served in the Army in Panama. Bill served in the infantry in Europe, arriving in France via Normandy's Omaha Beach. Manuel [not a member of the Quartet] fought and was taken prisoner in Germany.

After the war, there was a surge of interest in what are now called southern gospel quartets. Such phenomena as "county singings," "all night singings," and "all day singing with dinner on the ground" increased across the South. Quartet singers often visited other churches. In Appalachian communities, quartet singing dominated Sunday radio broadcasts.

Bill, Jim, Gale, and Archie regrouped. Instruments did not seem as important to them after the war, and they developed a fondness for unaccompanied singing. They sang at Chestnut Grove Church for several years before they began going to other churches and to singings that featured groups of singers.

At these gatherings, they attracted instant attention. Most groups of that period used piano accompaniment. A few used a single guitar. A very few used more than one instrument. But rarest of all was unaccompanied singing. Many Appalachian churches acquired their first musical instruments after World War II. Having just bought them, they put them to full use. The piano became as ubiquitous at rural churches as the organ was at "First Baptist" and "First Methodist" churches in towns.

Honed by years of brother-style singing and old ballads, the intense emotional edge of Chestnut Grove singing was made especially stark when delivered in a cappella arrangements. Some of their songs were performed in the "singing parts" quartet style that has evolved since Victorian times. Others derived their power from a straightforward harmony that echoed Sunday morning congregational singing during their youth at Chestnut Grove.

There were many compliments, and they were encouraged to try their voices on radio. This was made easy when radio station WBBI opened in Abingdon. They started on that station in the mid-1950s and remained there for over thirty years. Their program was from 2:00 until 2:30 on Sunday afternoons. They paid for the time through the sale of songbooks and LP recordings.

The reaction to their singing was enthusiastic, and it was impossible to meet all the requests for appearances. These were mostly from churches. They occasionally sang at community functions, but avoided most other secular appearances. (In the late seventies, this writer carried invitations to them from the Smithsonian's Festival of American Folklife, three National Folk Festivals at Wolf Trap, and a concert at the Library of Congress. They expressed appreciation for each invitation but begged to be excused.)

Archie Reynolds died on September 25, 1962. It was a devastating blow to the other members. They considered quitting. They sang as a trio, and it didn't seem right. They tried various replacements. After a year they met Ray Roe, of Chilhowie, Virginia, a community a dozen miles to the northeast. Ray had been reared in a singing family and was a fan of the Quartet's radio program. His singing of Archie's baritone part clicked. Ray became a part of the singing family and was with the group for twenty-five years, until his death in 1987.

By the sixties and seventies, the Chestnut Grove radio audience had become huge. It seemed that half the people within range of the WBBI signal tuned in. They traveled to rural churches in the mountain portions of Virginia, Tennessee, Kentucky, North Carolina, and West Virginia. They occasionally performed in other states and wore out five new vehicles. When the Stamps-Baxter Company went out of business, the Quartet bought a huge cache of leftover paperback hymnals and began selling them at appearances.

Announcer Ed Quinn of WBBI talked them into making their first LP recording. They were at first dubious. No one was selling a cappella LPs. Would people buy music without instruments? They made an appointment with the Arthur Smith Studios in Charlotte. Musician-businessman Smith expected them to be around for at least a day, and probably two days. To his consternation, they were finished in less than an hour, every song a "take" at first attempt. All their LPs were made with similar discipline.

In one eighteen-month period, they made four LPs and sold more than 50,000 copies, almost all at live appearances or to radio listeners. To those who know the recording and personal appearance business, that is an astonishing achievement.

Among the thousands who admired the Quartet during the sixties and seventies was Ralph Stanley, of nearby Dickenson County, Virginia. A pioneer of bluegrass music, Ralph had much in common with members of the Quartet. Like them, he grew up in the shadow of Clinch Mountain and under the influence of string bands, family balladry, and a cappella singing in church.

Ralph Stanley moved home to Virginia in the mid-sixties, when the Quartet was at the zenith of its influence. He had recently lost his singing partner and brother, Carter. Urban bluegrass bands were changing the sounds that had defined this post-war form of country music. Some bluegrass bands moved to Nashville. Others incorporated sounds from folk, rock, and modern country.

Ralph Stanley moved closer to the head of the hollow, both physically and musically. The influence of his mother's singing and banjo playing grew stronger in his music. And this Chestnut Grove Quartet fan added a cappella singing to the repertoire of his band, the Clinch Mountain Boys. It was good that Ralph did not ask the opinion of any experts before doing so. They would have told him that bluegrass is a music based upon instrumental virtuosity, and that anything as distant from superpicking as a cappella singing would surely flop.

The recordings Ralph Stanley made for Rebel Records in the early seventies set off a wave of a cappella singing. Other bluegrass bandleaders became admirers of the Chestnut Grove Quartet and adapted their songs.

Notable among these were Doyle Lawson, the Bluegrass Cardinals, and Ricky Skaggs. Suddenly, bluegrass bands from Tokyo to Prague were putting down their instruments and singing without accompaniment. Many skills of the Chestnut Grove Quartet are now essential parts of the international bluegrass resource bag.

The members of the Quartet grew up working on mountain farms before mechanization. They have always had work other than music. Bill was a steelworker, Jim a self-employed painter, Gale managed a Southern States Cooperative Store, Archie was a farmer, and Ray was a dairy farmer.

After Ray's death, the Quartet found a new member at home. Bill's wife, Ann Statzer Nunley, sang with them on radio and at personal appearances for seven years. A great singer, Ann already knew the words. Her children and grandchildren already reared, she was able to travel.

[In 1995] The Chestnut Grove Quartet no longer has its radio program and is not traveling, but its members still go to the little mountain church whose name they have worn and honored. Pinning down a date when this or that stopped is as hard as figuring out when it all started. At age seventy-nine, Bill is vigorously training and directing a group of young adult singers from the Chestnut Grove Church.

County Records released a CD of fifteen songs taken from nine LP recordings the Chestnuts made in the 1960s and 1970s. Included are songs that have since become standards in bluegrass gospel: "Lord Don't Leave Me Here," "Just Over Yonder," "Little Old Church By The Road," "The Great Beyond," and "Where The Roses Never Fade." It was their first recording to be nationally distributed.

The influence of the Chestnut Grove Quartet reached beyond bluegrass. Folk song groups from Portland to San Diego now include a cappella gospel songs in their repertoires. Generous givers, the Chestnuts are not concerned about credit. "It came to us free," Bill explains. "The best of everything has already been paid for."

Bill sometimes prefaces comments about the group by saying, "We come from a place . . ." They reflect the strength of that place and have made enormous contributions to it for over six decades. And who can doubt that a measure of the strength of our nation—in music, as in other affairs—comes from its small communities and the keepers of its deepest traditions?

Northern Plains Courting Flute
and Robert "Tree" Cody

· ·

The courting flute was once found throughout the Americas. In previous centuries, it was a solo instrument among almost all who played it, one used to express the deepest emotions of the individual performer.

It was called a "courting" flute because some tribes had a tradition of young men composing and playing songs and melodies for young women they hoped to persuade to become life partners. A remarkable range of sounds came from many different kinds of flutes.

Flute traditions were especially strong among the Dakota Indians who lived on the great "sea of grass" at the center of the North American continent. Sometimes called Sioux, the Dakota and Lakota people are the source of many of the emblems most associated with American Indians. These include the teepee and the eagle feather headdress. They were the Plains horse cavalry that briefly fought the U.S. Cavalry to a standstill under such leaders as Crazy Horse and Sitting Bull.

But by 1900, overt hostilities were over and the flute, an ancient emblem of Indian culture, seemed to be dying out. Among those who thought

Liner notes to Robert "Tree" Cody, *Siyotanka: Courting Flute of the Northern Plains*, Cracker Barrel Records, 2002.

it would soon be gone was writer and humorist Mark Twain, who described Indian flute as " . . . the only sound I've ever heard that is both pretty and spooky."

Younger musicians were not taking up the instrument. It was seldom heard outside Indian homes. But about three decades ago, just as cultural anthropologists expected the tradition to fully disappear, a powerful internal revitalization took place.

This revitalization came from within Native communities. In many tribal places, younger people began to explore the ancient tradition. They learned techniques, melodies, and flute making from grandfathers and great-grandfathers.

These elders encouraged the younger players to compose their own melodies and made clear that composing is a key part of the tradition, one that keeps it fresh and vital. Suddenly a sound that echoed across the Americas for more than a thousand years was heard again and a wave of new players appeared.

Although his tribal name is Oou Kas Mah Qwet (Thunder Bear), Robert Cody has been called "Tree" since his teens. At age sixteen, his height had reached six feet, ten inches, and his athleticism had made him the star of his high school basketball team. Tree is of Maricopa-Dakota heritage, and a familiar figure at scores of powwows and tribal gatherings across the nation. He is the adopted son of the late Iron Eyes Cody [a Sicilian-American screen actor], famous for the tear he shed on television after viewing the polluting of his nation.

Like many other young Indians, Tree grew up in two worlds. His athletic and language skills (Tree is multi-lingual) brought him scholarships at Bacone College in Oklahoma and Fort Lewis College in Colorado. He is trained in psychology and physical education, and is a respected teacher.

But he is also from the reservation, and was taught by committed keepers of traditions. He is an enrolled member of his mother's nation, the Salt River Pima-Maricopa community. His parents taught him to value ancient learning passed to the present by a succession of elders. He can't recall when he was not interested in the flute and the songs of the Dakota. They have been a daily passion since childhood.

Tree was a professional basketball player for seven years, but even then his tribal roots called him to study with the elders and go to cultural gatherings of his people. He imposed upon himself a long apprenticeship, learning from his father and keepers of flute, dance, and craft traditions he met as he grew up. Tree's amazing skills as a player and composer for the flute developed over a dozen years, and were honed in scores of meetings with great players on the powwow circuit. Soon, there were calls for him to share his knowledge.

Tree now works as a flutist, traditional dancer, artist, educator, actor, and emcee for Indian gatherings. He has recorded nine albums of his music, performed in films, and appeared live in Europe, Canada, Central and Latin America, Japan, Korea, Singapore, and Scandinavia. Though his travels range far, Tree continues to live in Phoenix, Arizona, adjacent to the Salt River Reservation. Tree and his wife Marlene have four sons; they are teaching them the old ways and the new ways, and to value their Indian and American heritage.

There is an oddity in the new popularity of Native American flute playing. This ancient form is now being embraced for the freshness of its sound rather than its antiquity or its place within Indian communities. Some "new age" flute fans are surprised when told it has an ancient history.

Tree Cody thinks that is okay. "This is a strong river of music from good times and hard times," he said. "The people and the animals will need water and trees and shade in all the summers to come."

Solás and a Story from the Bus

. . . .

Seamus Egan's new band, Solás, gets first billing. It took years to as-semble this gang and he is proud: Winnie Horan, fiddle; Karan Casey, vocals; John Doyle, guitar; and John Williams, accordion. It's okay to men-tion Egan's name, but just with the others, please.

His record company has assigned a flack to Egan and pals, an act com-parable to putting an altimeter on a submarine or socks on a rooster. She puzzles about their cheery confusion of performances.

"I don't have any information about that," she New York bristles. "Are you sure? Ohmigod, they never tell me anything."

The audience is young and appears to be returning from a sale of used classic clothing. Some are pierced and tattooed. One can learn to dress down this well only at a very good school.

Karan and John are Irish. The others are Irish-American, and it doesn't matter. This new Irish music has a taproot in the old music, but its feeder roots reach into many sounds here and in Ireland. The players grew up in the ethnic community, but they have heard it all.

Joe Wilson wrote: "This was written for an Irish music magazine on July 16, 1996, but I can't recall it being published."

John Doyle lays down a rolling thunder of background—rhythms like waves on the sea. Winnie's fiddle dips, soars, and rides the breakers. John Williams keeps an even keel; his choice of notes is so good that the wild ride becomes logical. Egan floats in and out on flute, tenor banjo, or guitar—like a pirating frigate bird, snatching the catch in mid-air.

Framed in this excitement of sound is Karan Casey's singing, beautifully ethereal and breathy, but with an edge of resonance. She believes these words. Karan has a toe in the new age, but she's also a traditionalist, committed to the old heartfelt ballads.

The usual comment is, "They're so young!" They are. But they've served long apprenticeships; these are young masters. They've been on the road; there are stories from the bus. Egan has been doing this since he was fourteen and he is now twenty-six.

Here's a bus story from a time when Egan was working in the Greenfields of America ensembles put together by Mick Maloney. It is about a musician who influenced Egan.

It was mid-May, but a torpid early summer had blasted Philadelphia. Seamus set out by air for the Rocky Mountains and a gig in the Grand Teton Lodge, south of Yellowstone, in his customary summer gear: flip-flops, short pants, and a circumcised tee shirt.

The aging Electra turboprop from Denver is a great mountain craft, but not for the faint of heart. It surges violently upward and roars to what seems a near stall high over the snow-capped mountains that surround Jackson Hole. Then it makes a precipitous sideways—and almost straight-down—drop for heart-stopping minutes, before rolling to a stop in front of a small terminal.

Egan stared open-mouthed at the foot of snow already on the ground and the giant flakes still falling. "Uh, I'm gonna need to go to a store and buy a coat, guys."

A coat turned out to be the least of his problems. The Electra had left Denver before luggage and instruments were transferred from the first airplane. They'd be back on the Electra tomorrow, but the gig was tonight.

The Jackson Hole music store had no problem supplying other band members. It had mandolins, fiddles, and guitars—but a tenor banjo? The owner had seen just one in the area. It was owned by an old-timer, a rancher named Sippy Wolf, who had once played at local dances and lived thirty miles to the north.

Mr. Wolf listened to the strange Eastern voice and odd story on the telephone. He thought it would be okay to stop by his place. His spread was at the end of a long dirt road near Grand Teton National Park, framed by towering pines, barns, a blacksmith and welding shop, and a long one-story ranch house almost hidden behind a giant woodpile.

An octogenarian old-timer with frosty hair and thick glasses ambled out. "You gotta be the boys that called." He greeted with outstretched hand and grin the long-haired Irish band clambering out of the big van. "Just call me Sippy."

There's an easygoing hospitality and gentility among rural people in the interior West. Sippy has those qualities and a fondness for musicians. "Let's go check out the living room."

He found soft drinks and a bottle of the hard stuff. "Which one of you is the banjo player?" he asked. "Oh, the young fellow." He pointed to a case at the left of a huge fireplace. "Let's hear what you can do."

Egan tuned the beautiful old antique Weymann tenor in the Irish way, replicating the tuning for the violin. Sippy had always used it for dance rhythms, tuned like a uke, an incisive beat slicing through ricky-tick piano and fiddles. He'd not heard Irish music.

Egan played "The Bird in the Tree," startling the dog from his snooze with an explosion of notes. Sippy listened intently as the old reel tripped from his instrument. "Would you know another one, son?"

When it came time to go to the gig, Sippy interrupted the carefully rehearsed question about renting the banjo: "Take it." Six strangers with long hair, odd accents, and a rented van drove off with a treasured and valuable possession.

Next day a local volunteered to return the banjo, but Seamus insisted on going along. "I'd like to see Sippy." The rest of the band tagged along. The second music session was intense. Sippy sent the group off with a quip: "Don't stay away so long this time, fellas."

And how did Sippy influence Egan? "I'd like to be that nice," Seamus says. "I'll never forget him."

The Memphis Sound

· ·

IN THE BEGINNING: LI'L DAVID ROCKS AND ROLLS

The late Mississippi comedian Brother Dave Gardner liked to sermonize to rock 'n' roll's first fans about the origins of their favorite music. Brother Dave's index finger would jab in the general direction of heaven, and his voice would modulate into the syncopated delivery of a hellfire and brimstone preacher.

As Brother Dave gesticulated and paced the stage, the inventor of rock 'n' roll was revealed as Li'l David, the youth who became King David, honored leader of ancient Israel. In Gardner's telling, Li'l David equipped himself with a smooth, round river rock and a slingshot for his battle with Goliath, a giant "Philadelphian":

> Li'l David's rock flew straight and true. It hit the giant between the eyes and made him fall.
>
> "He said 'Ouch!'" Brother Dave explained, staggering backward. "Because it hurt him, friends."

From *The Memphis Sound* tour program book, National Council for the Traditional Arts, 1995. *The Memphis Sound* examined the creation of new forms—early rockabilly and rock 'n' roll—from regional folk musics in and around Memphis in the early 1950s.

Gardner's voice modulated into the sincerity of a preacher's lesson as he explained that Li'l David then "leapt upon him and relieved him of his coin purse."

Brother Dave's finger shot toward heaven again as he delivered the promised point of his sermon in a resounding shout:

"So Li'l David was the first rock 'n' roller, because he taken the ROCK an' he ROLLED the giant."

Gardner's vignette delighted 1950s Southerners, reared on preachers and preacher jokes and weary of sermons and news stories about the supposed dangers and mysterious origins of rock 'n' roll. Both Gardner and his listeners knew that rock 'n' roll's birth, while mystical, was deeply imbedded in Southern culture and a multitude of American musical forms.

Folklorist Ralph Rinzler speculated that banjoist and songster Uncle Dave Macon's song, "Rock Around My Saro Jane" was the first song in which the ubiquitous "rock around" line was used, and that Macon thus deserved consideration as one of rock's founders.

Musicologist P.K. Reeves pointed to the career of "Harmonica Frank" Floyd, a street and medicine show performer, whose repertoire combined black and white music forms and who recorded for Sam Phillips's Sun Records. He speculated that Elvis and other musical youth in the Memphis area could hardly have avoided hearing Frank on the busy downtown street corners.

A plethora of other old coots and alternative-vision musicians have been cited as inspirational figures and founding fathers by a muddle of rock historians. All are interesting artists, but their influence upon rock 'n' roll seems as remote as that of Li'l David.

ROCKABILLY: LET'S GET HOT

In the early 1950s, Memphis was the birthplace of the music form today's listeners call "rockabilly." Back then, before the genre widened, the music was just called "rock 'n' roll." Memphis rockabilly performers included Elvis Presley, Jerry Lee Lewis, Carl Perkins, Johnny Cash, and Roy Orbison, among others.

Like other American popular music forms, rockabilly combined music from black and white communities. The young white performers who made these combinations drew upon media innovations (radio and 45 rpm records) as well as occasions where they actually saw black musicians at work.

Like many other musical movements of the past three centuries, rockabilly was created by adolescents rejecting the older music of their parents while unconsciously combining these creations with older music forms. Fueled by raging hormones and 3.2 beer, these youngsters developed this music for dancing, in the roadhouses that were their space.

There was a similar movement among black teenagers, at the same time and in the same region. Labeled as rhythm and blues (R&B), electric blues, "jook music," or Chicago blues, their creations drew upon many of the same older music forms.

These black and white teenagers heard each other over radio and via recordings. Chuck Berry called himself a "black hillbilly," and Elvis Presley learned the songs of Arthur "Big Boy" Crudup and "Big Mama" Thornton.

The three forms of music usually cited as being combined in rockabilly are country, rhythm and blues, and gospel. But each of these forms contained elements from complicated earlier musical borrowing and trading between black and white musicians.

GETTIN' DOWN EARLY: EUROPE MEETS AFRICA

The initial meeting of musical forms from Europe and Africa was during colonial times in North America. There are only a few contemporary descriptions, but it is clear that the European fiddle and African banjo met in the hands of black players in the Virginia Tidewater during the 1600s, and that the violin and banjo ensemble continued to provide music for white and black dancing through the 1700s and into the 1800s [see "The Blue Ridge: a Place near the Heart in American Musical History"].

Black string bands continued into the twentieth century, and a handful of musical veterans who got their start in them were still performing in the 1990s (most notably octogenarian jazz and blues fiddlers Claude Williams and Howard Armstrong). Some of the black string band material was adapted by Piedmont bluesmen and continued in the repertoire of such musicians as John Cephas [see "Cephas and Wiggins"] and John Jackson [see "John Jackson: Front Porch Blues"].

STEALING THEIR MUSIC, WEARING THEIR FACE:
THE FIRST POPULAR MUSIC FAD

The banjo and fiddle were key instruments in *minstrelsy*, the first and longest-running popular music fad. Minstrelsy's styles and formats became major popular music forces in the 1840s and continued into the twentieth century. In minstrel stage presentations, white performers blackened their faces, wore ragged clothing, and sang songs they claimed were from Southern black sources. A few minstrel songs were indeed from black sources (though most were not), and black instrumental styles were adopted, but the format was largely held together by racist caricatures and comedy [see "Minstrelsy (Or Why Blacks Gave up the Banjo)"].

Does all this sound remote from rockabilly and Memphis? It isn't. Elvis Presley's first hit single, "That's All Right, Mama," had on its reverse side "Blue Moon of Kentucky," a song he had learned from bluegrass musician Bill Monroe. Bluegrass is largely adapted from traditional Southern string band music, which in turn evolved in part from minstrelsy.

Rockabilly and minstrelsy have additional common ground. They and other popular music forms have allowed a larger public to embrace elements of black music without embracing blacks. This thought may jar in an era supposedly committed to diversity, but a color line is still obvious and very strong in commercial music. The great blues artist B.B. King said of Memphis in the 1950s, "Music was segregated then . . . but music is still segregated, because it comes from families and churches and communities where the color line is still in place."

Combinations and collisions of elements from black and white musical communities have fed the creation of other folk and popular music forms; jazz and blues are good examples. Even forms within forms—such as the cakewalk—have roots on both sides of the color line.

THE BLACK ANCESTRY OF COUNTRY MUSIC:
A FORK IN THE FAMILY TREE

That today's country music has a black as well as a white ancestry is not well known, but it is true. This can be seen in instruments, repertoire, styles, and even in the careers of many of its founders.

Mississippi blue yodeler Jimmie Rodgers, often cited as the "Father of Country Music," got his start in minstrel shows. Moreover, he was an avid fan of black music and used Louis and Lil Armstrong and the fine St. Louis bluesman Clifford Gibson on some of his Victor sessions.

Tennessee fiddler and string band leader Roy Acuff, usually cited as "the King of Country Music," worked in a blackface medicine show minstrel troupe as he was getting started.

One of commercial country music's earliest "stars," black harmonica virtuoso DeFord Bailey, spent over a decade performing on the Grand Ole Opry. While largely overlooked by today's multitudes of country music fans, his influence is still being felt. At least two versions of his famous "Pan American Boogie" were recorded and released by white country musicians in 1995.

Musical material and technology moved just as easily in the other direction. That the creation of the blues form by black artists at the end of the last century was strongly influenced by white parlor music fads sends some blues scholars into denial, but the evidence is compelling.

MOVING TO TOWN: ROCKING IN THE PROJECTS

The ever-evolving new combinations across racial barriers that make American folk and popular forms exciting are based upon far more than echoes from the past. Rockabilly was created during a period of immense social and economic change.

A huge rural-to-urban population shift happened during World War II. Many thousands of rural people moved to Memphis to work in industrial plants as part of the war effort. Among them was Vernon Presley, former farmer and handyman, who commuted home to Tupelo, Mississippi, on weekends to be with his wife and young son.

In having no electricity or indoor plumbing, the Presleys were like the majority of rural Southerners in the 1930s. The family moved to Memphis after the war, and Elvis was able to accomplish something that had not been within the reach of either of his parents: he graduated from high school.

Obtaining a high school diploma and a weekly paycheck for driving a delivery truck or being a stock clerk represented huge progress for families accustomed to living almost outside the cash economy.

Acquiring a "cash money" job at "public works" (anything other than farming or sawmilling) and an apartment with "flush plumbing" were major steps forward. Thousands came to town who had lived in two-room tarpaper shacks with newspapered interior walls and an outhouse out back—some shacks were bereft of even that minimal sanitary feature.

Streaming northward from the Mississippi and Arkansas Delta and other farming areas during the same period were black families. Displaced by agricultural mechanization, oppressive sharecropping systems, and a decade of disastrous weather, they fled the same grinding rural poverty that sent the Presleys and other whites to Memphis.

Memphis had an established black musical culture, and for a generation its Beale Street had accommodated black folk seeking a good time. But the musical presence of the newcomers was most evident in a new commerce involving radio and recordings.

RADIO MIXES THE MUSIC: MEMPHIS KIDS IGNORE THE OLD RULES

Radio is the most democratic of media. It cares not a whit about the race, creed, or place of origin of a listener or broadcaster. No other medium so effectively divorces sound from the context and culture that creates it. At the same time, radio creates a sense of intimacy. It places the listener within inches of singer, speaker, or instrument and allows the imagination to create visual images.

Blacks and whites shared the streets and workplaces in Memphis, but the color line was rigid in matters where there was even a hint of interracial socialization. The waiting rooms, water fountains, bus and train service, and even the zoo were rigidly segregated. (The zoo served black and white patrons on different days.)

If the city's Beale Street could indeed talk, it would tell how segregated live music was during its heyday. Black bands sometimes performed for segregated white audiences at private parties and clubs, but virtually all face-to-face performing across color lines was impromptu and on the street. Music moved across the color line in recordings—commerce often ignores social rules. But musical race mixing in Memphis was largely a radio phenomenon.

Madcap Memphis disc jockey Dewey Phillips (no relation to Sun Record Company owner Sam Phillips) had the ear of the white youth of the city. His grip resulted from his zany ways, the unexpected turns of his wit, and from his ability to choose music that had a pronounced dance beat and reasonably lucid lyrics.

Phillips had no format. His nine to midnight show was not defined by genre or sales. He dipped into various pop and country musics and sprinkled black music throughout. He was much like his audience—hearing music basically from a rural Southern country perspective but putting down new roots, welcoming new pop sounds, and being open to the black sounds suddenly available on radio and locally made recordings.

It was Dewey Phillips who "broke" Elvis Presley's rockabilly hits and those of other performers into the Memphis youth market.

SORRY, DUDE: IT WAS MAINLY A HILLBILLY THING

Nowadays, rock documentarians tend to emphasize the black roots of rock 'n' roll. While these roots are real and diverse, rock 'n' roll has been as sponge-like as most other popular forms, absorbing and reorganizing sounds from many places and many times.

Older forms of country music are the true bedrock of rockabilly. Elvis was initially called "The Hillbilly Cat," and his manager Colonel Tom Parker had been managing Nashville acts for years before taking a chance on the long-haired truck driver who sounded black but wasn't.

The Memphis rockabilly performers listened to B.B. King and Rufus Thomas, but they were more in tune with Hank Snow and the Delmore Brothers. Their music moved from tarpaper shack porches and kerosene circuit school programs in the early fifties. It began to be performed in urban "beer joints" and at dances in new school gyms in the post-World War II suburbs.

The Baptist ban on dancing was hard to maintain in this setting, and a louder sound was needed for the musicians to be heard over the chatter. So the music acquired a stronger beat than it had needed for front porch ballads, and electricity boosted the volume.

Their parents had preferred live radio broadcasts of the Grand Ole Opry and "farm and home hour" daily hillbilly shows. The kids preferred deejays who played hot records and mixed other sounds into the hillbilly matrix.

Rockabilly—the Memphis Sound—is essentially an offshoot of traditional country music. Rock 'n' roll largely evolved from it in the late fifties and early sixties.

A collision between country music and big band popular music in the 1930s had helped to set the stage. It resulted in western swing, a music that embraced electricity and combined two or three fiddles with electric and electric steel guitars, "doghouse" bass, piano, and drums, and perhaps even a saxophone or two.

Country honky-tonk music of the forties and fifties began dismissing the fiddles, but kept the rest of the instrumentation and tied it to a "country hit parade" of popular song balladry.

Rockabilly performers used the same instruments and story-song format. Their music was briefly popular, but the sponge-like quality of mass popularization fed new sounds into the mix and rockabilly was essentially finished by 1965.

Rockabilly is now a musical orphan in the contemporary commercial soundscape, a place once visited, the youth music of people now nearing retirement. It was the most sparkling of the fresh streams that fed the river of rock 'n' roll. It has maintained a devoted audience, and it reminds us that the youth of our nation determine the direction of much of our culture.

It also tells us that, while much has changed in three centuries, Europe is still meeting Africa in our culture and there are highly positive benefits from the meeting. And there's this oddity of a few thousand teenagers from greater Memphis setting off a sound that is still reverberating around the world almost fifty years later.

INDEX